Psychology: A Christian Perspective
High School Edition

Teachers' Guide

Originally published 2015
Revised 2018

© Copyright 2018 Timothy S. Rice
by Timothy (Tim) S. Rice, D. Min., LPC

www.homeschoolpsychology.com

Published by
Rocking R Ventures, Inc.
104 Goss Street
Epworth, GA 30541

ISBN 978-0-9815587-3-8

Table of Contents

Introduction

There are many resources available to help teach psychology. But there are few resources to help teach psychology from a Christian worldview perspective -- few that provide teachers with ideas for incorporating the Christian worldview into every lesson.

It's important. In college, Christian students may encounter professors and peers who do not believe in the Christian worldview. Students may encounter psychology professors who believe that the Christian worldview has no place in psychology – who ridicule Christianity as unscientific, irrational, and silly. This guide is about explaining why the Christian worldview is not silly – that instead, it provides the most logical and meaningful framework for understanding psychology. Students need not fear psychology professors. Psychology class should strengthen students' faith.

In every psychology class students learn about psychology's major school-of-thought – behaviorism, Freudian psychodynamic psychology, humanistic psychology, and evolutionary psychology. Each makes specific claims about human nature – what it means to be human. This guide is about understanding those claims and contrasting them with what the Bible says about human nature and what it means to be human.

In every psychology class students learn about the brain and nervous system, sensation and perception, motivation and emotion, abnormal and treatment psychology, and the rest of the 'fundamentals of psychology.' This guide is about how each topic points toward God. This guide is about positively asserting a Christian psychological apologetic so that students can boldly bring their Christian worldview to psychology class.

This guide is divided into fifteen chapters. Each includes:

LEARNING OBJECTIVES The textbook and this guide are intended to help prepare students for the psychology CLEP test.

KEY CONCEPTS AND PEOPLE

STUDY GUIDE Fill-in-the-blank statements intended for student to complete as they read the material. When completed, the study guide becomes -- a study guide – to review before the quizzes.

SHORT ESSAY QUESTIONS The short essay questions are an opportunity for students to demonstrate understanding at a deeper level. They are opportunities for students to demonstrate that they can write clearly and use the critical thinking skills that they've only recent acquired.

OPPORTUNITIES FOR FURTHER STUDY There are countless resources for studying Psychology on the Internet. Many are included in this section.

TOPICS FOR DISCUSSION Psychology class provides many opportunities to talk about important issues. Here are just a few.

WORLDVIEW ISSUES Lecture ideas. This section is intended to help teachers bring important worldview issues to their lectures.

MULIPLE CHOICE QUIZZES

Chapter 1 What is Psychology?

Chapter 1 Learning Objectives

Discuss the importance of worldviews in defining psychology and describe how psychology's definition has changed over time.

Describe the controversy among Christians about psychology.

Describe psychology's influence in academia, the culture, and the Christian Church.

Describe a Christian approach to the study of psychology.

Describe psychology's goals.

Describe psychology's subfields and careers.

Describe modern psychology's major approaches or schools of thought.

Identify possible career alternatives in psychology.

Describe areas of potential psychological research on topics of interest to Christians.

Key Concepts and People

Affect	Freedom	Philosophy
Behavior	Subjective	Agnosticism
Cognition	Objective	Atheism
Psyche	Freedom	Determinism
Dominion	Objective	Empiricism
Popular Psychology	Subjective	
Stigma	Modernism	

Short essay questions

1. Define psychology in your own words.
2. Describe reasons that psychology is controversial among Christians today.
3. Discuss the influence of psychology's theories in the culture and on the Christian Church.
4. Discuss the statement "psychology is not a harmless discipline nor is it inherently anti-Christian?"
5. Describe the impact of Darwin's theory of evolution on the study of the psychology.
6. Name and describe five of psychology subfields.
7. What advice does the text offer about a Christian approach to Psychology?
8. The text named four things psychologists do? Name and describe them.
9. The text named five main approaches to psychology. Name and describe them.

For Further Study

1. Web: Review the Divisions of the American Psychological Association at http://www.apa.org/about/division/
2. and visit the homepage for a few of the divisions to explore the extent of psychological topics.
3. Find word #5590 (psuche) in Strong's Exhaustive Concordance of the Bible (available at http://www.eliyah.com/lexicon.html) Review usage of psuche, read verses containing the word, and compare and contrast meanings of psuche.
4. Video: The Discovering Psychology: Updated Edition http://learner.org/resources/series138.html is an instructional series on introductory psychology for college and high school classrooms and adult learners comprised of 26 half-hour video programs. The series features demonstrations, classic experiments and simulations, current research, documentary footage, and computer animation and provides students plenty of opportunity to discern the worldview perspectives embedded in Dr. Zimbardo's narration.
5. Read: Christ, the Lord of Psychology, by Eric L. Johnson from the Journal of Psychology and Theology at https://journals.biola.edu/jpt/assets/9/25-011.pdf

6. Read: Select articles from the Neuroscience & Christianity section of the American Scientific Affiliation at http://www.asa3.org/ASA/topics/PsychologyNeuroscience/index.html where there are a number of resources for further study on neuroscience and the Christian worldview.
7. Read: The End of Christian Psychology at www.psychoheresy-aware.org/endofcp.html by Martin & Deidre Bobgan
8. Read: All Truth God's Truth? At www.psychoheresy-aware.org/truth92.html by Martin & Deidre Bobgan.
9. Read: Christian Psychology - Part I by Dave Hunt at www.thebereancall.org/node/5949. Hunt describes psychology as a dangerous, and, at the same time, an appealing and popular form of modernism.
10. Read: Christian Psychology - Part II by Dave Hunt at www.thebereancall.org/node/5950. Hunt describes Christian psychology as cult-like and calls desperately for a return to biblical Christianity.
11. Read: Biola University's Journal of Psychology & Theology. Free articles at http://journals.biola.edu/jpt/free-articles/
12. Read: Psychology and Faith, by David G. Myers at www.davidmyers.org/davidmyers/assets/Psych.and.Faith.pdf.

Topics for Discussion

1. What does it mean to love the Lord your God with all your heart, soul, and mind?
2. Why is it especially important to wear the full armor of God while studying psychology?
3. How could failing to recognize the worldview assumptions embedded in psychology's theories lead Christian students to inadvertently compromise their Christian worldview?
4. Why do many Christian students walk away from their faith after the first year of college?

Chapter 1 Worldview Issues

To bring the Christian worldview to psychology class, we need to accomplish several tasks.

- We need to have an expansive definition of psychology.
- We need to understand worldviews and to recognize the worldview beliefs underlying modern psychology's major theories.
- We need to understand what the Bible has to say about psychology's subject matter – the human mind.

Psychology is often defined narrowly – the scientific study of the human brain and behavior. Some people think psychology is all about mental illness, counseling, and psychiatric medications. We need an expansive definition because psychology is so much more. It is the study of God's grandest creation. You. Psychology is the study of your joys and your sorrows, your memories and your ambitions, your sense of personal identity and your free will. Psychology is the scientific study of every mental power and capacity you possess. But that is not all.

The origin of the prefix 'psych,' or more accurately, 'psyche' (pronounced sy-key) is the Greek word 'psuche.' Psuche had two meanings. In the first, psuche is defined as the 'life force' – that which animates all life on earth. It differentiates life from non-life. All life, at least all animal life, has psuche.

But psuche had a second meaning. Psuche also describes something uniquely human, something special, and something spiritual and uniquely human. A full definition of psuche recognizes that humans are unique on earth and it makes room for the human heart, soul, and mind. With a big definition, it becomes clear that psychology is interested in topics dear to a Christian worldview – topics dealt with extensively in the Bible.

Psychology Is Old

Who was the first person to wonder about the human mind? It may have been King David when he wrote in Psalm 8:4, "What is man that thou art mindful of him, and the son of man that thou dost care for him?" Job was very interested in the causes of and cures for mental pain and suffering. Moses himself struggled with fear and self-doubt.

It wasn't called psychology and it wasn't scientific, but there is a rich history of Christian theologians writing about psychology from the Christian perspective. The early church fathers wrote about, human nature, the mind, the soul, perceptions, emotions, and mental pain and suffering. Augustine wrote about love, sin, grace, memory, mental illumination, wisdom, volition, and the experience of time. Thomas Aquinas wrote about motivation, free- will, habits, virtues and vices, emotions, memory, and the intellect. Soren Kierkegaard, the most significant Christian psychologist since the Middle Ages, contributed profound psychological works. Jonathan Edwards and John of the Cross described spiritual development, sin, grace, knowledge, faith, and the nature of the Christian life.

The history of a Christian approach to psychology continues through the Protestant Reformation. Prior to Martin Luther nailing his theses to the door of the Wittenberg Castle church, the Catholic church had been the 'authority' on all matters. Prior to the reformation, the Bible, Church scholars were the astronomers, physicists, doctors, and psychologists. After the reformation, the fathers of science (the grandfathers of modern psychology) had rejected Church authority and used reason, logic, careful observation, and experimentation to discover truths about the world, and eventually, the human mind.

Psychology is Young

Psychology is an old interest, but a young science. Students learn that the birth of modern psychology dates to 1879 when Wilhelm Wundt established his laboratory at Leipzig University in Germany. It was a time when scientific methods were producing great discoveries and advancements in other disciplines. Wundt and the fathers of modern psychology employed scientific methods to study psychological phenomenon. That was new. Psychology, once a field for philosophers and theologians, became a science. As modern psychology developed, psychologists emphasized that it was a natural science – a 'hard' science like physics and chemistry. This occurred at a time when Charles Darwin's Origin of Species was changing each of the natural sciences. As we'll see, Darwin changed psychology, too.

Study Guide Chapter 1

1. Many Christians see psychology as a harmless academic discipline, not at all _____ with a Christian worldview.

2. Many Christians have serious objections to psychology and claim that psychology is a

   _____.

3. In the Greek language the word psyche meant _____.

4. The concepts of the _____are absent from most modern definitions of psychology.

5. Psychology is the scientific study of the ABCs _____

   _____.

6. Psychology and the Bible both deal with _____.

7. You need to recognize when worldview assumptions are _____ by sprinkling in a few Bible verses and mentioning Jesus.

8. You must evaluate psychology at the _____.

9. It is essential that Christians studying psychology respect the _____

   _____of the Bible.

10. We must not underestimate the corrupting, distorting, and destructive influence of_____ on human thinking.

11. Christians studying and working in psychology _____

    _____.

12. Christians studying and working in psychology can also help reduce the Church's misunderstanding and fear of psychology and help remove the _____ of seeking help for emotional problems.

13. Christians studying psychology must have excellent preparation in _____

    _____.

14. in addition to exemplary scholarship, Christians in every field must strive to _____

    _____.

15. Our goal is to have the _____, so we must reclaim psychology for Christ.

16. Many Christians believe that there is a _____, similar to the Great Commission that requires Christians to reclaim the culture, education, and by extension, psychology.

17. The Church risks _____ if Christians ignore their responsibility to reclaim the whole culture (including psychology).

18. As we study psychology, we must also distinguish fact from _____.

Chapter 1 Quiz

1) Which is not a main purpose for psychological research?
   a) Psychologists observe and describe psychological phenomena.
   b) Psychologists test theories and hypotheses explaining the phenomena.
   c) Psychologists attempt to identify ways to control people's thoughts and read their minds.
   d) Psychologists develop and implement techniques to predict and change thoughts, feelings, and behavior.

2) Cognitive psychologists study:
   a) the mental processes involved in perception, decision-making, problem solving, and the ways we construct meaning.
   b) study the brain, how nerve cells communicate and transmit information, and the role of genetics in psychology.
   c) unconscious mental activity
   d) study the way that people interact with other people and in groups.

3) Neuroscientists _____
   a) study the brain and the ways neurons communicate and transmit information.
   b) measure and compare people according to personality characteristics.
   c) develop strategies to improve teaching and learning.
   d) study the way that people interact with other people and in groups.

4) Personality psychologists study:
   a) study the causes of mental and behavioral disorders
   b) the unique characteristics of people.
   c) the brain, how nerve cells communicate and transmit information
   d) the mental processes involved in sensation and perception, learning and memory, decision-making, and problem solving.

5) What psychology specialty studies changes in behavior and mental processes across the life span?
   a) Social Psychology
   b) Developmental psychology
   c) Biologic psychology
   d) Cognitive psychology

6) What psychology specialty studies the way that people interact with other people and in groups?

   a) Social Psychology
   b) Developmental psychology
   c) Cognitive psychology
   d) Biologic psychology

7) Which approach focuses on biological structures and electro-chemical processes?
   a) Biologic approach
   b) Cognitive approach
   c) Behavioral approach
   d) Developmental psychology

8) Which approach to psychology emphasizes the relationship between environmental influences and behavior?
   a) Behavioral approach
   b) Biologic approach
   c) Cognitive approach
   d) Humanistic approach

9) Which approach to psychology emphasizes thoughts, feelings, and innate human goodness and potential?
   a) Humanistic approach
   b) Psychodynamic approach
   c) Behavioral approach
   d) Behavioral approach

10) Which of psychology's perspectives/schools of thought sees all human behavior is determined by the environment in a closed cause and effect system?
   a) Humanism
   b) Behaviorism
   c) Scientism
   d) Mechanism

Answer Key Chapter 1

Chapter 1 Study Guide (Answers)

1. Many Christians see psychology as a harmless academic discipline, not at all **inconsistent** with a Christian worldview.
2. Many Christians have serious objections to psychology and claim that psychology is **a dangerous, idolatrous, and ungodly rival religion.**
3. In the Greek language the word psyche meant **soul and mind.**
4. The concepts of the **soul and mind** are absent from most modern definitions of psychology.
5. Psychology is the scientific study of the ABCs – **affect (emotions), behavior, and cognition (mental processes).**
6. Psychology and the Bible both deal **with human nature and the human condition.**
7. You need to recognize when worldview assumptions are **Christianized** by sprinkling in a few Bible verses and mentioning Jesus.
8. You must evaluate psychology at the **worldview level.**
9. It is essential that Christians studying psychology respect the **inspiration and authority** of the Bible.
10. We must not underestimate the corrupting, distorting, and destructive influence of **sin** on human thinking.
11. Christians studying and working in psychology **must be faithful to Scripture, not compromise their Christian worldview assumptions, and must understand modern psychology's historical roots, philosophical assumptions, and empirical methods.**
12. Christians studying and working in psychology can also help reduce the Church's misunderstanding and fear of psychology and help remove the **stigma** of seeking help for emotional problems.
13. Christians studying psychology must have excellent preparation in **theology, biblical interpretation, and the principles of Christian discipleship.**
14. In addition to exemplary scholarship, Christians in every field must strive to **live exemplary lives.**
15. Our goal is to have the **mind of Christ**, so we must reclaim psychology for Christ.
16. Many Christians believe that there is a **cultural commission**, similar to the Great Commission that requires Christians to reclaim the culture, education, and by extension, psychology.
17. The Church risks **marginalization** if Christians ignore their responsibility to reclaim the whole culture (including psychology).
18. As we study psychology, we must also distinguish fact from **philosophy.**

Chapter 1 Short Essay Questions (Answers)

1. The scientific study of the brain and behavior. The science of human affect, behavior, and cognition. The study of the soul, the mind, and the relationship of mind to the brain and the body.
2. Some Christians see psychology as a harmless academic discipline and other Christians believe that psychology (especially counseling psychology) represents a secular, humanistic, and idolatrous replacement for Biblical anthropology and Biblical models of caring for problems of living.
3. Psychological theories influence sermons across the country. Some pastors leave the pulpit for jobs in pastoral counseling or social work. Christian authors and speakers sometimes take popular secular self-help books, theories, and speaker and "Christianize" them by mentioning the Bible and Jesus.
4. Modern psychology's worldview assumptions are not harmless, but they do not define or limit psychology.
5. Beginning with Charles Darwin's Origin of Species psychology, underwent a transformation. Data was interpreted in ways that excluded supernatural beliefs and assumptions. Psychology, once the study of the soul, became the study of the brain and behavior Darwinian macro-evolution is now imposing itself on the Christian understanding of Man (psychology) and trying to exclude anything Christian.
6. Cognitive psychologists study mental processes. Physiological psychologists study the brain, how nerve cells communicate and transmit information, and the role of genetics in mental disorders. Personality psychologists study the unique characteristics of people. Developmental psychologists study changes in behavior and mental processes across the life span. Counseling, clinical, and community psychologists study the causes of mental and behavioral disorders and devise techniques to help people recover from those problems. Educational psychologists study teaching and learning and develop strategies to improve teaching and learning. School psychologists testing for, diagnose, and treat learning and academic problems. Social psychologists study the way that people interact with other people and in groups.
7. Christians studying psychology must; Respect the inspiration and authority of the Bible. Not underestimate the distorting, and destructive influence of sin on human thinking. Remember that there will be no conflict between true psychology and a Christian worldview. Not compromise their Christian worldview assumptions
8. Psychologists observe and describe psychological phenomena. Psychologist test theories and hypotheses explaining the phenomena. Psychologists attempt to identify the factors that influence our thoughts, feelings, and behaviors. Psychologist develop and implement techniques to predict and change thoughts, feelings, behavior.

9. The biological approach views mental processes and behaviors in terms of biological structures and electro-chemical processes. The behavioral approach emphasizes the relationship between environmental influences and behavior. The cognitive approach emphasizes conscious thought processes. Cognition refers to perception, problem solving, memory, thinking, and any mental process that transforms sensory input. The psychoanalytic approach emphasizes unconscious processes. The humanistic approach emphasizes the influence of our thoughts, feelings, and experiences on the environment and emphasizes innate goodness and potential.

Chapter 1 Quiz Answers

1. Which is not a main purpose for psychological research? c) Psychologists attempt to identify ways to control people's thoughts and read their minds.
2. Cognitive psychologists study: a) the mental processes involved in perception, decision-making, problem solving, and the ways
3. Neuroscientists a) study the brain and the ways neurons communicate and transmit information.
4. Personality psychologists study: b) the unique characteristics of people.
5. What psychology specialty studies changes in behavior and mental processes across the life span? b) Developmental psychology
6. What psychology specialty studies the way that people interact with other people and in groups? a) Social Psychology
7. Which approach to psychology focuses on mental processes and behaviors in terms of biological structures and electro-chemical processes? a) Biologic approach
8. Which approach to psychology emphasizes the relationship between environmental influences and behavior? a) Behavioral approach
9. 9) Which approach to psychology emphasizes the influence of our thoughts, feelings, and experiences on the environment and innate human goodness and potential? a) Humanistic approach
10. 10) Which of psychology's perspectives/schools of thought sees all human behavior is determined by the environment in a closed cause and effect system? b) Behaviorism

Chapter 2 A Christian Worldview

Chapter 2 Learning Objectives

Define "worldview."
Describe the intersection of psychology and the Bible.
Describe a Christian view of moral absolutes.
Describe a Christian perspective of the causes for mental pain and suffering.
Describe the history and influence of naturalism on psychology and other sciences.
Describe the history and influence of Darwinian evolution on psychology.
Define Biblical anthropology.
Define epistemology. Describe a Christian view of knowledge.
Describe the "faith/Science dichotomy" and discuss a Christian view of science.
Describe general and natural revelation in relation to knowledge about the nature of Man.
Describe the ways that 'sin' is relevant to psychology class.

Key Concepts and People

Vis-à-vis	Epistemology	Freedom vs. Determinism
Psyche	Faith/science dichotomy	Heredity vs. Environment
Mind	God-likeness	Cultural Commission
Soul	Naturalism	
Theism	Popular Psychology	

Short essay questions

1. What is a worldview?
2. What is epistemology?
3. What is natural revelation? What is special revelation?
4. What do you believe about God?
5. What do you believe about the nature of Mankind?
6. What do you believe about moral absolutes?
7. What do you think causes mental pain and suffering?
8. Describe a monistic, dualistic, and tripartite view of human nature.
9. Describe the faith/science dichotomy. Do you believe there is a dichotomy between science and a Christian worldview? Explain your answer.
10. Have your thoughts and opinions about psychology and worldviews changed?

For Further Study

1. Read: The Spheres of Revelation and Science. What Are Their Limitations in Relation to Each Other? Clark, R. E. (1953) in The Journal of the American Scientific Affiliation at https://asa3.org/ASA/PSCF/1953/JASA6-53Clark.html
2. Web: Historical Studies of Science and Christianity https://asa3.org/ASA/topics/history/index.html
3. Read: How Sin Affects Scholarship: A New Model by Stephen K. Moroney at https://asa3.org/ASA/topics/ethics/CSRSpring-1999Moroney.html
4. Web: Summit Ministries https://www.summit.org/

Topics for Discussion

1. It this statement true or false? Support your answer. "The foundational beliefs of a Christian worldview, of an atheist's worldview, and of a psychology professor's worldview are matters of faith and philosophy and not of data and science."
2. Do we have a mind that is greater than the sum of our brain activity?

3. Why do Christians disagree about proper approaches to caring for mental suffering?
4. How does God use guilt, pain, and suffering as tools to conform Christians to Christ's image?
5. In what ways are we like animals, psychologically. Psychologically, in what ways are humans unique among life?
6. In what ways are we different from the animals?
7. Do we have free-will? Are people basically good or bad?
8. Is 'all truth God's Truth?'
9. Why do many people believe that faith and science are enemies?

Chapter 2 Worldview Issues

What is a worldview?

Sigmund Freud, known as the father of psychiatry, defined worldview (weltanschauung) as an intellectual construction which gives a unified solution for all the problems of our existence… a comprehensive hypothesis in which no question is left open and that everything in which we are interested finds a place.

Worldviews are big. Worldviews leave no question unanswered. Worldviews answer ultimate questions, like:

Is there a God?
How did we get here?
What does it mean to be human?
Is there truth and how can we know what is true?

Everyone has a worldview. Christians, Muslims, Jews, atheists, agnostics, and psychology professors have worldviews. Each of us hold core foundational beliefs – convictions – through which we perceive and understand the world. Those foundational beliefs define one's worldview. A worldview is, as the word suggests, a way of looking at the world. Worldview is the conceptual framework that give meaning to the world. It is made of your core beliefs and your most fundamental assumptions about the world.

You may not think about your worldview very often, but all intellectual activities, including scientific research, are interpreted and understood through one's worldview. Ultimately, truth is only discernible from error at the worldview level. The Apostle Paul instructed Christians to submit every thought to the obedience of Christ. In psychology class, that means examining everything you learn through your worldview.

What is the Christian Worldview?

The first step toward examining psychology in light of the Christian worldview is to have a solid understanding of the Christian worldview. At its core, the Christian worldview is a biblical worldview. It begins with the Biblical account of God, creation, the fall, and the plan for redemption. It is the Biblical account of where we came from, our nature, and how we should live.

But the Christian worldview, like psychology, is big. It includes your beliefs about theology, epistemology, biblical anthropology, sin, the Church, end times, marriage, the family, standards of behavior, and much more. You could spend your career studying psychology or the Christian worldview, but our interest is in four questions where the Christian worldview and modern psychology intersect.

Where did we come from?

What are the sources of truth and knowledge?
What is human nature?
What are the causes of and cures for mental pain and suffering?

It is important that we get this right. The Bible warns us to be wary of philosophies and empty deceptions in the tradition of men and the world. It tells us to demolish arguments and pretensions that set themselves against the knowledge of God. That's very relevant in psychology class.

This is important because psychology class provides students with warnings, an opportunity to understand the real-world pressures students will face in and after college. Stanley Milgram's famous research on obedience to authority is an example.

The Solomon Asch conformity study is also famous in the history of psychology because it demonstrated the power of conformity – the pressure to change our thoughts, feelings, or behavior to match those of the group. Asch demonstrated that not conforming is difficult. Subjects in his study denied what they saw with their own eyes to not stand out. Bringing the Christian worldview to psychology class is an act of nonconformity. It will make Christian students stand out. Without God as your ultimate authority, you will feel pressure to conform to psychology's worldviews.

What are the beliefs to which students will feel pressure to conform?

Theism
Students will feel pressure to conform to a belief that God is not real – to a philosophy of naturalism. God exists, or He does not. He created the universe, or He did not. A fundamental part of your worldview is your belief about God, the origin of the universe, and how we came to be. A Christian approach is theistic. It begins with the belief that God is real. There is one triune God who created the universe and everything in it – including the human mind. He is personal, loving, just, infinite, self-revealing, all-powerful, all knowing, ever present, self-existent, sovereign, eternal, and active in the world today. Our minds were designed and created by God and by His grace we reflect His likeness.

If God does exist, what are His attributes? Theology proper, the study of God's attributes, is a big topic, too. Some of God's attributes are more relevant to psychology than others. We are interested in God's immutability. His unchanging nature and His designs for the world are foundational to all sciences, including psychology. In as much as psychology is a science, it is grounded in God's unchanging nature and His design for us. We are also interested in God's truth, goodness, purpose, righteousness, love, healing, and provision. These qualities are foundational to our understanding of human nature, morality, the causes and cures of mental pain and suffering, and more.

Naturalism
Modern psychology's major theories are not theistic. They are naturalistic. Naturalism is a worldview, a belief that natural causes and only natural causes created and can explain everything that exists – including the human mind. Naturalism demands a small definition of psyche – it excludes the possibility of the supernatural. From this perspective, all behavior and mental

processes, every topic every psychology textbook, without exception, are the result of the operation of natural forces.

Natural and Special Revelation

From a Christian perspective, we can know truth with certainty from more than one source. The relationship between worldviews, psychology, and science can be described in terms of natural and special revelation. A Christian worldview believes that God reveals things to us in two ways: natural (general) revelation and special revelation.

Natural revelation refers to truths revealed through nature. Natural revelation refers to the discoveries made using scientific methods. We can learn about the world by observing it, testing it, and by logic and reason (any technique apart from reading the Bible or the working of the Holy Spirit). God reveals His existence in what we observe – in the stars and in psychology class. The laws of nature have their origin in God's creation, and creation reveals God's power and order. Scientific psychology's sole focus is natural revelation.

But from a Christian perspective, there are other ways to know truth -- special revelation. The Bible contains special revelation. It is an inspired, infallible, and completely valid source of information. Special revelation refers to the biblical account of God's character, His purpose, our nature, His plan for us, and our relationship with Him. Special revelation refers to God's works in history and the work of the Holy Spirit in humanity.

In Genesis we learn that God formed man of the dust of the ground. We are part of the natural order. As such, to be human means having much in common with the animals. We, like animals, have brains and bodies. We share DNA and psychological characteristics with animals. Therefore, psychology is the study of the human mind as part of the natural order. But the Bible is clear that we are made in the image of God. We are special - distinct from the animals. Therefore, psychology is also the study of the human mind as a unique and supernatural creation of God.

Natural and special revelation are parts of an overarching and non-contradictory whole. We can learn psychological truths through both special and natural revelation. Ultimately, they are harmonious. There can be no faith/science dichotomy. True science and true faith must agree. In terms of psychology, the appearance of a disagreement is the result of bad science, bad interpretation, or bad theology.

Proximate and Ultimate Cause

The relationship between worldviews, psychology, and science can also be described in terms of proximate and ultimate causes. Proximate means the cause that is closest to the event – how something happens. Worldviews aren't crucial to understanding the mechanics of the human brain and behavior. Scientific psychology is interested in proximate causes. How do we see? What happens when neurons fires? How do people behave in social situations? The goal of scientific psychology is to discover how every mental power and capacity works.

Ultimate cause refers to the original link in the chain of events. Science cannot answer ultimate cause question. Why do we see? Why do we have language? Why do humans behave badly in social situations? Why is there mental pain and suffering? Science can describe the ways people *do* think, feel, and behave, but it cannot tell us why. Science cannot tell us how we *should* think, feel, and behave. We can examine every topic in psychology in terms of proximate and ultimate causes.

Sin

The concept of sin doesn't get much attention in most introductory psychology classes. From a naturalistic perspective, in which morality is a subjective human invention, the word 'sin' is meaningless. Students will feel pressure to conform to humanism, a belief that to be human means to have an inherent goodness. A Christian approach to psychology must deal with the problem of sin.

A central piece of the Christian worldview is known as the doctrine of sin. When Adam sinned, it changed everything. The Fall also had psychological consequences. Jeremiah 17:9 describes the 'noetic' effect of sin, that it difficult to even comprehend how sin corrupts and distorts our minds. When the Bible describes the human 'heart,' it is describing the essence of our being. It is from the heart that our thoughts, emotions, and behavior flow. The heart is mentioned hundreds of times in the Bible, but not to mean the organ that pumps blood. When the Bible uses the word heart, it means, among other things, our motives and our emotional lives. A Christian approach to psychology is both informed by and marred by the effect of sin on our hearts.

The 'natural' or 'carnal' man is alienated from God and blinded to truth. But God's grace brings freedom from many of the secondary effects of the Fall – namely the darkening of our minds. Jesus came to transform our minds – to change our behavior, social relationships, motives, and our emotions. By God's grace our minds are renewed, and we can pursue the mind of Christ.

Morality

In Romans 2:15 we are told that there is a moral code written on the human heart. That is a bold psychological claim that probably sounds silly to a naturalist.

Part of being human is to have God's law written on one's heart. A Christian approach to psychology begins with the belief that there are universal, moral absolutes that flow from God's righteousness and form the basis of our conscience. Fascinating research from the Infant Cognition Center at Yale University seems to have demonstrated that children as young as 9 months old make moral judgments, exhibit bias, and have a sense of justice. They seem to have a moral core, a sense of good and evil written somewhere.

The Christian view of moral absolutes written on our hearts stands in stark contrast to naturalistic beliefs that morality is a human invention or that it evolved to solve our ancient ancestor's problems of living in small groups. From this perspective, there are no absolute standards of right or wrong, and that all viewpoints, lifestyles, and behaviors are equally valid.

Sexuality and Gender

In psychology class students learn the sexual response cycle, sexual disorders, and the physiological, neurological, and psychological processes involved in sex. Human sexuality is a reproductive necessity, but it is a lot more. Worldview beliefs are revealed in attitudes about male and female roles, marriage, divorce, re-marriage, sexual preference, and gender identity.

Christians view sexuality and gender from a biblical moral perspective. Sex is a natural reproductive necessity, but it is also a sacred gift – a type of mystical union.

Most psychology classes present sexuality and gender from the perspective of naturalism, humanism, and moral relativism. Sexuality is interpreted in terms of non-religious factors. Students will feel pressure to conform to a belief about sex that says, 'if it feels good, do it' and 'if it feels right, it is right for you.'

Study Guide Chapter 2

1. Complicated mental processes like "thoughts" and "feelings" involve complex interactions between the _____, _____, and the _____.

2. One's worldview is a complex system of core _____, _____, and _____.

3. All human intellectual activities, including _____ research and _____, happen in a worldview context and are guided by one's worldview.

4. The Christian worldview begins with the Biblical account of _____, _____, _____, and _____.

5. The most basic piece of your worldview includes whether you believe _____ exists, what you believe about _____, and the extent to which _____.

6. A Christian view of Mankind is known as _____.

7. _____, the traditional Christian belief, is that because God is spiritual (non-material), we must also have a non-material nature in order to have that relationship.

8. _____ is the study of the nature, sources, and limits of knowledge.

9. Many believe that the Bible has no place in science and that science is the Bible's enemy. In other words, they believe that there is a _____.

10. The historical Christian approach to science was that faith and science were _____.

11. A Christian worldview believes that God reveals things to us in two ways: general or _____ revelation and _____ revelation.

12. _____ refers to truths revealed through the world. We can learn truth by observing creation, by scientific experiments, by logic, and by the study of history.

13. _____ refers to biblical details about God's character, His purpose, our nature, His plan for us, and our relationship with Him.

14. God's natural and special revelation have _____, they are parts of an overarching and non-contradictory whole.

15. A Christian worldview includes the understanding of the effect of sin on our behavior and our thinking called the _____ of sin.

16. Our _____ and _____ should cause us to maintain a sense of humility and hold our conclusions tentatively.

17. A Christian worldview recognizes moral absolutes described _____ and _____ by Jesus Christ.

18. The Christian worldview believes that _____ and _____ make us "whole" but that "wholeness" does not necessarily equal ease and comfort.

19. The foundational beliefs of a Christian worldview, of an atheist's worldview, and of a psychology professor's worldview are matters of _____ and _____ and not of data and science.

20. A Christian worldview emphasizes _____ as the primary (if not exclusive) cause of mental and emotional pain.

Chapter 2 Quiz

1) The study of the nature, sources, and limits of knowledge is called:
   a) Teleology
   b) Epistemology
   c) Ontology
   d) Hermeneutics

2) The Christian approach to the study of the nature Mankind is known as:
   a) Theology
   b) Biblical anthropology
   c) Hermeneutics
   d) Epistemology

3) The traditional Christian belief that Mankind has physical (material) and spiritual (non-material) natures is known as:
   a) Monsim
   b) Humanism
   c) Dualism
   d) Anthropology

4) Those who believe that the Bible has no place in science, and that science is the Bible's enemy believe there is a(n)
   a) faith/science dichotomy
   b) separation of church and state
   c) moral relativism
   d) anti-science bias

5) The historical Christian approach to science (though not without exception) was that faith and science were;
   a) enemies
   b) complementary
   c) divergent realities
   d) incompatible

6) Truth revealed through the world, via observing creation, scientific experiments, logic, and the study of history is known as:
   a) natural revelation
   b) general revelation
   c) empiricism
   d) the book of revelation

7) Biblical details about God's character, His purpose, our nature, His plan for us, our relationship with Him. and the work of the Holy Spirit is known as:
   a) special revelation
   b) general revelation
   c) natural revelation
   d) the book of revelation

8) A Christian worldview belief that sin affects our behavior and our thinking is known as:
   a) carnal knowledge
   b) the noetic effect of sin
   c) discipleship
   d) Christian maturity

Answer Key Chapter 2

Chapter 2 Study Guide (Answers)

1. Complicated mental processes like "thoughts" and "feelings" involve complex interactions between **the brain, the body, and the outside world**.
2. One's worldview is a complex system of core **attitudes, beliefs, and values**.
3. All human intellectual activities, including **scientific** research and **theories**, happen in a worldview context and are guided by one's worldview.
4. The Christian worldview begins with the Biblical account of **God, Creation, The Fall**, and **Redemption**.
5. The most basic piece of your worldview includes whether you believe **God** exists, what you believe about **His nature**, and the extent to which **He influences your life**.
6. A Christian view of Mankind is known as **biblical anthropology**.
7. **Dualism**, the traditional Christian belief, is that because God is spiritual (non-material), we must also have a non-material nature in order to have that relationship.
8. **Epistemology** is the study of the nature, sources, and limits of knowledge.
9. Many believe that the Bible has no place in science and that science is the Bible's enemy. In other words, they believe that there is a **faith/science dichotomy**.
10. The historical Christian approach to science was that faith and science were **complementary**.
11. A Christian worldview believes that God reveals things to us in two ways: general or **natural** revelation and **special** revelation.
12. **Natural revelation** refers to truths revealed through the world. We can learn truth by observing creation, by scientific experiments, by logic, and by the study of history.
13. **Special revelation** refers to biblical details about God's character, His purpose, our nature, His plan for us, and our relationship with Him.
14. God's natural and special revelation have **convergent validity**; they are parts of an overarching and non-contradictory whole.
15. A Christian worldview includes the understanding of the effect of sin on our behavior and our thinking called the **noetic effect** of sin.
16. Our **personal bias** and **depravity** should cause us to maintain a sense of humility and hold our conclusions tentatively.
17. A Christian worldview recognizes moral absolutes described **in the Bible** and **lived** by Jesus Christ.
18. The Christian worldview believes that **redemption** and **restoration** make us "whole" but that "wholeness" does not necessarily equal ease and comfort.
19. The foundational beliefs of a Christian worldview, of an atheist's worldview, and of a psychology professor's worldview are matters of **faith** and **philosophy** and not of data and science.
20. A Christian worldview emphasizes **sin** as the primary (if not exclusive) cause of mental and emotional pain.

Chapter 2 Short Essay Questions (Answers)

1. One's worldview is a complex system of core attitudes, beliefs, and values.
2. Epistemology is the study of the nature, sources, and limits of knowledge.
3. Natural revelation refers to truths revealed through the world. We can learn truth by observing creation, by scientific experiments, by logic, and by the study of history (that is, any technique apart from reading the Bible or the working of the Holy Spirit). Special revelation refers to biblical details about God's character, His purpose, our nature, His plan for us, and our relationship with Him. Special revelation refers to God's works in history and the work of the Holy Spirit in humanity. A Christian approach to the study of psychology rests on a worldview that God reveals truths through both special and natural revelation.
4. God exists or He does not. Either He created you and the universe or not. The most basic piece of your worldview includes whether you believe God exists, what you believe about His nature, and the extent to which He influences your life. The Christian worldview is that there is one true triune God who is personal, loving, just, infinite, self-revealing, all-powerful, all-knowing, ever-present, self-existent, sovereign, eternal, and active in the world today.
5. A Christian view of Mankind, or biblical anthropology, describes us as the purposeful creation of God, made in His image and likeness, and as sinners in rebellion against Him by nature and by choice. We were made from the dust of the earth and are part of the natural order. As such, we have much in common with the animals. We are born, we grow old, and our bodies eventually die. However, like God, we are spiritual beings. Unlike the animals, we have moral discernment, freedom to choose, and responsibility for our behavior. We experience guilt, grace, and love. We are relational beings. We have consciousness, a mind, and a soul.
6. A Christian worldview recognizes moral absolutes described in the Bible and lived by Jesus Christ.

7. A Christian worldview holds that through pain we are refined and made more Christ-like. The Christian worldview believes that redemption and restoration make us "whole" but that "wholeness" does not necessarily equal ease and comfort. Christians disagree about whether extra-biblical techniques (e.g., medication) are ever proper approaches to caring for abnormal thoughts, feelings, and behaviors. A Christian worldview emphasizes sin as the primary, if not exclusive, cause of abnormal thoughts, feelings, and behaviors. A Christian worldview sees guilt, pain, and suffering as tools God uses to conform us to Christ's image. Jesus himself was a "man of sorrows."

8. In that monistic worldview, all mental life is nothing more than complex brain activity. There is no mind or soul. Dualism, the traditional Christian belief, is that because God is spiritual (non-material), we must also have a non-material nature in order to have that relationship. Dualists believe that our brains and our minds are distinct in essence but operate in interaction. A trichotomous worldview describes Mankind in terms of body, mind, and soul.

9. Many people believe that a Christian worldview and science are inherently in conflict – that the Bible has no place in science and that science is the Bible's enemy. Some historians have made the case that the Church (especially the Catholic church) fought every new scientific idea. Though it is true that through history the Church disputed many major scientific discoveries, it is not correct that the Christian church is necessarily "anti-science." In fact, science (and by extension, psychology) was born of the Christian worldview. A Christian worldview sees God as immutable, sees the world as orderly and rational, and believes that we can and should seek to understand creation. The historical Christian approach to science (though not without exception) was that faith and science were complementary.

10. Your discretion.

Chapter 2 Quiz Answers

1. The study of the nature, sources, and limits of knowledge is called: b) Epistemology
2. The Christian approach to the study of the nature Mankind is known as: b) Biblical anthropology
3. The traditional Christian belief that Mankind has physical (material) and spiritual (non-material) natures is known as: c) Dualism
4. Those who believe that the Bible has no place in science, and that science is the Bible's enemy believe there is a(n) a) faith/science dichotomy
5. The historical Christian approach to science (though not without exception) was that faith and science were; b) complementary
6. Truth revealed through the world, via observing creation, scientific experiments, logic, and the study of history is known as: a) natural revelation
7. Biblical details about God's character, His purpose, our nature, His plan for us, our relationship with Him. and the work of the Holy Spirit is known as: a) special revelation
8. A Christian worldview belief that sin affects our behavior and our thinking is known as: a) the noetic effect of sin

Chapter 3 Psychology's History and Worldview

Chapter 3 Learning Objectives

Describe Cartesian Dualism.
Describe the emergence of experimental psychology.
Describe the study of psychology pre-dating the establishment of modern scientific psychology.
Describe examples of ancient psychological research and theories.
Describe the development of psychology as an empirical science.
Describe phrenology.
Trace the history of psychology through each of its five major schools-of-thought.
Describe Freudian/psychodynamic psychology.
Describe behaviorism's claims about the nature of Mankind.
Describe the structuralists.
Explain the contribution of Dr. Charles Bell, Franz Gall, Gustave Fechner, Wilhelm Wundt, Edward Titchener to the development of modern psychology.
Describe reductionism and its implications on the nature of Mankind.
Describe the functionalists.
Describe the influence of Herbert Spencer, Charles Darwin, and William James on modern psychology.
Describe humanism and contrast humanism's beliefs about the nature of Man with a Christian view.
Define self-esteem. Evaluate "selfism" in comparison to Biblical anthropology.
Describe cognitive psychology.
Describe neuro-biology
Describe various explanations for mental illness in terms of underlying worldview assumptions.

Key Concepts and People

Naturalism
Atheism
Church authority
The Reformation
Martin Luther
Rationalism
Renee Descartes
Deductive reasoning
Monism
Cartesian dualism
The Conarium
Reflex arc
Empiricism
Francis Bacon
Inductive reasoning
Hippocrates

Four humors
Wilhelm Wundt
Phrenology
Franz Gall
Psychophysics
Paul Broca
Gustav Fechner
Structuralism
Herman von Helmholtz
Introspection
Charles Bell
Edward B. Titchener
Charles Darwin
Evolutionary psychology
Functionalism
Herbert Spencer

William James
Proximate and ultimate
Neuro-biology
Reductive (reductionism)
Behavioral Genetics
Francis Galton
Behaviorism
Sigmund Freud
Cognitive psychology
Humanism
Self-psychology
Feminist psychology

Short essay questions

1. What is Cartesian dualism?
2. How did a naturalistic worldview effect modern psychology?
3. How did rationalism contribute to the development of modern psychology?
4. What are some criticisms of modern psychology's reliance on empirical methods?
5. What is phrenology and how are phrenology and modern neurobiology similar?
6. How did Sigmund Freud's view of Mankind differ from a Christian view?
7. What were radical behaviorism's assumptions about the nature of Mankind?
8. In what ways is secular humanism inconsistent with a Christian worldview?

For Further Study

1. Web: History of Psychology, in conjunction with Dr. Donald Pozella of the University of Dayton at http://www.elvers.us/hop/welcome.asp
2. Read: the affirmations of the Humanist Manifesto I at the American Humanist Association at https://americanhumanist.org/what-is-humanism/manifesto1/
3. Read: the affirmations of the Humanist Manifesto I at the American Humanist Association at https://americanhumanist.org/what-is-humanism/manifesto2/
4. Read about ancient philosophers' influence in the history of psychology.
5. Democritus at http://www.iep.utm.edu/democrit/
6. Epicurus at http://www.iep.utm.edu/epicur/
7. Galen at http://www.iep.utm.edu/galen/
8. Read Marko Marulic -The Author of the Term "Psychology" at www.psychclassics.yorku.ca/Krstic/marulic.htm
9. Read John Locke – An Essay Concerning Human Understanding at http://www.gutenberg.org/ebooks/10615
10. Read David Hume – An Enquiry Concerning Human Understanding at https://www.gutenberg.org/files/9662/9662-h/9662-h.htm
11. Read Gustav Fechner -- Elements of Psychophysics at http://www.psychclassics.yorku.ca/Fechner/
12. Read Why Freud Survives: He's been debunked again and again—and yet we still can't give him up. https://www.newyorker.com/magazine/2017/08/28/why-freud-survives
13. Web: Classics in the History of Psychology an internet resource at psychclassics.yorku.ca/links.htm
14. Read: Darwin's Dirty Secret by Nancy R. Pearcey from World Magazine 3/13/2000 at
15. http://www.leaderu.com/orgs/arn/pearcey/np_world-rape0300.htm
16. Read: Non-bizarre delusions as strategic deception, by Edward H. Hagen. Hagen suggests that delusions are an evolved adaptive survival benefit at anthro.vancouver.wsu.edu/media/PDF/Delusions_revised_Aug_2007.pdf
17. Read: Leaving Psychology Behind, by Paul Vitz at https://www.summit.org/resources/articles/essays/leaving-psychology-behind/
18. Web: The Psychology of Religion pages at http://psywww.com/psyrelig/

Topics for Discussion

1. Is psychology old or is it new?
2. Are there limits to what science can explain about the human mind?
3. What is the nature of the human "heart"?
4. Why did Christians at the time call phrenology a heresy?
5. How might psychologists explain human aggression – murder and mayhem -- from behavioral, psychodynamic, humanistic, and Christian perspectives?

Chapter 3 Worldview Issues

The Problem of Dualism

In every psychology class students learn about 'the problem of dualism.' The problem of dualism highlights a major difference between Christian and naturalist approaches to psychology. The problem of dualism is about human nature – our substance.

Hippocrates thought that to be human was to be one substance -- he was a naturalist. Students today will feel pressure to conform to naturalistic philosophies that say to be human is to be of one physical substance.

Unlike Hippocrates, many ancient philosopher and theologians were dualists. René Descartes is famous for 'Cartesian dualism,' the idea that that we have two natures – physical and spiritual. The body and the soul.

The Bible is clear that we are physical and spiritual beings. We have a brain and a body, but we also have a mind, a heart, and a soul. For Christians, the problem of dualism is about how our body, heart, soul, and mind exist in unity in this life.

For the naturalist, the problem of dualism is different. It is about why people believe they are spiritual. It is about how physical processes (neurons) give rise to the subjective experience of consciousness. For the naturalist, there is nothing supernatural. The physical brain gives rise to the mind. You are your brain.

Evolutionary Psychology

Darwin's distant future has arrived. Today, evolutionary psychology is the 'new' psychology. Students will feel pressure to conform to a belief in evolution. The culture demands obedience to the evolutionary worldview. That is why it is important to understand evolutionary psychology.

Believing in evolution means different things to different people. Some define evolution simply as the change over time in living structures or as the increase in gene frequency over time. Some definitions differentiate micro evolution from macro. There is divergent, convergent, and parallel evolution. Some evolutionists define evolution in a way that includes the origins of life and others do not. We want a big definition.

For our purposes, evolution is a grand theory that explains the origins and diversity of all life, including human life. Evolutionary psychology (EP) is a grand theory that explains the origins and diversity of all mental life, including human mental life.

It seems silly to think that the most complex structure in the known universe, the human brain, evolved by numerous and successive slight modifications – adaptations that provided survival and reproductive advantages. According to evolutionary theory, the human mind was designed by evolution, not by an intelligent designer.

Darwin wrote, "in the distant future" because he understood the world wasn't ready for evolutionary psychology. Today, many people claim to be evolutionists, but they haven't really thought deeply about evolution. If there is an organism whose existence can't be explained by the principles of evolution, it disproves the theory. You are that organism. You, your mind, proves evolution wrong.

Evolutionary Psychology – Stone-aged minds

As a result of evolution, we have 'stone-aged minds in the modern world.' The human mind, in its current form, is said to have appeared about 300,000 years ago during the Pleistocene epoch. Because evolution works slowly, we haven't evolved very much since then. The key to human psychology today is found in challenges faced by our ancient ancestors. What was life like and what things were dangerous to early humans? What psychological characteristics would have helped them survive? Our minds evolved 'mental modules' (brain aps) as solutions to the problems of finding food and shelter, identifying a mate, raising children, living with others, avoiding predators, and surviving in a hostile environment.

Evolutionary Psychology –The Mechanics

Evolution is evolution. The evolutionary processes that are said to have designed our bodies – variations, adaptations, selection, random genetic noise, and epiphenomena – must also have designed our minds.

Variations are small genetic changes. Adaptive variations increase an organism's chance of surviving and reproducing. Evolution selects 'for' adaptive variations and selects 'against' variations that are not adaptive. Adaptations are transmitted from one generation to the next through inheritance.

Sometimes evolution produces epiphenomena, or 'by-products' of adaptations. Consciousness is thought to be an epiphenomenon – a by-product of having really big brains. Sometimes evolution acts through noise or random effects – variations that are not adaptive. Sometimes evolution acts through 'horizontal gene transfer' in which genes are transmitted in ways other than through inheritance.

Evolutionary Psychology – The Tree of Life

In evolutionary biology, The Tree of Life is used to illustrate the belief that of all life descended from a common ancestor. It demonstrates the concept of continuity – that all biological structures have their origins in increasingly simpler physical structures. The theory of evolution requires that every species' evolutionary history traces back to an original single-celled ancestor. If the theory of evolution is true, then there must be continuity in terms of physical characteristics.

The ideas of continuity and common descent were once illustrated by the recapitulation theory. Ernst Haeckel's recapitulation theory, once taught as a principle of evolution, has long been debunked. Haeckel suggested that the gestational development of an individual organism parallels the species' entire evolutionary history – all the way back to its original single-celled ancestor. A chicken embryo was thought, in the 28 days of its gestation, to recapitulate the entire evolutionary history of chickens. In the 9 months of human gestation, we were thought to move through the numerous stages of human evolution. The recapitulation theory has been demonstrated as false. Human embryos do not develop and then lose gill slits or prehensile tails during gestation.

If the theory of evolution is true, there must be a Psychological Tree of Life. The 'necessary acquirement…by gradation' of mental capacities means that each has its origins in simpler capacities. The human mind, including our 'highest' mental capacities, must have their origins in the ever increasingly less complex mental lives of our ancestors.

For example, Jean Piaget's stages of cognitive development are taught in every psychology class. It is useful to understand how thinking changes as children mature. But Piaget understood Darwin's theory. Piaget thought that the stages of cognitive development we see in children were once seen in human evolution. Piaget believed he was describing the origins of knowledge. At one time, our ancestors never developed past the sensorimotor stage. We must have had an ancestor who first understood object permanence. We must have had an ancestor who first saw the world through another's eyes, did math and logic, and who first had an abstract thought.

Evolutionary Psychology — Human Nature

Evolutionary psychology makes bold claims about human nature and our purpose. Human nature is to survive and reproduce. The ultimate purpose of the mind is survival and reproduction. Period. The mind is a collection of adaptations – mental modules – designed by evolution, to solve problems of finding food, avoiding predators, finding a mate, raising offspring, and living in small groups.

Evolutionary Psychology -- Emotions

If the theory of evolution is true, it must be true for human emotions as well. Darwin wrote extensively about emotions in The Expression of the Emotions in Man and Animals (1872). He believed that emotions in animals (e.g. fear, anger, and surprise) were evidence of a shared evolutionary history.

Life must have been dangerous for our ancestors 300,000 years ago. They needed to adapt to survive. Anger, fear, surprise, disgust, happiness, and sadness are said to be adaptions that helped them survive.

Evolutionary Psychology -- Anger

Anger is a powerful emotion that may have evolved to help our ancestors fight off predators. Or, anger and aggression may have evolved as a bargaining tactic, a way to keep rivals from stealing their mates or a way to punish cheaters. Humans evolved to be aggressive – murderous, warlike, and genocidal.

Evolutionary Psychology -- Fear

Similarly, fear is a powerful emotion. What frightens you? Whatever your answer is, your fear was formed in the minds of your ancient ancestors. If you fear spiders, snakes, heights, storms, large animals, darkness, blood, strangers, humiliation, deep water, or speaking in public, it is because those things were a threat to survival. Our responses to fear evolved too. We freeze so the predator might not see us. We flee or fight – depending on the predator. We submit, play dead, or faint in hopes that the predator will lose interest.

Evolutionary Psychology -- Happiness

Happiness, like fear, exists because it solved an adaptive problem. It is a mental state that caused our ancestors to do things that lead survival and/or reproduction – a type of positive reinforcement. Perhaps smiling, a sign of happiness, evolved to signal that you are not a threat. Happy smiles evolved to solve the problem of knowing who was friendly and who was going to kill you and steal your mate.

Evolutionary Psychology -- Sadness

Sadness and depression evolved as a type of negative reinforcement. It motivated our ancestors to pull themselves up by their bootstraps and pray harder. to communicate that they needed help. Perhaps it evolved as a by-product of attachment – a type of withdrawal symptom.

Evolutionary Psychology -- Disgust

Disgust evolved to prevent us from eating or touching gross things like rotted meat, blood, and poop. Taboos and morality today are the byproducts of the disgust adaptation.

Evolutionary Psychology – Food and Shelter

A major problem for all animals is finding food. Our minds were designed by evolution to solve the problems of finding nutritious food and avoiding toxins. Our ancestors did not have grocery stores and had to evolve the capacity to hunt and gather. Females evolved to be gatherers. Women today are thought to prefer pink because their ancestors had to be good at foraging bright ripe berries. Males evolved to be big strong hunters and to like big trucks and high-powered rifles.

The mental capacities that evolved during the Pleistocene Epoch are not well-suited to the modern world of 24-hour grocery stores. The same capacities that helped humans survive in history are killing us today. Obesity, heart disease, diabetes, and alcohol abuse are said to be the be the result of our stone-aged minds making modern food choices.

It was important for our ancient ancestors to evolve the capacity to recognize good places to live. They needed safety, shelter, and access to food and water. In the modern world, that capacity is revealed in our 'love' of art that depicts expansive vistas, running water, and lush vegetation.

Evolutionary Psychology -- Sex

Because reproduction drives evolution, evolutionary psychologists, like the Freudians, think a lot about sex. To understand the differences between males and females today, you must understand the problem of sex during the Pleistocene. The problem of sex for our caveman ancestors was different than for the cavewomen. Males and females evolved differently to solve their different problems related to reproduction. The differing sexual calculus produced the differences between men and women today.

You may believe that attraction and 'mate selection' is personal – an exercise of your free-will, personal preferences and tastes, and God's will for your life. But evolutionary naturalism explains mate selection differently. Mate selection is about finding a high value mate – one who is fit – who has good genes and a good chance of producing offspring and the resources and commitment to the offspring to raise them to maturity. We 'think' we 'want' certain characteristics in a husband or wife, but our choices are actually evolved 'mate selection strategies.' We evolved to recognize the best possible mate.

Females have a fixed number of eggs. Conceiving, carrying, and caring for a child requires significant maternal commitment. Our ancient female ancestors had limited opportunities to reproduce, so they had to be picky. Females evolved a preference for males who were protective, stable, dependable, and willing to help with the children.

Males, on the other hand, could father many children and not be involved with the offspring. But because the females were being picky, males had to compete with other males. They had to learn to act stable, dependable, and willing to help with the children. Males evolved to recognized and prefer females who had clear skin, full lips, clear eyes, and a certain body shape – signs of health and fertility. Some evolutionary psychologists suggest that sexual harassment, promiscuity, infidelity, and even rape evolved as 'short-term' mate selection strategies.

Evolutionary Psychology -- Jealousy
From an evolutionary perspective, the experience of jealousy is adaptive and is different for males and females. For our caveman ancestors, one of the worst things that could happen, was to invest his resources to protect and provide for kids who were not his genetic offspring. That was the problem. How could they be sure that their mates weren't messing around with other cavemen? The adaptive solution was jealousy – man style – controlling, suspicious, and violent.

One of the worst things that could have happened to our ancient female ancestors was for her mate to withdraw his support and protection and provide it for someone else. So, for cavewomen, the adaptive solution was jealousy – woman style -- focused on emotional, rather than sexual infidelity.

Our ancient ancestors couldn't help but notice when their neighbor had a better shelter or a mate with more signs of fertility. Humans evolved to be envious and proud.

Evolutionary Psychology –Difficult Questions
Some mental capacities, like sleep and dreams, our social nature, and mental illness, are said to provide both survival and reproductive advantages. Some, like altruism, homosexuality, and suicide, seem counter-intuitive and require an expanded definition of 'adaptive.'

Some mental powers can't be explained by survival and reproduction and present deep challenges to the theory of evolution. Consciousness, language, religion, love, and creativity are epiphenomena – byproducts of adaptations.

Evolutionary Psychology -- Sleep and Dreams
Sleep is puzzling to evolutionary psychologists because it is counter-intuitive. It does not make evolutionary sense for an animal to spend long periods of time in a vulnerable, unprotected, and non-alert state. Perhaps it evolved to protect our ancestors from predators. They were more likely to survive and reproduce if they slept while man-eaters were on the prowl. Dreams evolved as a way to safely rehearse strategies to elude man-eaters – a real survival advantage.

Evolutionary Psychology -- Socialization
As mentioned earlier, social psychology provides many examples of the ways humans behave badly and of ways we behave admirably. From an evolutionary perspective, human social interactions must have evolved to solve problems of living together in small groups of close relatives. The origins of social

interactions today are found in the simpler social interactions of our ancestors. There must be a continuum of social behaviors that extend continuously backwards. From an evolutionary perspective, our social behavior, attitudes, tendencies, biases, and prejudices each provided a survival and/or reproductive advantage.

Evolutionary Psychology -- Mental illness

Evolutionary psychology struggles to explain serious mental illnesses. People with schizophrenia and other serious mental illnesses reproduce at a lower rate and often die and younger ages. Why hasn't evolution selected against the genes for mental illness?

To overcome the paradox, evolutionary psychology suggests that perhaps what we call mental disorders, though detrimental today, might have once served an adaptive purpose. Or, perhaps mental illnesses are vestiges -- leftovers from an earlier stage of human evolution.

Evolutionary Psychology -- Theory of Inclusive Fitness

Evolutionary psychology takes a 'gene-centered' perspective. Think about it. From an evolutionary perspective, it is not about you, it is about your genes. 'You' are not important – your genes are. You are a vehicle for the survival and propagation of genes. Genes are selfish in that they make you do things that benefit your genes. But you share genes with your close relatives. If you reproduce, that is good. If your kin reproduce, that is good, too. If your actions lead to your kin reproducing, that is also good. Evolution designed our minds to facilitate the reproduction of genes, and it doesn't really matter if your genes get passed on by you or by your brother or sister or cousin. The theory of inclusive fitness says that some psychological adaptations served to increase the reproductive 'fitness' of your relatives. For example, the gay-uncle theory of homosexuality suggests that although gay uncles do not reproduce at high rates, they provide inclusive fitness by somehow facilitating more reproduction by their close relatives.

Evolutionary Psychology -- Altruism

Why did altruism evolve? Altruism seems to contradict the importance of survival. Why would any organism risk itself, its genes, to save another organism's genes? For offspring, maybe, but or not for strangers. But stories of heroic self-sacrifice are common, and they present a problem for EP. From an evolutionary perspective, survival of the fittest makes sense, altruism and helping strangers does not.

The answer is inclusive fitness. Helping behavior is determined by the extent one perceives a genetic similarity to the person in need of help. From the perspective of genes, it might make sense to risk your life to save another, based on a cold-blooded calculation that the genes in your kin will survive.

Evolutionary Psychology -- Suicide

Why would any organism intentionally take its own life? Evolutionary psychology suggests a depressing answer – a kind of inverse inclusive fitness. When we can no longer reproduce, when we can no longer contribute to inclusive fitness, when we become a burden to our kin, with no hope, we evolved to commit suicide.

Evolutionary Psychology -- Consciousness

The theory of evolution hinges on human consciousness, and it is in the context of consciousness that evolution seems most silly. Conscious self-awareness serves no clear survival or reproductive advantages. It seems more likely that evolution would have designed humans to be like zombies – soulless survivors. Consciousness, therefore must be a by-product of other adaptations.

Humans evolved large brains because our ancestors had to outwit and elude predators, use language, learn to use fire, and develop complex social structures. The smart ones, with the biggest brains, survived. At some point in the past, when the brain was sufficiently large, consciousness just happened. It was a byproduct of evolving really big brains.

Evolutionary Psychology -- The Unconscious Mind

Evolutionary psychology must account for the unconscious mind. Perhaps the unconscious mind evolved to help us deceive other. In the struggle to survive and reproduce, good liars had an advantage. To get the best mate, our ancestors stood up straight, sucked in their bellies, and put on makeup to look healthy and attractive. They lied. That was a problem, so they evolved lie detection skills. As liars got better at lying, our lie-detection skills improved, too. There was a type of lying / lie-detection arms race. What are the best lies? They're are the lies we believe. That's where the unconscious is useful. It is a part of the mind that evolved so that we can hide the truth from ourselves, so that we can deceive each other, so that we can have an honest shot at reproducing.

Evolutionary Psychology -- Language

The emergence of human language is said to have occurred through a series of small successive variations that produced the physical structures (e.g. the larynx and vocal chords) and a series of small successive variations that produced the packs of neurons that in turn, produced the mental processes required for language. In other words, human language is a more complicated version of the postures, gestures, and vocalizations of other primates.

Evolutionary Psychology -- Parental Love

Why do parents love their children? From an evolutionary perspective, love is just another mental capacity. It is an adaptation that provided our ancestors a survival advantage. The experience of love is simply the activation of the pleasure center brain – a way to make parents want to care for children. The subjective feeling of love is an illusion. It's all about the genes.

From an evolutionary perspective, adoption makes little sense. Adoption favors someone else's genes over one's own. Perhaps kin selection and inclusive fitness gone awry causes adoptive parents to feel love for children with unrelated genes – a kind of double illusion.

Evolutionary Psychology -- Religion

If evolutionary naturalism is true, it must account for religious beliefs. What survival and/or reproductive advantage did religious beliefs and experiences provide? One theory suggests that religious beliefs evolved as a social tool. The idea that an all-powerful being, an eye in the sky, unseen but watching, evolved to make our ancestors behave better. Watched cavemen are nice cavemen. The idea of god helped our ancestors cooperate and to not kill each other and steal each other's mates. Prayers and offerings and other religious rituals evolved to distinguish trustworthy true believers from the untrustworthy unbelievers.

Another theory suggests that religious beliefs are a byproduct of agency detection. Our Pleistocene ancestors needed to know as soon as possible when saber-toothed tigers were around. They evolved the ability to recognize agency – the capacity to wonder, when a twig breaks or the grass moves, 'what was the cause?' Was that a predator, enemy, or a friend? Religious beliefs are agency detection gone awry – creating supernatural explanations for things our ancestors hadn't yet evolved enough to understand.

Evolutionary Psychology – Alfred Russell Wallace

Have you heard of Alfred Russell Wallace? He is the most famous evolutionist that most people have never heard of. Everyone knows Charles Darwin, but Wallace is less well-know. Alfred Russell Wallace is the 'co-discoverer' of evolution by natural selection. Darwin published On the Origin of Species first. But Wallace was a close second with his work, On the Tendency of Varieties to Depart Independently from the Original Type. Wallace independently developed a theory of evolution.

Wallace's obscurity has less to do with being published second and more to do with his worldview. Wallace has been called 'Darwin's heretic' because of his ideas about the human mind. Wallace thought his theory could explain the diversity of life on earth but did not believe that it could explain Mankind. Wallace wasn't a Christian -- he was a spiritualist who dabbled in the occult. Wallace's heresy was his believing that that humans had a supernatural nature that evolution couldn't explain.

When students feel pressure to conform to a belief in evolution, they should remember Alfred Russell Wallace. They should remember that evolution hinges, not on geology and the fossil record, but on psychology. Evolution hinges on Darwin's dangerous idea -- the necessary acquirement of every mental power and capacity by gradation. If evolution fails to explain psychology, it fails as a grand theory.

Chapter 3 Study Guide

1. Most histories of psychology date its beginning to 1879 with _____ laboratory in Germany.

2. _____ is the worldview assumption that defines the difference between the old and new psychology.

3. Modern psychology traces its roots to the Reformation (16th century) and the rejection of _____ as the sole source of knowledge about God and the world.

4. Descartes believed that the soul interacted with the body in the _____.

5. Renee Descartes believed that we can use _____ to know things about the world with certainty.

6. _____ has been called the father of modern science.

7. Wilhelm Wundt, like many psychologists today, differentiated psychology from philosophy and religion by limiting their study to _____ phenomena.

8. About 400 B. C., the Greek doctor and philosopher _____ proposed an early theory of human personality types.

9. Hippocrates thought that personality types were determined by levels (balance) of body fluids called _____.

10. Around 1800, Dr. Franz Gall, popularized a "science" called _____.

11. In the first half of the 19th century, most psychologists studied _____, the measurement of sensations, perceptions, and motor responses.

12. Francis Crick, co-discoverer of DNA, proposed what he called _____.

13. _____ hypothesized that our mental life, consciousness, morality, decision-making, and judgment is the product of a material physical brain.

14. Psychologists like _____ explored the "structure" of mental processes.

15. Herman von Helmholtz was the first to measure the _____.

16. Wilhelm Wundt's interest was the structure of consciousness. His goal was to identify the components, or _____ in a type of periodic table of mental elements.

17. Wundt's used was _____, meaning looking inward to describe subjective mental experiences.

18. Franz Mesmer promoted mesmerism, now known as _____.

19. _____ suggests that human psychology and animal psychology differed only in degrees and not in essence.

20. Darwin's theory requires that psychology explain and interpret everything about us in terms of _____ passed down from one generation to the next according to natural selection.

21. _____ refers to the mechanics of a behavior or cognitive process – what happens and how?

22. _____ refers to the "why" of behavior and mental processes.

23. The ultimate cause of any behavior or mental process, in terms of evolutionary psychology, is always a _____.

24. Darwin's theory led to a new focus in psychology called _____.

25. _____ saw human behavior and mental processes as complex combinations of increasingly simple component behaviors and processes.

26. Herbert Spencer a famous evolutionist and contemporary of Charles Darwin, coined the phrase _____.

27. Williams James, known as the _____.

28. Many modern psychologists see in evolution a _____ theory and a reason for all behavior and mental processes.

29. For many, _____ is the "new" psychology.

30. Though evolutionary psychologists assert evolution as fact, it is nonetheless a _____ ultimately grounded in faith.

31. _____, also called psychobiology and neuro-anatomy, is the study of the nervous system's structures and processes.

32. Modern neuro-biology is _____, meaning that each mental structure and behavior consists of ever simpler component structures and behaviors.

33. A reductive perspective is behind descriptions of Man as _____. We are complicated but reducible to simpler underlying parts.

34. A _____ perspective explains all mental processes, including love, hope, prayer, and worship, as ultimately nothing more than electrical and biochemical processes occurring in a very advanced neural network.

35. _____ psychology was also known as psychology's Third Force.

36. _____ first described the heritability of physical characteristics.

37. The goal of _____ is to explain the natural laws of behavior.

38. As a worldview, _____ saw Mankind as nothing other than very complicated machines that react to stimuli or input in predictable ways.

39. According to B. F. Skinner, Ivan Pavlov, and John Watson, all human behavior is determined by the environment in a _____.

40. Radical behaviorism is a _____ worldview in which _____ is an illusion.

41. A Christian worldview balances God's _____ with human _____ and _____.

42. The Bible provides many examples of God's use of _____.

43. _____ emphasize the ways we acquire and process information and construct meaning from the world.

44. _____ describes a set of principles for living a fulfilled life.

45. _____ places human values, reason, free-will, meeting needs, and individual self-worth above all else.

46. Humanism presume that Mankind is the self-existent culmination of evolutionary development.

47. Humanist psychology claims that are _____.

48. Humanism presents a stark contrast to the Christian beliefs in original sin, depravity, and the need for _____.

49. _____ means achieving personal fulfillment and full potential.

50. A Christian worldview sees personal fulfillment and full potential in terms of the extent to which we have _____.

51. _____ focuses on the study of positive emotions, strengths, and virtues.

52. As a worldview, _____ believes that high self-esteem, personal fulfillment, self-expression, self-acceptance, and self-fulfillment are what it means to be human.

53. Some Christians equate high self-esteem with _____.

54. Some Christian integrate _____ into their theology by balancing our sinfulness with our special status in creation.

55. The Christian worldview sees _____ as glorifying God through obedient service.

56. Psychology's naturalistic foundation requires that abnormality be explained in terms of anything except _____.

57. _____ is a worldview in which standards of behavior are based on

some temporal framework of values and beliefs and not on any moral absolutes.

58. A Christian worldview recognizes that the Bible prescribes _____.

59. _____ grew out of the feminist movement of the late 1960s.

Chapter 3 Quiz

1) _____ is the worldview assumption that marks the difference between old and new psychology.
   a) Atheism
   b) Naturalism
   c) Marxism
   d) Humanism

2) Descartes' belief that we can use reason to know things about the world with certainty. Descartes believed that our physical senses were less trustworthy than reason. Descartes was a(n):
   a) rationalist
   b) philosopher
   c) empiricist
   d) naturalist

3) Descartes used _____ reasoning. It involves beginning from a premise or truth that is certain and deducing one conclusion from another.
   a) deductive
   b) inductive
   c) rational
   d) emotional

4) Descartes believed that the physical and spiritual connected at the _____, now known as the pineal gland.
   a) hippocampus
   b) conarium
   c) pituitary gland
   d) third eye

5) Descartes thought that sensations traveled from the body, via nerves, to the conarium, where animal spirits were released. The animal spirits traveled back to the body along nerves causing muscles to inflate. The cycle came to be known as:
   a) the reflex arc
   b) action potential
   c) voluntary behaviors
   d) involuntary behaviors.

6) Descartes, like people of faith through the ages, believed that Mankind consisted of both a material and non-material nature. Descartes was a(n):
   a) atheist
   b) dualist
   c) humanist
   d) monist

7) Francis Bacon's philosophy is called empiricism. It method is known as:
   a) inductive reasoning
   b) deductive reasoning
   c) rationalization
   d) logic

8) A rigid belief that only by controlled experimentation can one know things with certainty is known as:
   a) empiricism
   b) rationalism
   c) existentialism
   d) objectivism

9) Dr. Franz Gall popularized a "science" called _____ that suggested that the shape of the skull was an indicator of a person's character and personality.
   a) psychophysics
   b) psychology
   c) psychoanalysis
   d) phrenology

10) _____ was an early approach to psychology interested in describing mental experiences in terms of complex structures made from increasingly simpler component structures.
   a) Structuralism
   b) Phrenology
   c) Functionalism
   d) Gestalt

11) _____ gets the credit as the founder of scientific psychology with the establishment of a psychology laboratory at the University of Leipzig in Germany in 1879.
   a) Sigmund Freud
   b) Wilhelm Wundt
   c) William James
   d) Rene Descartes

12) The structuralists' goal was to identify the elements of mental experiences. Their method was:
   a) introspection
   b) phrenology
   c) psychoanalysis
   d) experimentation

13) _____ refers to the mechanics of a behavior or cognitive process – what happens and how?
   a) Ultimate cause
   b) Proximate cause
   c) Evolutionary psychology
   d) Structuralism

14) _____ refers to the "why" of behavior and mental processes.
   a) Proximate cause
   b) Ultimate cause
   c) General revelation
   d) Special revelation

15) _____ focused on discovering the survival and reproductive advantages behaviors and mental functions provided.
   a) Phrenologist
   b) Psychophysicists
   c) Functionalists
   d) Structuralists

16) _____, known as the father of American psychology, theorized that consciousness and emotions evolved as a complex mix of physical processes that equipped our ancestors for the challenges of survival.
   a) Sigmund Freud
   b) Wilhelm Wundt
   c) Rene Descartes
   d) Williams James

17) _____ means that mental structures and behaviors consist of ever simpler component structures and behaviors.
   a) Reductive
   b) Inductive
   c) Deductive
   d) Lucrative

18) _____ psychology, known as psychology's "Third Force," rejected the determinism in both psycho-analysis and behaviorism, in favor of an emphasis on human autonomy and potential.
   a) Humanistic
   b) Evolutionary
   c) Feminist
   d) Cognitive

19) _____ psychologists emphasize the ways we acquire and process information and construct meaning from the world.
   a) Cognitive
   b) Humanistic
   c) Behavioral
   d) Freudian

20) _____ is a philosophy that describes a set of principles for living a fulfilled life. It appeared in psychology around the 1970s when Skinnerian behaviorism and Freudian psycho-analysis were falling from favor.
   a) Humanism
   b) Self-psychology
   c) Atheism
   d) Feminism

21) _____ means achieving personal fulfillment and full potential.
   a) Self-actualization
   b) Potentiation
   c) The meaning of life
   d) Being a Christian

22) _____ is a worldview in which standards of behavior are based on some temporal framework of values and beliefs and not on any absolutes.
   a) Moral relativism
   b) Humanism
   c) Rationalism
   d) Atheism

23) Which approach to psychology emphasizes unconscious processes?
   a) Psychoanalytic approach
   b) Behavioral approach
   c) Cognitive approach
   d) Unconscious approach

Answer Key Chapter 3

Chapter 3 Study Guide (Answers)

1. Most histories of psychology date its beginning to 1879 with **Wilhelm Wundt's** laboratory in Germany.
2. **Naturalism** is the worldview assumption that defines the difference between the old and new psychology.
3. Modern psychology traces its roots to the Reformation (16th century) and the rejection of **authority** as the sole source of knowledge about God and the world.
4. Descartes believed that the soul interacted with the body in the **pineal gland**.
5. Renee Descartes believed that we can use **reason** to know things about the world with certainty.
6. **Francis Bacon** has been called the father of modern science.
7. Wilhelm Wundt, like many psychologists today, differentiated psychology from philosophy and religion by limiting their study to **observable and quantifiable** phenomena.
8. About 400 B. C., the Greek doctor and philosopher **Hippocrates** proposed an early theory of human personality types.
9. Hippocrates thought that personality types were determined by levels (balance) of body fluids called **humors**.
10. Around 1800, Dr. Franz Gall, popularized a "science" called **phrenology**.
11. In the first half of the 19th century, most psychologists studied **psychophysics**, the measurement of sensations, perceptions, and motor responses.
12. Francis Crick, co-discoverer of DNA, proposed what he called **The Astonishing Hypothesis**.
13. **Francis Crick** hypothesized that our mental life, consciousness, morality, decision-making, and judgment is the product of a material physical brain.
14. Psychologists like **Fechner, Herman von Helmholtz, Wilhelm Wundt, and Edward B. Titchener** explored the "structure" of mental processes.
15. Herman von Helmholtz was the first to measure the **speed of nerve impulses**.
16. Wilhelm Wundt's interest was the structure of consciousness. His goal was to identify the components, or **elements of mental experiences** in a type of periodic table of mental elements.
17. Wundt's used was **introspection**, meaning looking inward to describe subjective mental experiences.
18. Franz Mesmer promoted mesmerism, now known as **hypnosis**.
19. **Evolutionary psychology** suggests that human psychology and animal psychology differed only in degrees and not in essence.
20. Darwin's theory requires that psychology explain and interpret everything about us in terms of **adaptive traits** passed down from one generation to the next according to natural selection.
21. **Proximate Cause** refers to the mechanics of a behavior or cognitive process – what happens and how?
22. **Ultimate Cause** refers to the "why" of behavior and mental processes.
23. The ultimate cause of any behavior or mental process, in terms of evolutionary psychology, is always a **survival and reproductive advantage**.
24. Darwin's theory led to a new focus in psychology called **functionalism**.
25. **Functionalists** saw human behavior and mental processes as complex combinations of increasingly simple component behaviors and processes.
26. Herbert Spencer a famous evolutionist and contemporary of Charles Darwin, coined the phrase **survival of the fittest**.
27. Williams James, known as the **father of American psychology**.
28. Many modern psychologists see in evolution a **grand unifying psychological** theory and a reason for all behavior and mental processes.
29. For many, **evolutionary psychology** is the "new" psychology.
30. Though evolutionary psychologists assert evolution as fact, it is nonetheless a **worldview assumption** ultimately grounded in faith.
31. **Neuro-biology**, also called psychobiology and neuro-anatomy, is the study of the nervous system's structures and processes.
32. Modern neuro-biology is **reductive**, meaning that each mental structure and behavior consists of ever simpler component structures and behaviors.
33. A reductive perspective is behind descriptions of Man as **complex machines or computers**. We are complicated but reducible to simpler underlying parts.
34. A **reductive** perspective explains all mental processes, including love, hope, prayer, and worship, as ultimately nothing more than electrical and biochemical processes occurring in a very advanced neural network.
35. **Humanistic** psychology was also known as psychology's Third Force.
36. **Sir Francis Galton** first described the heritability of physical characteristics.

37. The goal of **behaviorism** is to explain the natural laws of behavior.
38. As a worldview, **behaviorism** saw Mankind as nothing other than very complicated machines that react to stimuli or input in predictable ways.
39. According to B. F. Skinner, Ivan Pavlov, and John Watson, all human behavior is determined by the environment in a **closed cause and effect system**.
40. Radical behaviorism is a **deterministic** worldview in which **free-will** is an illusion.
41. A Christian worldview balances God's **sovereignty** with human **freedom** and **responsibility**.
42. The Bible provides many examples of God's use of **rewards and punishments**.
43. **Cognitive psychologists** emphasize the ways we acquire and process information and construct meaning from the world.
44. **Humanism** describes a set of principles for living a fulfilled life
45. **Humanism** places human values, reason, free-will, meeting needs, and individual self-worth above all else.
46. **Humanism** presume that Mankind is the self-existent culmination of evolutionary development.
47. Humanist psychology claims that are **inherently good**.
48. Humanism presents a stark contrast to the Christian beliefs in original sin, depravity, and the need for **redemption, justification, and sanctification**.
49. **Self-actualization** means achieving personal fulfillment and full potential.
50. A Christian worldview sees personal fulfillment and full potential in terms of the extent to which we have **the mind of Christ**.
51. **Positive psychology** focuses on the study of positive emotions, strengths, and virtues.
52. As a worldview, **self-psychology** believes that high self-esteem, personal fulfillment, self-expression, self-acceptance, and self-fulfillment are what it means to be human.
53. Some Christians equate high self-esteem with **idolatrous pride**.
54. Some Christian integrate **self-esteem** into their theology by balancing our sinfulness with our special status in creation.
55. The Christian worldview sees **self-actualization** as glorifying God through obedient service.
56. Psychology's naturalistic foundation requires that abnormality be explained in terms of anything except **sin and disunity with God**.
57. **Moral relativism** is a worldview in which standards of behavior are based on some temporal framework of values and beliefs and not on any moral absolutes.
58. A Christian worldview recognizes that the Bible prescribes **moral absolutes**.
59. **Feminist psychology** grew out of the feminist movement of the late 1960s.

Chapter 3 Short Essay Questions (Answers)

1. Descartes concluded that we are made of body and soul, and that though distinct, the body and soul interact with one another. Descartes believed that the physical and spiritual connected at the conarium, now known as the pineal gland.
2. Early scientific psychologists worked during a time of major worldview shifts. Naturalism sought to exclude God, creation, and the Bible from all sciences, A naturalistic worldview leads to the conclusion that if the mind exists, it evolved within the structures of the brain and it is in no way "special." Naturalism, the worldview, means that all mental activity (including love, hope, prayer, worship, etc.) MUST ultimately be nothing more than biochemical processes.
3. Rationalism was a new way of knowing. Descartes believed that we can use "reason" to know things about the world with certainty.
4. The difficulties applying empirical methods to psychological research (e.g., inability to control variables, bias, placebo effects) have even led many to argue that psychology does not fit the definition of a true empirical science. A psychology that leaves out intangibles like the mind, love, and faith is seen as sterile and trivial. Strict empiricism only allows psychologists to study our creatureliness, it makes no meaningful contribution to what it means to be human, and it relegates Christian beliefs to a topic of study, along with mysticism, rituals, and other primitive belief systems.
5. Mainstream science rejected phrenology as fakery. Phrenology was right, however, in its basic belief that the brain is involved in mental activity and that many mental functions are localized in specific parts of the brain. In that sense, phrenology was an important step toward modern day neuro-biology.
6. The Christian and Freudian worldviews could hardly differ more and criticisms of his theories by Christians are not surprising. Freud presumed that God did not exist. Despite his Jewish heritage, Freud was an atheist who made it clear that his theories were an alternative to theistic beliefs. Freud believed that Mankind invented gods and religions as ways to cope with psychic fears. Freud's was a deterministic worldview that emphasized sex and aggression as the prime motivations for human behavior and personality development. Freud believed Mankind is tripartite in nature (id, ego, and superego) and that we are not consciously aware of most of the influences on our thoughts, feelings, and behavior. According to Freud, our consciousness is like the tip of an iceberg. The bulk of who we are is below the surface and unconscious, meaning we cannot bring it to conscious awareness except by psycho-analytic techniques.
7. As a worldview, behaviorism radically redefined what it meant to be human. As a worldview, behaviorism saw Mankind as nothing other than very complicated machines that react to stimuli or input in predictable ways. According to B. F. Skinner,

Ivan Pavlov, and John Watson, each a "radical behaviorist," all human behavior is determined by the environment in a closed cause and effect system. Radical behaviorism is a deterministic worldview; free-will is an illusion.

8. Humanism specifically rejects God and relies on reason and science to define morality. Humanism promises to help people live happy and fulfilled lives. Secular humanism presumes not only that God does not exist, but that Mankind is the self-existent culmination of evolutionary development. Humanist psychology claims that people in their "natural state" are inherently good and that in accepting and nonjudgmental environments we can recover that original goodness through a process of "self-actualization." Humanism presents a stark contrast to the Christian beliefs in original sin, depravity, and the need for redemption, justification, and sanctification.

Chapter 3 Quiz Answers

1. _____ is the worldview assumption that marks the difference between old and new psychology. b) Naturalism

2. Descartes' belief that we can use reason to know things about the world with certainty. Descartes believed that our physical senses were less trustworthy than reason. Descartes was a(n)   a) rationalist

3. Descartes used _____ reasoning. It involves beginning from a premise or truth that is certain and deducing one conclusion from another. a) deductive

4. Descartes believed that the physical and spiritual connected at the _____, now known as the pineal gland. b) conarium

5. Descartes thought that sensations traveled from the body, via nerves, to the conarium, where animal spirits were released. The animal spirits traveled back to the body along nerves causing muscles to inflate. The cycle came to be known as: a) the reflex arc

6. Descartes, like people of faith through the ages, believed that Mankind consisted of both a material and non-material nature. Descartes was a(n): b) dualist

7. Francis Bacon's philosophy is called empiricism. It method is known as: a) inductive reasoning

8. A rigid belief that only by controlled experimentation can one know things with certainty is known as: a) empiricism

9. Dr. Franz Gall popularized a "science" called _____ that suggested that the shape of the skull was an indicator of a person's character and personality. d) phrenology

10. _____ was an early approach to psychology interested in describing mental experiences in terms of complex structures made from increasingly simpler component structures. a) Structuralism

11. _____ gets the credit as the founder of scientific psychology with the establishment of a psychology laboratory at the University of Leipzig in Germany in 1879. b) Wilhelm Wundt

12. The structuralists' goal was to identify the elements of mental experiences. Their method was: a) introspection

13. _____ refers to the mechanics of a behavior or cognitive process – what happens and how? b) Proximate cause

14. _____ refers to the "why" of behavior and mental processes. b) Ultimate cause

15. _____ focused on discovering the survival and reproductive advantages behaviors and mental functions provided. c) Functionalists

16. _____, known as the father of American psychology, theorized that consciousness and emotions evolved as a complex mix of physical processes that equipped our ancestors for the challenges of survival. d) Williams James

17. _____ means that mental structures and behaviors consist of ever simpler component structures and behaviors. a) Reductive

18. _____ psychology, known as psychology's "Third Force," rejected the determinism in both psycho-analysis and behaviorism, in favor of an emphasis on human autonomy and potential. a) Humanistic

19. _____ psychologists emphasize the ways we acquire and process information and construct meaning from the world.   a) Cognitive

20. _____ is a philosophy that describes a set of principles for living a fulfilled life. It appeared in psychology around the 1970s when Skinnerian behaviorism and Freudian psycho-analysis were falling from favor. a) Humanism

21. _____ means achieving personal fulfillment and full potential.   a) Self-actualization

22. _____ is a worldview in which standards of behavior are based on some temporal framework of values and beliefs and not on any absolutes.   a) Moral relativism

23. Which approach to psychology emphasizes unconscious processes?   a) Psychoanalytic approach

Chapter 4 Brain and Nervous System

Chapter 4 Learning Objectives

Describe the structure and function of the neuron
Recognize that specific functions are centered in specific lobes of the cerebral cortex
Describe the organization of the nervous system
Describe the function of the CNS, PNS, and the sympathetic and parasympathetic systems
Describe techniques for studying the brain
Describe the function of the endocrine system and how the endocrine glands are linked to the nervous system
Classify the major divisions and subdivisions of the nervous system
Differentiate the functions of the various subdivisions of the nervous system
Identify the structure and function of the major regions of the brain
Describe lateralization of brain functions
Describe the divisions of the brain
Identify and describe the cerebrum, cerebellum, and medulla
Describe how brain injury contributed to our understanding of brain function
Describe how brain stimulation studies contributed to our understanding of brain function
Describe how imaging contributes to our understanding of brain function
Describe lobotomy

Key Concepts and People

Neuro-psychology
Nervous system
Central nervous system
Peripheral nervous system
Somatic division
Autonomic division
Sympathetic nervous system
Parasympathetic nervous system
Sensory neurons
Motor neurons
Interneurons

Neurotransmission
Peter Milne
James Olds
Walter Penfield
Phrenology
Blood-brain barrier
Localization of functioning
Phineas P. Gage
Galen
Franz Gall
Cortical mapping
Cerebral cortex

Thalamus
Hypothalamus
Amygdala
Hippocampus
Bi-lateral symmetry
Hemispheric specialization
Brain lateralization
Brain plasticity
Brain imaging
Endocrine system
Limbic system
Neurotransmitters

Short essay questions

1. Respond to the following statement from a Christian worldview perspective. "All mental experience is nothing more than brain activity."
2. Describe important historical discoveries about the structure and function of the brain.
3. Describe "the god spot" from a naturalistic perspective and from a Christian perspective.

For Further Study

1. Read: The Human Nervous System: Evidence of Intelligent Design [Part I]
   http://www.apologeticspress.org/apcontent.aspx?category=12&article=1581 by Brad Harrub, Ph.D at Apologetics Press
2. Read: The Human Nervous System: Evidence of Intelligent Design [Part II]
   http://www.apologeticspress.org/apcontent.aspx?category=12&article=1697 by Brad Harrub, Ph.D. at Apologetics Press

3. Read: Mind Life http://www.asa3.org/ASA/PSCF/2001/PSCF6-01Glanzer.html by P. David Glanzer at The American Scientific Affiliation
4. Web: Disorder Index http://www.ninds.nih.gov/disorders/disorder_index.htm National Institute of Neurological Disorders and Stroke.
5. Video: The Lobotomist http://www.pbs.org/wgbh/americanexperience/films/lobotomist/ American Experience on PBS.
6. Web: The Divisions of the Nervous System Neuroscience for Kids, Eric H. Chulder, PhD. http://faculty.washington.edu/chudler/nsdivide.html
7. Web: Neuroscience for Kids Eric H. Chulder, PhD. http://faculty.washington.edu/chudler/introb.html
8. Web: The Wada Test https://www.epilepsy.com/learn/treating-seizures-and-epilepsy/surgery/pre-surgery-tests/wada-test at Epilepsy.com.
9. Read: The Split-Brain Experiments at Nobel.org. http://nobelprize.org/educational_games/medicine/split-brain/background.html
10. Web: Neuroscience Online http://nba.uth.tmc.edu/neuroscience/ An electronic textbook for the neurosciences. University of Texas.
11. Video: Kim Gorgens: Protecting the brain against concussion, at TED. http://www.ted.com/talks/kim_gorgens_protecting_the_brain_against_concussion.html
12. Read: Damaged, by Malcolm Gladwell, from The New Yorker. https://www.newyorker.com/magazine/1997/02/24/damaged What are the article's implication for understanding free will and moral responsibility?
13. Read: Is God and Accident? By Dr. Paul Bloom from The Atlantic. http://www.theatlantic.com/magazine/archive/2005/12/is-god-an-accident/4425/
14. Read about brain activity in frozen Artic Salmon – a critique of neuromania. http://www.npr.org/2012/09/22/161604476/study-on-dead-fishs-thoughts-snags-ig-nobel-prize

Topics for Discussion

1. Respond to this statement; "though experiencing God may correlate with brain activity, it does not disprove or diminish the experience."
2. Why do you think that Phineas Gage's accident was such an important event in the history of psychology?

Chapter 4 Worldview Issues

A Dangerous Idea and The Astonishing Hypothesis

Students taking psychology today do so at a time predicted by Charles Darwin in the closing pages of On the Origin of Species. In what has been called his "Dangerous Idea," Darwin wrote: "In the distant future I see open fields for far more important researches. Psychology will be based on a new foundation, that of the necessary acquirement of each mental power and capacity by gradation. Light will be thrown on the origin of man and his history."

That day has come. Evolutionary psychology is called 'The New Psychology.' Evolutionary psychology presumes that every mental power and capacity, even those we think of as uniquely human, special, or God-like, were acquired, bit by bit, over a very long time, through variation and natural selection.

When Darwin wrote, 'every mental power and capacity' he meant everything – every topic in every psychology book. He meant your motivation, your emotions, your joys and sorrows – he meant your memories and ambitions, sense of self and free will, consciousness, morality, your capacity to make decisions, judgments, and plan. Darwin was predicting that evolution would someday explain obedience, empathy, altruism, prejudice, love, and hate. Evolution alone would account for art and music, greed, religious beliefs, dreams, language and song, and everything else that makes us human.

Darwin also wrote "the necessary acquirement." He understood that if his theory was true, it had to be true for humans, too. It had to be true of human psychology, too. If his theory failed to explain the fullness of human psychology, it would fail completely.

Darwin didn't know much about the brain and the nervous system or about genetics. But Dr. Crick did when he made his astonishing hypothesis – "You are nothing but a pack of neurons.'"

Taken together, The Astonishing Hypothesis and Darwin's prediction are bold worldview claims. They represent evolutionary naturalism applied to psychology and taken to its logical conclusions. The most complex structure in the known universe, the human brain, must have evolved by numerous and successive slight modifications – adaptations that provided survival and reproductive advantages. The fullness of our mental lives is just neurons in the brain.

A Christian approach to neuroscience begins with a sense of awe and wonder. The human brain and nervous system is at the center of the most complex and coordinated communication network in the universe. There are billions of neurons communicating via complex chemical and electrical processes in perfect synchronization. We have conscious control over the voluntary nervous system and an involuntary system that regulates itself. The brain, weighing in at about two pounds, is at the center of both. Every aspect of life involves the brain. Every mental power and capacity, every breath we take, our organs and glands, and every beat of our hearts involves the nervous system. The brain has plasticity – the capacity to 're-wire' itself in response to damage or changing conditions. The complexity and precision of the nervous system is a staggering wonder that points unmistakably toward God. It is God's grandest creation.

The history of neuroscience is rich with important discoveries, but underneath each new discovery there is an old worldview struggle between theism and naturalism. The old theory of phrenology illustrates that struggle. Students in every psychology class learn about phrenology. The phrenologists were wrong about almost everything, but their naturalistic worldview is evident today. In the early 1800s, before the establishment of Wundt's laboratory, phrenology was psychology. Phrenologist studied the brain and its relationship to mental life. The phrenologists believed that mental powers and capacities were located in mental 'organs' and that the skull mirrored the shape and size of those organs. Phrenologists believed that they could pinpoint, or localize, the parts of the brain responsible for qualities like reverence, individuality, and hope.

Christians in the early 1800s struggled with phrenology. It was controversial. Many Christians condemned phrenology as heretical for claiming that any characteristics of the 'mind'-- the part of humans created in the image of God, should have a seat in brain matter. The 'science' of the day was saying that what had been thought of as part of our immaterial nature was not – the problem of dualism, 19th century version.

Neuro-mania and the god spot
Today, brain imaging techniques allow neuroscientists to 'see' the living brain at work. Technology allows neuroscientists to examine individual neurons and collections of neurons

across the brain. At the worldview level, there isn't a meaningful difference between 'packs of neurons' and the phrenologist's brain organs.

Students will feel pressure to join in neuro-mania. Neuro-mania refers to a belief that today, we are at the brink of being able to explain every mental power and capacity in terms of brain activity. Neuro-maniacs presume that Dr. Crick's hypothesis is true – we ARE our brains. With better technology and a little more time, neuroscientists will map each of the billions of neural connections, second by second, and 'see' consciousness, reason, love, and even the experience of God. Neuro-mania is like phrenology on steroids.

From this perspective, belief in God must be the operation of a pack of neurons. Because believing in gods is common across peoples and throughout history, it must be 'hard-wired' in our brains. There must be a 'god spot' somewhere in the brain. A part of the left temporal lobe was thought hold the god spot after the it was discovered that people with temporal-lobe epilepsy were prone to religious hallucinations.

It has been suggested that the god spot is in the frontal cortex and that the god spot is not a spot, but a network of spots spread across the brain. Students will be asked to conform to a belief that God is merely a product of brain activity.

Christians interested in psychology today, like those in the 1800s, must wrestle with the problem of dualism – the 21st century version. We should boldly use science to seek greater understanding while humbly accepting that God's ways are greater than our understanding. We must be confident that if God chooses to operate through brain processes, it does not diminish Him or us.

Study Guide Chapter 4

1. The study of the brain and the nervous system is called _____, _____, and _____.

2. The _____ is the most complex structure in the known universe and a wonder of God's creation.

3. All activities of the mind, _____, involve the brain.

4. Many psychologists believe that all activities of the mind are nothing more than _____.

5. _____, the worldview, means that all mental activity (including love, hope, prayer, worship, etc.) must ultimately be nothing more than biochemical processes.

6. The near-infinite complexity of the brain represents the single biggest _____ necessary to hold an evolutionary worldview.

7. We must be confident that if God chooses to operate through brain processes, it does not _____.

8. The human nervous system consists of two sub-systems: the _____ and _____.

9. The central nervous system consists of the _____ and the _____.

10. The _____ consists of those nerves outside of the brain and the spinal cord.

11. The peripheral nervous system is divided into two main divisions called the _____ divisions in a network of nerves traveling throughout the entire body.

12. The _____ is the most basic building block of the nervous system.

13. Neurons differ from other cells in that they communicate with each other via specialized extensions called _____.

14. The _____ extends from the cell body much like the branches of a tree.

15. The axon has appendages called _____ or _____.

16. There are three types of neurons: _____.

17. At rest, a neuron has a slightly _____.

18. The neuron's membrane is selectively _____ with channels that open and close allowing positively charged ions to pass through.

19. _____carry signals from the brain and spinal cord to the muscles and glands. Sensory and motor neurons are present throughout our bodies.

20. _____, the third type of neuron, exist exclusively in the brain and spinal cord and make up about 90% of all human neurons.

21. _____ make the connection between sensory and motor neurons and are involved in all mental activity.

22. _____, though technically not neurons, support neural functioning by digesting dead neurons, producing the myelin sheathing, and providing nutrition to neurons.

23. The process by which neurons communicate is known as _____.

24. Neurotransmission is an electro-chemical process that occurs _____

_____.

25. Within the neuron, neurotransmission describes the movement of an _____.

26. _____, neurotransmission describes the process of one neuron sending chemical signals to other neurons across the synaptic cleft, or the gap between neurons.

27. When a neuron is sufficiently excited, it sends an electrical impulse known as the

_____.

28. The axon is covered in a fatty _____that insulates the axon and enables signals to move more quickly.

29. The recovery time after firing is called the _____.

30. When the electrical impulse reaches the axon, appendages called terminal buttons release chemical signals called _____ to other nearby neurons.

31. Neurons do not communicate directly. The chemical signal must cross the _____, the gap between the axon of one neuron and the dendrite of another.

32. Neurotransmitters are either _____ or _____.

33. _____ means that the chemical signal increases the likelihood that neighboring neurons will fire.

34. _____ means the signal lowers the likelihood that other neurons will fire.

35. The PNS controls _____ of the body.

36. The peripheral system is made up of three subsystems: _____, _____, and

_____.

37. The somatic nervous system controls _____.

38. The _____makes the connection between the motor cortex of the brain and the skeletal muscles used in movement.

39. The autonomic or involuntary nervous system controls _____.

40. The autonomic nervous system is further subdivided into the _____.

41. The _____is a network of nerve fibers in the stomach, intestines, pancreas, and gall bladder controlling the digestive process.

42. The sympathetic and parasympathetic systems _____.

43. The _____creates an excited state and mobilizes the body for action by accelerating some functions and decelerating others.

44. The _____restores the body to a state of rest and relaxation.

45. Ancient peoples performed _____; surgically opening the skull to expose the brain, perhaps to release evil spirits causing mental disorders.

46. The part of the brain responsible for speech production is known as _____.

47. _____ operate at the level of neurotransmitters.

48. The phrase _____refers to a belief that mental health problems are due to imbalances in neurotransmitter levels.

49. Psychotropic medications affect the supply of _____ or the way in which _____.

50. _____ make more of a neurotransmitter available in the synapse.

51. _____ decrease the amount of a neurotransmitter or block it from delivering its signal.

52. An aphasia in _____results in impairments in understanding written and spoken language.

53. _____means that different parts of the brain carry out different functions.

54. The _____ shows the areas of the brain that control movement of specific body parts.

55. The _____ is involved in the experience of fear.

56. The case of Phineas Gage suggested a connection between _____ and the brain.

57. Egas Moniz developed of a type of psycho-surgery known as _____.

58. _____ is involved in movement and the experience of pleasure. Dopamine plays a role in the addictiveness of drugs like cocaine.

59. Dopamine levels are associated with the shakiness of patients with _____ _____.

60. _____ affects sleep and mood. Medications like Prozac, Zoloft, and Paxil increase the availability of serotonin.

61. _____records electrical voltage produced when neurons fire.

62. The Electroencephalograph (EEG) shows _____.

63. _____involves rotating an x-ray machine around the brain to produce a series of images.

64. Computer axial tomography CT scans show _____.

65. _____ produce real-time three-dimensional images of the brain at work.

66. Positron Emission Tomography (PET scan) show both

_____.

67. _____ uses powerful magnetic fields and radio waves to create detailed images of the brain.

68. Magnetic Resonance Imaging (MRI) show _____.

69. _____ uses the magnetic properties of blood to produce pinpoint images of blood flow as it is occurring.

70. The brain is shielded by the _____, cushioned and nourished in

_____, and protected from toxins by the _____.

71. The _____is a separation that protects the brain by allowing glucose from the blood to enter the brain, and by keeping out other substances and some toxins.

72. The _____connects the brain with the body and transmits signals from the brain to the body and back again.

73. The brain consists of three major divisions – the

_____.

74. The _____ is the largest part of the brain making up about two-thirds of the brain's size.

75. The forebrain includes the _____.

76. The outer layer of the forebrain, just under the skull and forehead is the _____.

77. The _____contains the majority of the brain's neurons.

78. A deep fissure called the _____splits the cerebral cortex down the middle into the left and right hemispheres.

79. The cerebral cortex has _____, meaning that each hemisphere is a mirror image of the other.

80. The left and right hemispheres are connected by a dense bundle of nerve fibers called the

_____.

81. The _____allows the two halves of the brain to communicate.

82. _____ refers to the different roles each hemisphere plays in mental life.

83. Each hemisphere is further divided into _____ named for the parts of the skull under which they are located.

84. The _____ plays an important role in sensory processing and movement, serving as a type of relay station by receiving sensory information from the senses and sending it to the cerebral cortex.

85. The _____, a small structure resting under the thalamus, plays a major role in the autonomic nervous system, the experience of pleasure, and in control of body temperature, hunger, and thirst.

86. The _____ is an almond shaped structure located deep in the temporal lobe and plays a role in fear and other emotions, learning, memory, attention, and perception.

87. The _____ is a seahorse-shaped structure in the temporal lobe involved in processing memories, emotion, and spatial navigation.

88. The _____ sits under the cerebral cortex at the base of the skull and the top of the spinal cord and is comprised of the cerebellum, pons, and medulla.

89. The _____ is the second largest structure in the brain and is associated with movement, co-ordination, balance, and motor-related memory.

90. The _____ is a mesh-like network of neurons involved in sleep and consciousness, arousal and attention, coordinating signals from the senses, and pain modulation.

91. The _____ (Latin for "bridge") serves in coordinating communication between the two cerebral hemispheres and between parts of the brain and the spinal cord.

92. The _____, is located at the top of the spinal cord and is associated with breathing, temperature regulation, and some aspects of speech.

93. The _____ is a small area of the brain (approximately 2 cm long) that sits between the forebrain and the hindbrain.

94. The midbrain is comprised of the _____.

95. The tectum is involved in processing _____.

96. The _____ is a network of neurons involved in reflexes, involuntary body functions, and attention.

97. The _____ are large fiber bundles of neurons that connect the midbrain and the cerebellum.

98. The _____ is a collection of glands that secrete hormones into the blood stream.

99. The pineal gland produces _____ which helps regulate the sleep cycle.

100. _____ are types of chemical messengers that work with the nervous system to control growth and development, mood, metabolism, and reproduction.

Chapter 4 Quiz

1) The study of the brain and the nervous system is called:
   a) neuro-psychology
   b) neuro-anatomy
   c) neuro-biology
   d) all of the above

2) At rest, a neuron has a:
   a) slightly negative electrical charge
   b) neutral electrical charge
   c) slightly positive electrical charge

3) Neurons differ from other cells in that they communicate with each other via specialized extensions called:
   a) dendrites and axons
   b) synapses
   c) myelin sheaths
   d) terminal buttons

4) The axon is a long, very thin tube leading away from the cell body. The axon has appendages called:
   a) dendrites and axons
   b) neurons
   c) axon terminals

5) The cell body contains the nucleus, which in turn contains _____, which provide the neuron's energy.
   a) mitochondria
   b) dendrites
   c) terminal buttons

6) _____ neurons carry signals from the brain and spinal cord to the muscles and glands.
   a) Efferent
   b) Sensory
   c) Inhibitory
   d) Afferent

7) _____ carry signals from the sense receptors in the body to the brain.
   a) Afferent neurons
   b) Motor neurons
   c) Interneurons
   d) Cranial neurons

8) _____ exist exclusively in the brain and spinal cord and make up about 90% of all human neurons.
   a) Sensory neurons
   b) Motor neurons
   c) Interneurons
   d) Glia cells

9) _____ is an electro-chemical process that occurs within and between neurons.
   a) Neurotransmission
   b) Refractory period
   c) Action potential
   d) Transduction

10) Neurotransmitters are either excitatory or inhibitory. _____ means that the chemical signal increases the likelihood that neighboring neurons will fire.
    a) excitatory
    b) inhibitory

11) Neurotransmitters are either excitatory or inhibitory. _____ means the signal lowers the likelihood that other neurons will fire.
    a) excitatory
    b) inhibitory

12) The _____ consists of the neurons running throughout the body outside of the brain and the spinal cord.
    a) peripheral nervous system
    b) central nervous system
    c) somatic nervous system
    d) autonomic nervous system

13) The _____ nervous system controls body functions like circulation, respiration, perspiration, and digestion.
    a) Autonomic
    b) Voluntary
    c) Central
    d) Peripheral

14) _____ was an early attempt to localize psychological traits and characteristics in specific brain areas.
    a) Phrenology
    b) Behaviorism
    c) Psychotherapy
    d) None of the above

15) In 1848 Phineas Gage's accident demonstrated that there is a connection between the brain and _____.
   a) Intelligence
   b) Memory
   c) Personality
   d) Visual hallucinations

16) In 1861 Paul Broca discovered the connection between an area of the brain (which bears his name today) and speech _____.
   a) Production
   b) Reception
   c) Understanding
   d) All of the above

17) _____ refers to the localization of some brain activity in the right or left hemisphere.
   a) Brain lateralization
   b) Localization of function
   c) Corpus Callosum
   d) None of the above

18) The near-infinite complexity of the brain is one of the biggest leaps of faith necessary to hold an evolutionary worldview.
   a) True
   b) False

19) Psychotropic medications affect the supply of _____ or the way in which they are absorbed.
   a) Neurons
   b) Endorphins
   c) Neurotransmitters
   d) None of the above

20) The central nervous system consists of the brain and the:
   a) sensory neurons
   b) spinal cord
   c) cranial nerves
   d) peripheral nervous system

21) The _____ is the most basic building block of the nervous system.
   a) neuron
   b) brain
   c) spinal cord
   d) neurotransmitters

22) The _____ extends from the cell body much like the branches of a tree.
   a) synapse
   b) dendrite
   c) myelin sheath
   d) mitochondria

23) The axon has appendages called _____.
   a) the cell body
   b) the synaptic cleft
   c) axon terminals
   d) arms and legs

24) _____ support neural functioning by digesting dead neurons, producing the myelin sheathing, and providing nutrition to neurons.
   a) Interneurons
   b) Neurotransmitters
   c) Glial cells
   d) The myelin sheaths

25) The axon is covered in _____ that insulates the axon and enables signals to move more quickly.
   a) nodes of Ranvier
   b) a myelin sheath
   c) a neurotransmitter
   d) a semi-permeable membrane

26) Neurons do not communicate directly. The chemical signal must cross the _____, the gap between the axon of one neuron and the dendrite of another.
   a) nodes of Ranvier
   b) synaptic cleft
   c) cell membrane
   d) soma

27) The _____ controls voluntary muscle movement and makes the connection between the motor cortex of the brain and the skeletal muscles used in movement.
   a) enteric nervous system
   b) parasympathetic nervous system
   c) somatic nervous system
   d) autonomic nervous system

28) The autonomic nervous system controls:
   a) voluntary body functions
   b) higher cognitive functions
   c) unconscious mental activity
   d) involuntary body functions

29) The _____ is further subdivided into the sympathetic and parasympathetic nervous systems.
a) autonomic nervous system
b) voluntary nervous system
c) enteric nervous system
d) vestibular nervous system

30) The _____is a network of nerve fibers in the stomach, intestines, pancreas, and gall bladder controlling the digestive process.
a) enteric nervous system
b) peripheral nervous system
c) parasympathetic system
d) sympathetic system

31) The _____creates an excited state and mobilizes the body for action by accelerating some functions and decelerating others.
a) parasympathetic system
b) sympathetic system
c) limbic system
d) endocrine system

32) The _____restores the body to a state of rest and relaxation.
a) parasympathetic system
b) sympathetic system
c) limbic system
d) endocrine system

33) _____is involved in movement and the experience of pleasure. It also plays a role in the addictiveness of drugs like cocaine.
a) Serotonin
b) Dopamine
c) melatonin
d) opium

34) _____affects sleep and mood and is the active ingredient in medications like Prozac, Zoloft, and Paxil.
a) serotonin
b) melatonin
c) dopamine
d) GABA

35) The Electroencephalograph (EEG) records electrical voltage produced when neurons fire. It shows:
a) both brain structure and activity
b) brain activity but not brain structure
c) brain structure but not brain activity
d) none of the above

36) Computer axial tomography (CT scan) involves rotating an x-ray machine around the brain to produce a series of images. It shows:
a) brain structure but not brain activity
b) brain activity but not brain structure
c) both brain structure and activity
d) none of the above

37) Positron Emission Tomography (PET scan) produce real-time three-dimensional images of the brain at work. It shows:
a) brain structure but not brain activity
b) brain activity but not brain structure
c) both brain structure and activity
d) none of the above

38) Magnetic Resonance Imaging (MRI) uses powerful magnetic fields and radio waves to create detailed images of the brain. It shows:
a) both brain structure and brain activity
b) brain structure but not brain activity
c) brain activity but not brain structure
d) none of the above

39) The brain is shielded by the skull, cushioned and nourished in cerebrospinal fluid, and protected from toxins by the _____.
a) myelin sheath
b) blood-brain barrier
c) cell membrane
d) dendrites

40) The _____is the largest part of the brain making up about two-thirds of the brain's size.
a) midbrain
b) forebrain
c) hindbrain
d) cerebellum

41) The _____includes the cerebral cortex, thalamus, hypothalamus, amygdala, and hippocampus.
a) forebrain
b) midbrain
c) hindbrain
d) brain stem

42) The outer layer of the forebrain, just under the skull and forehead is the

_____.
a) cerebral cortex
b) cerebellum
c) temporal lobe
d) occipital lobe

43) A deep fissure called the

_____ splits the cerebral cortex down the middle into the left and right hemispheres.
a) longitudinal sulcus
b) reticular formation
c) corpus callosum
d) pons

44) The left and right hemispheres are connected by a dense bundle of nerve fibers called the _____.
a) reticular formation
b) corpus callosum
c) longitudinal sulcus
d) brain stem

45) The _____ plays an important role in sensory processing and movement, serving as a type of relay station by receiving sensory information from the senses and sending it to the cerebral cortex.
a) thalamus
b) amygdala
c) pons
d) hippocampus

46) The _____, a small structure resting under the thalamus, plays a major role in the autonomic nervous system, the experience of pleasure, and in control of body temperature, hunger, and thirst.
a) hypothalamus
b) amygdala
c) pons
d) hippocampus

47) The _____ is an almond shaped structure located deep in the temporal lobe and plays a role in fear and other emotions, learning, memory, attention, and perception.
a) amygdala
b) pons
c) hippocampus
d) hypothalamus

48) The _____ is a seahorse-shaped structure in the temporal lobe involved in processing memories, emotion, and spatial navigation.
a) pons
b) hippocampus
c) hypothalamus
d) thalamus

49) The _____ sits under the cerebral cortex at the base of the skull and the top of the spinal cord and is comprised of the cerebellum, pons, and medulla,
a) hindbrain
b) cerebral cortex
c) midbrain
d) forebrain

50) The _____ is the second largest structure in the brain and is associated with movement, co-ordination, balance, and motor-related memory.
a) cerebellum
b) forebrain
c) medulla oblongata
d) brain stem

51) The _____ is a mesh-like network of neurons involved in sleep and consciousness, arousal and attention, coordinating signals from the senses, and pain modulation.
a) pons
b) reticular formation
c) peduncles
d) brain stem

52) The _____ (Latin for "bridge") serves in coordinating communication between the two cerebral hemispheres and between of the brain and the spinal cord.
a) medulla oblongata
b) pons
c) reticular formation
d) corpus callosum

53) The _____ is located at the top of the spinal cord and is associated with breathing, temperature regulation, and some aspects of speech.
   a) medulla
   b) cerebral cortex
   c) cerebellum
   d) occipital lobe

54) The _____ is comprised of the tectum, tegmentum, and cerebral peduncles.
   a) midbrain
   b) hindbrain
   c) forebrain
   d) brain stem

55) The _____ is a collection of glands that secrete hormones into the blood stream.
   a) limbic system
   b) endocrine system
   c) circulatory system
   d) digestive system

56) The thalamus, hypothalamus, amygdala, and hippocampus make up the _____ which plays an important role in our sense of smell and in memory and emotions.
   a) olfactory system
   b) limbic system
   c) endocrine system
   d) nervous system

Chapter 4 Study Guide (Answers)

1. The study of the brain and the nervous system is called **neuro-psychology, neuro-anatomy,** and **neuro-biology.**
2. The **human nervous system** is the most complex structure in the known universe and a wonder of God's creation.
3. All activities of the mind, **including our experience of God,** involve the brain.
4. Many psychologists believe that all activities of the mind are nothing more than **brain activity.**
5. **Naturalism,** the worldview, means that all mental activity (including love, hope, prayer, worship, etc.) must ultimately be nothing more than biochemical processes.
6. The near-infinite complexity of the brain represents the single biggest **leap of faith** necessary to hold an evolutionary worldview.
7. We must be confident that if God chooses to operate through brain processes, it does not **diminish Him or us.**
8. The human nervous system consists of two sub-systems: the **central nervous system (CNS)** and the **peripheral nervous system (PNS).**
9. The central nervous system consists of the **brain** and the **spinal cord.**
10. The **peripheral nervous system** consists of those nerves outside of the brain and the spinal cord.
11. The peripheral nervous system is divided into two main divisions called the **somatic** and **autonomic** divisions in a network of nerves traveling throughout the entire body.
12. The **neuron** is the most basic building block of the nervous system.
13. Neurons differ from other cells in that they communicate with each other via specialized extensions called **dendrites** and **axons.**
14. The **dendrite** extends from the cell body much like the branches of a tree.
15. The axon has appendages called **axon terminals** or **terminal buttons.**
16. There are three types of neurons: **sensory, motor, and interneurons**
17. At rest, a neuron has a slightly **negative electrical charge.**
18. The neuron's membrane is selectively **permeable,** with channels that open and close allowing positively charged ions to pass through.
19. **Motor (efferent) neurons** carry signals from the brain and spinal cord to the muscles and glands. Sensory and motor neurons are present throughout our bodies.
20. **Interneurons,** the third type of neuron, exist exclusively in the brain and spinal cord and make up about 90% of all human neurons.
21. **Interneurons** make the connection between sensory and motor neurons and are involved in all mental activity.
22. **Glial cells,** though technically not neurons, support neural functioning by digesting dead neurons, producing the myelin sheathing, and providing nutrition to neurons.
23. The process by which neurons communicate is known as **neurotransmission.**
24. Neurotransmission is an electro-chemical process that occurs **within and between neurons.**
25. Within the neuron, neurotransmission describes the movement of an **electrical impulse.**
26. **Between neurons,** neurotransmission describes the process of one neuron sending chemical signals to other neurons across the synaptic cleft, or the gap between neurons.
27. When a neuron is sufficiently excited, it sends an electrical impulse known as the **action potential.**
28. The axon is covered in a fatty **myelin sheath** that insulates the axon and enables signals to move more quickly.
29. The recovery time after firing is called the **refractory period.**
30. When the electrical impulse reaches the axon, appendages called terminal buttons release chemical signals called **neurotransmitters** to other nearby neurons.
31. Neurons do not communicate directly. The chemical signal must cross the **synaptic cleft,** the gap between the axon of one neuron and the dendrite of another.
32. Neurotransmitters are either **excitatory or inhibitory.**
33. **Excitatory** means that the chemical signal increases the likelihood that neighboring neurons will fire.
34. **Inhibitory** means the signal lowers the likelihood that other neurons will fire.
35. The PNS controls voluntary and involuntary muscle movement, sensory information, and automatic functions of the body.
36. The peripheral system is made up of three subsystems: the somatic, autonomic, and enteric systems.
37. The somatic nervous system controls **voluntary muscle movement.**

38. The **somatic system** makes the connection between the motor cortex of the brain and the skeletal muscles used in movement.
39. The autonomic or involuntary nervous system controls **automatic body functions**.
40. The autonomic nervous system is further subdivided into the **sympathetic and parasympathetic nervous systems**.
41. The **enteric nervous system** is a network of nerve fibers in the stomach, intestines, pancreas, and gall bladder controlling the digestive process.
42. The sympathetic and parasympathetic systems **operate as opposites**.
43. The **sympathetic system** creates an excited state and mobilizes the body for action by accelerating some functions and decelerating others.
44. The **parasympathetic system** restores the body to a state of rest and relaxation.
45. Ancient peoples performed **trepanation**; surgically opening the skull to expose the brain, perhaps to release evil spirits causing mental disorders.
46. The part of the brain responsible for speech production is known as **Broca's Area**.
47. **Psychiatric or psychotropic medications** operate at the level of neurotransmitters.
48. The phrase **chemical imbalance of the brain** refers to a belief that mental health problems are due to imbalances in neurotransmitter levels.
49. Psychotropic medications affect the supply of **neurotransmitters** or the way in which **neurotransmitters are absorbed**.
50. **Agonists** make more of a neurotransmitter available in the synapse.
51. **Antagonists** decrease the amount of a neurotransmitter or block it from delivering its signal.
52. An aphasia in **Wernicke's Area** results in impairments in understanding written and spoken language.
53. **Localization of functioning** means that different parts of the brain carry out different functions.
54. The **homonculous** shows the areas of the brain that control movement of specific body parts.
55. The **amygdala** is involved in the experience of fear.
56. The case of Phineas Gage suggested a connection between **personality** and the brain.
57. Egas Moniz developed of a type of psycho-surgery known as **lobotomy.**
58. **Dopamine** is involved in movement and the experience of pleasure. Dopamine plays a role in the addictiveness of drugs like cocaine.
59. Dopamine levels are associated with the shakiness of patients with **Parkinson's disease**.
60. **Serotonin** affects sleep and mood. Medications like Prozac, Zoloft, and Paxil increase the availability of serotonin.
61. **The Electroencephalograph (EEG)** records electrical voltage produced when neurons fire.
62. The Electroencephalograph (EEG) shows **brain activity but not brain structure**.
63. **Computer axial tomography (CT scan)** involves rotating an x-ray machine around the brain to produce a series of images.
64. Computer axial tomography CT scans show **brain structure but not brain activity**.
65. **Positron Emission Tomography (PET scan)** produce real-time three-dimensional images of the brain at work.
66. Positron Emission Tomography (PET scan) show both **brain structure and activity**.
67. **Magnetic Resonance Imaging (MRI)** uses powerful magnetic fields and radio waves to create detailed images of the brain.
68. Magnetic Resonance Imaging (MRI) show **brain structure and brain activity**.
69. **Functional Magnetic Resonance Imaging (fMRI)** uses the magnetic properties of blood to produce pinpoint images of blood flow as it is occurring.
70. The brain is shielded by the **skull**, cushioned and nourished in **cerebrospinal fluid**, and protected from toxins by the **blood-brain barrier**.
71. The **blood-brain barrier** is a separation that protects the brain by allowing glucose from the blood to enter the brain, and by keeping out other substances and some toxins.
72. The **spinal cord** connects the brain with the body and transmits signals from the brain to the body and back again.
73. The brain consists of three major divisions – the **forebrain, midbrain**, and **hindbrain**.
74. The **forebrain** is the largest part of the brain making up about two-thirds of the brain's size.
75. The forebrain includes the **cerebral cortex, thalamus, hypothalamus, amygdala**, and **hippocampus**.
76. The outer layer of the forebrain, just under the skull and forehead is the cerebral cortex.
77. The cerebral cortex contains the majority of the brain's neurons.
78. A deep fissure called the **longitudinal sulcus** splits the cerebral cortex down the middle into the left and right hemispheres.
79. The cerebral cortex has **bilateral symmetry**, meaning that each hemisphere is a mirror image of the other.

80. The left and right hemispheres are connected by a dense bundle of nerve fibers called the **corpus callosum**.
81. The **corpus callosum** allows the two halves of the brain to communicate.
82. **Hemispheric specialization** refers to the different roles each hemisphere plays in mental life.
83. Each hemisphere is further divided into **four lobes** named for the parts of the skull under which they are located.
84. The **thalamus** plays an important role in sensory processing and movement, serving as a type of relay station by receiving sensory information from the senses and sending it to the cerebral cortex.
85. The hypothalamus, a small structure resting under the thalamus, plays a major role in the autonomic nervous system, the experience of pleasure, and in control of body temperature, hunger, and thirst.
86. The **amygdala** is an almond shaped structure located deep in the temporal lobe and plays a role in fear and other emotions, learning, memory, attention, and perception.
87. The **hippocampus** is a seahorse-shaped structure in the temporal lobe involved in processing memories, emotion, and spatial navigation.
88. The **hindbrain** sits under the cerebral cortex at the base of the skull and the top of the spinal cord and is comprised of the cerebellum, pons, and medulla
89. The **cerebellum** is the second largest structure in the brain and is associated with movement, co-ordination, balance, and motor-related memory.
90. The **reticular formation** is a mesh-like network of neurons involved in sleep and consciousness, arousal and attention, coordinating signals from the senses, and pain modulation.
91. The **pons** (Latin for "bridge") serves in coordinating communication between the two cerebral hemispheres and between parts of the brain and the spinal cord.
92. The **medulla**, or **medulla oblongata**, is located at the top of the spinal cord and is associated with breathing, temperature regulation, and some aspects of speech.
93. The **midbrain** is a small area of the brain (approximately 2 cm long) that sits between the forebrain and the hindbrain.
94. The midbrain is comprised of the **tectum**, **tegmentum**, and **cerebral peduncles**.
95. The tectum is involved in processing **visual and auditory signals**.
96. The **tegmentum** is a network of neurons involved in reflexes, involuntary body functions, and attention.
97. The **cerebral peduncles** are large fiber bundles of neurons that connect the midbrain and the cerebellum.
98. The **endocrine system** is a collection of glands that secrete hormones into the blood stream.
99. The pineal gland produces **melatonin** which helps regulate the sleep cycle.
100. **Hormones** are types of chemical messengers that work with the nervous system to control growth and development, mood, metabolism, and reproduction.

Chapter 4 Short Essay Question (Answers)

1. A Christian worldview understands that Mankind is material, made from the dust of the earth, but that we are also something more. The Bible is clear that there is something about us that makes us distinct from the animals – a non-material, spiritual God-likeness. The naturalistic monistic worldview underlying the statement "All mental experience is nothing more than brain activity" is a worldview assumption not supported or supportable by scientific psychology.
2. In the 1st century AD Hippocrates suggested that the brain was the seat of the mind. In the 17th century, Renee Descartes described the role played by the conarium (pineal gland) in the reflex arc. During the Renaissance, knowledge of the structure of the brain increased dramatically, and scientists began to understand the importance of the brain. Andreas Vesalius produced one of the first known neuro-anatomy textbooks, containing descriptions and illustrations of the workings of the nerves and the brain. In the early 1800s, Dr. Franz Gall, the founder of phrenology, proposed that various mental functions and personality traits were linked to specific locations in the brain. Also, in the early 1800s, Dr. Charles Bell published Idea of a New Anatomy of the Brain in which he described the connection between the mind (seated in the cerebrum), the senses, and motor activity. In 1848 Phineas Gage's accident demonstrated that there is a connection between the brain and personality. In 1861 Paul Broca discovered the connection between the brain and speech production. In the 1940s Wilder Penfield mapped the motor cortex.
3. Many psychologists believe that belief in God is programmed into our brains. Because beliefs in gods are common across peoples and throughout history, it must be programmed or "hard-wired" in our brains. If so, there must be a highly-evolved structure somewhere in the brain. The god spot, in the left temporal lobe, is said to be that structure. The discovery that some people with temporal-lobe epilepsy were prone to religious hallucinations led to the discovery that electrical stimulation to the temporal-lobe induced a religious-like experience. fMRIs show that the same area of the brain is active when subjects engage in religious activities. It should come as no surprise that our brains are involved in our experiences with God. The God spot may be the region of the brain where we experience God; it is not a region of the brain that creates that experience. The naturalism, reductionism, and atheism underlying the suggesting that God is nothing more than brain activity is a worldview position not supported or supportable by scientific psychology.

Chapter 4 Quiz Answers

1. The study of the brain and the nervous system is called: d) all of the above
2. At rest, a neuron has a: a) slightly negative electrical charge
3. Neurons differ from other cells in that they communicate with each other via specialized extensions called: a) dendrites and axons
4. The axon is a long, very thin tube leading away from the cell body. The axon has appendages called: c) axon terminals
5. The cell body contains the nucleus, which in turn contains _____, which provide the neuron's energy. a) mitochondria
6. _____neurons carry signals from the brain and spinal cord to the muscles and glands.   a) Efferent
7. _____ carry signals from the sense receptors in the body to the brain.   a) Afferent neurons
8. _____ exist exclusively in the brain and spinal cord and make up about 90% of all human neurons. a) Interneurons
9. _____is an electro-chemical process that occurs within and between neurons.
10. Neurotransmitters are either excitatory or inhibitory. ___means that the chemical signal increases the likelihood that neighboring neurons will fire. a) excitatory
11. Neurotransmitters are either excitatory or inhibitory. _____ means the signal lowers the likelihood that other neurons will fire.   b) inhibitory
12. The _____ consists of the neurons running throughout the body outside of the brain and the spinal cord.   a) peripheral nervous system
13. The _____ nervous system controls body functions like circulation, respiration, perspiration, and digestion.   a) Autonomic
14. _____ was an early attempt to localize psychological traits and characteristics in specific brain areas.   a) Phrenology
15. In 1848 Phineas Gage's accident demonstrated that there is a connection between the brain and __. c) Personality
16. In 1861 Paul Broca discovered the connection between an area of the brain (which bears his name today) and speech _____.   a) Production
17. _____ refers to the localization of some brain activity in the right or left hemisphere. a) Brain lateralization
18. The near-infinite complexity of the brain is one of the biggest leaps of faith necessary to hold an evolutionary worldview.   a) True
19. Psychotropic medications affect the supply of _____ or the way in which they are absorbed. c) Neurotransmitters
20. The central nervous system consists of the brain and the: b) spinal cord
21. The _____ is the most basic building block of the nervous system. a) neuron
22. The _____extends from the cell body much like the branches of a tree. b) dendrite
23. The axon has appendages called _____. c) axon terminals
24. _____ support neural functioning by digesting dead neurons, producing the myelin sheathing, and providing nutrition to neurons. c) Glial cells
25. The axon is covered in _____that insulates the axon and enables signals to move more quickly. b) a myelin sheath
26. Neurons do not communicate directly. The chemical signal must cross the _____, the gap between the axon of one neuron and the dendrite of another.   b) synaptic cleft
27. The _____controls voluntary muscle movement and makes the connection between the motor cortex of the brain and the skeletal muscles used in movement. c) somatic nervous system
28. The autonomic nervous system controls _____. d) involuntary body functions
29. The _____ is further subdivided into the sympathetic and parasympathetic nervous systems. a) autonomic nervous system
30. The _____is a network of nerve fibers in the stomach, intestines, pancreas, and gall bladder controlling the digestive process.   a) enteric nervous system
31. The _____creates an excited state and mobilizes the body for action by accelerating some functions and decelerating others.   b) sympathetic system
32. The _____restores the body to a state of rest and relaxation.   a) parasympathetic system
33. _____is involved in movement and the experience of pleasure. It also plays a role in the addictiveness of drugs like cocaine.   b) Dopamine
34. _____affects sleep and mood and is the active ingredient in medications like Prozac, Zoloft, and Paxil. a) serotonin

35. The Electroencephalograph (EEG) records electrical voltage produced when neurons fire. It shows: b) brain activity but not brain structure

36. Computer axial tomography (CT scan) involves rotating an x-ray machine around the brain to produce a series of images. It shows: a) brain structure but not brain activity

37. Positron Emission Tomography (PET scan) produce real-time three-dimensional images of the brain at work. It shows: c) both brain structure and activity

38. Magnetic Resonance Imaging (MRI) uses powerful magnetic fields and radio waves to create detailed images of the brain. It shows: a) both brain structure and brain activity

39. The brain is shielded by the skull, cushioned and nourished in cerebrospinal fluid, and protected from toxins by the _____. b) blood-brain barrier

40. The _____ is the largest part of the brain making up about two-thirds of the brain's size. b) forebrain

41. The _____ includes the cerebral cortex, thalamus, hypothalamus, amygdala, and hippocampus.   a) forebrain

42. The outer layer of the forebrain, just under the skull and forehead is the _____.   a) cerebral cortex

43. A deep fissure called the _____ splits the cerebral cortex down the middle into the left and right hemispheres. a) longitudinal sulcus

44. The left and right hemispheres are connected by a dense bundle of nerve fibers called the _____. b) corpus callosum

45. The _____ plays an important role in sensory processing and movement, serving as a type of relay station by receiving sensory information from the senses and sending it to the cerebral cortex.   thalamus

46. The _____, a small structure resting under the thalamus, plays a major role in the autonomic nervous system, the experience of pleasure, and in control of body temperature, hunger, and thirst. a) hypothalamus

47. The ____ is an almond shaped structure located deep in the temporal lobe and plays a role in fear and other emotions, learning, memory, attention, and perception. a) amygdala

48. The _____ is a seahorse-shaped structure in the temporal lobe involved in processing memories, emotion, and spatial navigation. b) hippocampus

49. The _____ sits under the cerebral cortex at the base of the skull and the top of the spinal cord and is comprised of the cerebellum, pons, and medulla,   a) hindbrain

50. The _____ is the second largest structure in the brain and is associated with movement, co-ordination, balance, and motor-related memory.   a) cerebellum

51. The _____ is a mesh-like network of neurons involved in sleep and consciousness, arousal and attention, coordinating signals from the senses, and pain modulation. b) reticular formation

52. The _____ (Latin for "bridge") serves in coordinating communication between the two cerebral hemispheres and between of the brain and the spinal cord. b) pons

53. The _____ is located at the top of the spinal cord and is associated with breathing, temperature regulation, and some aspects of speech. a) medulla

54. The _____ is comprised of the tectum, tegmentum, and cerebral peduncles.   a) midbrain

55. The _____ is a collection of glands that secrete hormones into the blood stream.   b) endocrine system

56. The thalamus, hypothalamus, amygdala, and hippocampus make up the _____ which plays an important role in our sense of smell and in memory and emotions.   b) limbic system

Chapter 5 Sensation and Perception

Chapter 5 Learning Objectives

Define and contrast sensation and perception
Define sensory threshold, just noticeable difference, and Weber's Law
Explain the concepts of sensory adaptation
Describe the visual system, the auditory system, the olfactory system, the gustatory system, the cutaneous system, and the kinesthetic system
List forms of energy for which we have sensory receptors
Explain Gestalt concepts such as figure-ground, continuity, similarity, proximity, and closure.
Describe binocular and monocular depth cues
Describe the influence of motivation, past experiences, culture, and expectations on perception
Explain what is meant by "attention"
Explain extrasensory perception and paranormal psychology

Key Concepts and People

Photo receptors	Visual system	Kinesthetic system
Chemoreceptors	Trichromatic theory of color	Vestibular system
Mechanoreceptors	vision	Perception
Mechanoreceptors	Opponent-process theory of	Top-down and bottom-up
Signal detection theory	color vision	processing
Absolute threshold	Auditory system	Gestalt
Sensory adaptation	Olfactory system	Stimulus factors
Just noticeable difference	Gustatory system	Personal factors
Ernst Weber	Cutaneous system	Extrasensory perception
Weber's Law	Proprioception system	Paranormal psychology

Short Essay Questions

1 Define sensation and perception.
2. Define sensory threshold, just noticeable difference, absolute threshold, and Weber's Law.
3. Describe the major structures and processes of the visual system.
4. Describe the trichromatic and opponent-process theories of color vision.
5. Describe the major structures and processes of the auditory system.
6. Describe the place and volley theories of coding sounds.
7. Describe the major structures and processes of the olfactory system.
8. Describe the major structures and processes of the gustatory system.
9. Describe the major structures and processes of the cutaneous system.
10. Describe the kinesthetic system.
11. Name the three primary types of receptor cells.
12. Describe top-down and bottom-up processing.
13. Explain Gestalt concepts and principles, such as figure-ground, continuity, similarity, proximity, closure, and so on.
14. Describe the influence of environmental variables, motivation, past experiences, culture, and expectation on perception.
15. Explain extrasensory perception and paranormal psychology.

For Further Study

1. Web: The blind spot and other vision demonstrations,
    http://faculty.washington.edu/chudler/chvision.html

2. Web: How does your eye work?
    http://www.exploratorium.edu/learning_studio/cow_eye/how.html
3. Web: National Institute on Deafness and Other Communication Disorders.
4. http://www.nidcd.nih.gov/Pages/default.aspx
5. Slide show: How you hear. http://www.mayoclinic.com/health/ear-infections/EI00027&slide=1
    Mayo Clinic.
6. Web: Tactile illusions: Seven ways to fool your sense of touch.
    http://www.newscientist.com/special/tactile-illusions
7. Web: Tips for Tricking Your Senses http://hms.harvard.edu/news/harvard-medicine/tips-tricking-your-senses
8. Web: National Federation of the Blind, student resources. https://nfb.org/students
9. Read Laws of Organization in Perceptual Forms by Max Wertheimer (1923) at
    http://psychclassics.yorku.ca/Wertheimer/Forms/forms.htm

Topics for Discussion

1. Appreciate your senses by giving one up for 24 hours.
2. Explain at the worldview level why naturalists and Christians both dismiss ESP and parapsychology.
3. What is the relationship (if any) between our sensation and perception as described by psychologists, and the "heart" as described by the Bible?

Chapter 5 Worldview Issues

EXTRA SENSORY PERCEPTION

Extra sensory perception (ESP) is defined as the sensation of an energy that we can't measure with known techniques. People with extrasensory perception are said to be psychic. People who are psychic, by definition, can sense and perceive 'extra' sensory, or supernatural forms of energy.

Some psychics are said to have a supernatural extension of their regular senses – like seeing or feeling ghosts. Some can receive information directly into the brain, bypassing the regular senses. Some psychics claim clairvoyance – the ability to see or predict the future, or mental telepathy – the ability to send and receive of thoughts through brain waves. Some claim they can affect physical objects with their mind. Parapsychologists have performed numerous 'studies' purported to be evidence of ESP.

Most psychologists and scientists do not believe that ESP is real. Scientific research has failed to demonstrate ESP. But research results aside, most psychologists reject ESP at the worldview level. Because extra sensory ESP has not been observed and measured, because it is not 'natural,' it does not exist. Naturalism demands it.

Most Christians also dismiss ESP at the worldview level, but for different reasons. Modern psychology dismisses parapsychology because it denies the existence of the supernatural, but Christians believe in the supernatural. Christians believe in a spiritual realm, that our consciousness survives after death, and that we can receive messages through 'extra sensory' means. The Christian worldview distinguishes between good spiritual forces (of God) and Satanic forces. Those who believe in ESP often attribute the ability to some benign universal consciousness or power, but Christians must remember that there is no middle ground and should approach ESP with extreme caution.

Study Guide Chapter 5

1. _____ are systems that transforms information about the outside world into nervous system activity and transmits it to the brain.

2. _____ are the subjective experience of sensations, the ways that we organize, interpret, and give meaning to raw neural impulses.

3. Photoreceptors are activated by _____.

4. _____ respond to chemicals substances.

5. Mechanoreceptors respond to _____.

6. _____ refers to the minimum intensity of a stimulus that will stimulate a sense organ to operate.

7. _____, a simple type of learning, refers to the tendency of neurons to become less sensitive to constant or familiar stimuli.

8. _____ refers to receptor cells' ability to detect subtle changes in stimulus strength.

9. The relationship of sensation to change in stimulus strength is known as _____.

10. Human _____ is the sensation of reflected electromagnetic radiation.

11. The retina is lined with specialized receptors called _____.

12. _____ are most sensitive to low levels of light and cones are sensitive to high light levels of light and are responsible for color vision and vision acuity.

13. Cones are most concentrated in the _____, the center of the field of vision.

14. The _____ extends from the eye, across the optic chiasm, to the cerebral hemisphere.

15. There are no rods or cones at the _____ where the optic nerve leaves the eye.

16. _____ is the sensation and perception of sounds.

17. The _____ detects airborne chemicals.

18. The _____ detects chemicals that come into contact with the tongue.

19. The _____ provide the brain with information about the body, its condition, and the body's relationship with the outside world.

20. _____ receptors respond to pressure, shape, texture, movement, and temperature.

21. _____ extend from the spinal cord to the body and are involved in the experience of pain.

22. The _____provides the brain with information about body position and movement.

23. The _____provides information about the position of our body relative to gravity and movement.

24. _____ is the process through which we select, organize, interpret, and give meaning to sensations.

25. _____describes reasons we select of some sensory inputs for attention and ignore others.

26. _____are those characteristics of objects that affect our perception of the object.

27. _____including experience, values, expectations, context, and mental and emotional states affect our perception.

Chapter 5 Quiz

1) _____ is the subjective experience of sensations, the ways we organize, interpret, and give meaning to the raw neural impulses
   a) Sensation
   b) Perception
   c) Attention
   d) Cognition

2) _____ is the process of converting physical stimuli into neural energy.
   a) Transduction
   b) Neuro-transmission
   c) Action potential
   d) Potentiation

3) _____ refers to the minimum intensity of a stimulus that will stimulate an organ to operate. In other words, the lowest intensity of a light, sound, touch, taste, or smell that we can sense.
   a) Just noticeable difference
   b) Weber's Law
   c) Absolute threshold
   d) Sensory adaptation

4) _____ refers to the tendency of neurons to become less sensitive to constant or familiar stimulus.
   a) Habituation
   b) Sensory adaptation
   c) Stimulus generalization
   d) Tolerance

5) _____ are most sensitive to low levels of light and give us our night vision.
   a) Rods
   b) Cones

6) _____ are photoreceptor cells that operate best at high levels of light and are responsible for color vision and vision acuity.
   a) Rods
   b) Cones

7) The _____, at the center of our field of vision and where we have our highest visual acuity, is densely packed with cones.
   a) optic nerve
   b) retina
   c) iris
   d) fovea

8) _____ psychologists focus on the ways that we create a "whole" experience from the many and varied sensory inputs.
   a) Cognitive
   b) Gestalt
   c) Psycho-dynamic
   d) Freudian

9) _____ is said to be the sensation of energy that cannot be measured or studied in replicable experiments.
   a) Extrasensory perception
   b) Paranormal psychology
   c) Quantum physics
   d) Déjà vu

10) Photoreceptors are activated by
    _____.
    a) electromagnetic energy
    b) chemical substances
    c) mechanical energy
    d) nuclear energy

11) Chemoreceptors respond to
    _____.
    a) electromagnetic energy
    b) chemical substances
    c) mechanical energy
    d) nuclear energy

12) Mechanoreceptors respond to
    _____.
    a) electromagnetic energy
    b) chemical substances
    c) mechanical energy
    d) nuclear energy

13) _____ refers to receptor cells' ability to detect subtle changes in stimulus strength.
a) Habituation
b) Weber's Law
c) Stimulus generalization
d) Just noticeable difference (JND)

14) The relationship of sensation to change in stimulus strength is known as _____.
a) Just noticeable difference (JND)
b) Habituation
c) Weber's Law
d) Stimulus generalization

15) The olfactory system detects
a) electromagnetic energy
b) mechanical energy
c) nuclear energy
d) airborne chemicals

16) The gustatory system detects _____
a) electromagnetic energy
b) chemical substances
c) mechanical energy
d) nuclear energy

17) _____ extend from the spinal cord to the body and are involved in the experience of pain.
a) Nociceptors
b) Photoreceptors
c) Chemoreceptors
d) Mechanoreceptors

18) The _____ provides the brain with information about body position and movement.
a) kinesthetic system
b) vestibular system
c) motor cortex

19) The _____ provides information about the position of our body relative to gravity and movement.
a) kinesthetic system
b) vestibular system

20) _____ are those characteristics of objects that affect our perception of the object.
a) Stimulus factors
b) Personal factors

21) _____ include experience, values, expectations, context, and mental and emotional states that affect our perception.
a) Stimulus factors
b) Personal factors

Answer Key Chapter 5

Chapter 5 Study Guide (Answers)

1. **Senses** are systems that transforms information about the outside world into nervous system activity and transmits it to the brain.
2. **Perceptions** are the subjective experience of sensations, the ways that we organize, interpret, and give meaning to raw neural impulses.
3. Photoreceptors are activated by **electromagnetic energy**.
4. **Chemoreceptors** respond to chemicals substances.
5. Mechanoreceptors respond to **mechanical energy**.
6. **Absolute threshold** refers to the minimum intensity of a stimulus that will stimulate a sense organ to operate.
7. **Habituation**, a simple type of learning, refers to the tendency of neurons to become less sensitive to constant or familiar stimuli.
8. **Just noticeable difference (JND)** refers to receptor cells' ability to detect subtle changes in stimulus strength.
9. The relationship of sensation to change in stimulus strength is known as **Weber's Law**.
10. Human **sight** is the sensation of reflected electromagnetic radiation.
11. The retina is lined with specialized receptors called **rods and cones**.
12. **Rod**s are most sensitive to low levels of light and cones are sensitive to high light levels of light and are responsible for color vision and vision acuity.
13. Cones are most concentrated in the **fovea**, the center of the field of vision.
14. The **optic nerve** extends from the eye, across the optic chiasm, to the cerebral hemisphere.
15. There are no rods or cones at the **blind spot** where the optic nerve leaves the eye.
16. **Hearing** is the sensation and perception of sounds.
17. The **olfactory system** detects airborne chemicals.
18. The **gustatory system** detects chemicals that come into contact with the tongue.
19. The **somatic senses** provide the brain with information about the body, its condition, and the body's relationship with the outside world.
20. **Cutaneous** receptors respond to pressure, shape, texture, movement, and temperature.
21. **Nociceptors** extend from the spinal cord to the body and are involved in the experience of pain.
22. The **kinesthetic system** provides the brain with information about body position and movement.
23. The **vestibular system** provides information about the position of our body relative to gravity and movement.
24. **Perception** is the process through which we select, organize, interpret, and give meaning to sensations.
25. **Perceptual selectivity** describes reasons we select of some sensory inputs for attention and ignore others.
26. **Stimulus factors** are those characteristics of objects that affect our perception of the object.
27. **Personal factors** including experience, values, expectations, context, and mental and emotional states affect our perception.

Chapter 5 Short Essay Questions (Answers)

1. A sense is a system that transmits to the brain, information about the world outside of the brain. A sense converts characteristics of the physical world into nervous system activity. Sensations are processes by which external physical energy and chemicals stimulate our sense organs to transmit neural signals to the brain. Sensation refers to the experience of the environment through touch, taste, sight, sound, and smell and to our experience of ourselves in the world. Our sensory organs and sensory neural pathways to the brain are similar to those of other mammals. Perception, on the other hand, is the process through which we organize, interpret, and give meaning to the raw neural impulses. Perception is tied to our consciousness. It involves an awareness and understanding unlike any animal.
2. Sensory threshold, also known as absolute threshold, refers to the minimum intensity of a stimulus that will stimulate an organ to operate. In other words, the absolute threshold is the lowest intensity of a light, sound, touch, taste, or smell that we can sense. Because the absolute threshold varies from person to person and from time to time for the same person, absolute threshold is defined as the point at which a very weak stimulus could be detected 50% of the time. The just noticeable difference (JND) refers to receptor cells' ability to detect subtle changes in stimulus strength. How much brighter, louder, warmer, or smellier must a stimulus be before we notice the change? The just noticeable difference is the smallest change in a stimulus which a person can detect 50% of the time. Ernst Weber discovered the relationship between signal strength and JND. Weber found that we cannot detect changes in signal strength unless the magnitude of the change is more than a fixed proportion. The relationship of sensation to change in stimulus strength is known as Weber's Law.
3. The cornea refracts (bends and concentrates) the light into the iris. The anterior chamber is filled with a transparent liquid called the aqueous humor, which further refracts and focuses the image. The iris, the colored part of the eye behind the cornea, contains small muscles that open or close the pupil to allow in more or less light. The lens, located behind the iris, has primary responsibility for focusing the image onto the retina. The retina is comparable to a rounded screen at the back

of the eye. The retina contains specialized photoreceptors called rods and cones. Rods and cones are named for their shapes. They are photoreceptors, meaning they contain chemicals that respond to light energy, triggering the neuron to send fire. Rods are most sensitive to low levels of light and give us our night vision. Rods, named for their rod-like shape, do not respond to different wavelengths of light, so they do not sense color. The human eye has over 100 million rod cells concentrated around the outer edges of the retina. Rods provide peripheral vision and detect motion. Cones are photoreceptor cells that operate best at high levels of light and are responsible for color vision and vision acuity. Cones are concentrated in the center of the retina, most densely in an area called the fovea. The fovea is at the center of our field of vision. It is a small area, densely packed with cones, in the center of the retina. The fovea only contains cones and is where we have our highest visual acuity. Rods and cones transmit their signal to ganglion cells. The ganglion cells' axons (over 1 million of them) exit the eye and form the optic nerve. The optic nerve is a bundle of nerve fibers that travel from the eye, crossing at the optic chiasm.

4. The trichromatic, or three-color theory of color vision, one of psychology's oldest, suggests that we experience all colors as mixtures of red, green, and blue light. Later research showed that there are three types of cones, each responding to red, green, or blue light. Each type of cone contains chemicals designed to respond to light in the red, green, or blue light range of the spectrum. The opponent-process theory of color vision suggests that in addition to the mixing of three colors, we sense color through the activity of two opponent systems – a blue-yellow system and a red-green mechanism. Cones respond to opposing colors with excitatory or inhibitory responses. The ratio and combination of cones responding to colors in an excitatory/inhibitory blend is thought to best explain color vision.

5. The funnel-shaped outer-ear, also called the auricle or pinna, gathers sound pressure waves and directs them down the auditory canal to the eardrum or tympanic membrane. The auricle, auditory canal, and tympanic membrane, also called the eardrum, make up the outer ear. The eardrum is a thin, skin-like stretched membrane, much like the skin of a drum. When the sound waves hit the eardrum, it vibrates. Those vibrations pass through a series of small bones or ossicles in the middle ear. The ossicles consist of the hammer or malleus, anvil or incus, and the stirrup or stape. The ossicles are the smallest bones in your body and work to magnify the eardrum's vibrations and to transmit them to the inner ear. Those magnified vibrations enter the inner ear at the oval window. The cochlea is a hard, snail-shaped fluid-filled structure lined with the basilar membrane. The basilar membrane is covered with microscopic hair-like cells called stereocilia that connect with the auditory nerve. As vibrations enter the cochlea, the fluid moves, bending the stereocilia and stimulating a neural impulse that travels along the auditory nerve to the auditory cortex of the temporal lobe. The stereocilia are mechanoreceptors; they convert mechanical stimulation (vibrations) into neural activity.

6. Place theory suggests that the stereocilia in specific parts of the cochlea fire in response to specific frequencies. Volley theory suggests that neurons along the cochlea fire in a wave that matches the frequency of the sound.

7. At the roof of your nasal cavity is a lining of specialized tissue known as the olfactory epithelium (mucous membrane). The olfactory epithelium holds the olfactory receptors. Olfactory receptors are designed to respond to particular chemicals. The receptors join the olfactory nerve and feed directly into the olfactory bulb in the brain (not through the thalamus as with other senses). From the olfactory bulb, signals travel to other parts of the brain including the amygdala, which processes emotion, which may be why the link between smells and memories is so strong.

8. Taste begins with taste receptor cells called gustatory cells clustered primarily in the papillae, commonly called the taste buds. Papillae are open to the surface of the tongue and contain clusters of taste receptors. Taste receptors are specialized and respond best to a single taste. We can sense sweet, salty, bitter, and sour. Some psychologists suggest that we have unique receptor cells that respond to two other tastes called umani (glutamates) and astringent (tannins).

9. Our sense of touch is extremely complex and involves several types of receptor cells. One square inch of skin contains nearly 20 million cells. Your fingertips are especially densely packed with cutaneous receptors, which makes them very sensitive to touch. Specialized cutaneous receptors respond either to pressure, shape, texture, movement, and temperature. Touch receptors fire at varying rates and combinations to signal characteristics of touch. Specialized neurons called nociceptors extend from the spinal cord to the skin or any other part of the body that can experience pain. Specialized nociceptors respond to sharp pricking pain or to dull gnawing pain.

10. Our kinesthetic sense informs us about the position and movement of parts of the body. Without this sense, we could not control voluntary movements like walking. The kinesthetic sense allows you to know where your foot is, relative to the rest of your body, even when your eyes are closed. The kinesthetic sense plays a big part in allowing you to stumble but not fall. Neurons in muscle fibers and joints send information via the thalamus to the sensory cortex.

11. Photoreceptors are activated by electromagnetic energy (i.e., light). Chemoreceptors respond to chemical substances (i.e., odors). Mechanoreceptors respond to mechanical energy (i.e., touch, movement, vibrations).

12. Along each sensory pathway, sensory information is automatically sorted, organized, identified, selected, and grouped before it reaches the cerebral cortex in a process psychologists call bottom-up processing. When sensory information arrives in the cerebral cortex, our "higher level" mental processes, past experience, expectations, context, and mental and emotional states affect how we perceive the information in a process.

13. Early psychologists recognized that we group the characteristics of sensations into a "whole" experience. The word gestalt means overall, whole, and totality. Gestalt psychologists focus on the ways that we create a "whole" experience from the many and varied sensory inputs. When describing perception, gestalt refers to the ways we perceive stimuli by grouping sensations together in meaningful ways. Gestalt principles (also called laws) by which we automatically group stimuli. Proximity. When objects and events appear close to one another (in space or in time), they are perceived as though they belong together. Similarity. We tend to group objects with similar properties (i.e., color, shape, texture). • Continuity. We tend to group objects according to smooth lines or curves. Common fate. We tend to group objects moving in the same direction and perceive them as a single object. Closure. We tend to fill in the gaps in incomplete figures.

14. Your worldview affects your perceptions. Mental set and schema are terms psychologists use to describe the effect of our beliefs, knowledge, and assumptions on perception. Our mental set predisposes us to perceive new experiences in

predictable ways. Past experience, values, expectations, context, and mental and emotional states affect our perception. We do not just passively receive stimuli; we are actively engaged in perceiving the world. Psychologists have shown that one's cultural background influences perception, too. A Christian worldview believes that sin affects perception (Jeremiah 17:9).

15. Extrasensory perception is said to be the sensation of energy that cannot be measured or studied in replicable experiments. People with extrasensory perception are said to be psychic. The study of ESP is part of parapsychology. Parapsychology is the study of paranormal psychological phenomena. Paranormal refers to any phenomena that is not replicable, "physically" impossible, not explainable by natural processes, or beyond the range of normal experience.

Chapter 5 Quiz Answers

1. _____ is the subjective experience of sensations, the ways we organize, interpret, and give meaning to the raw neural impulses   b) Perception
2. _____ is the process of converting physical stimuli into neural energy.   a) Transduction
3. _____ refers to the minimum intensity of a stimulus that will stimulate an organ to operate. In other words, the lowest intensity of a light, sound, touch, taste, or smell that we can sense.   c) Absolute threshold
4. _____ refers to the tendency of neurons to become less sensitive to constant or familiar stimulus. a) Habituation
5. _____ are most sensitive to low levels of light and give us our night vision.   a) Rods
6. _____ are photoreceptor cells that operate best at high levels of light and are responsible for color vision and vision acuity.   b) Cones
7. The _____, at the center of our field of vision and where we have our highest visual acuity, is densely packed with cones. d) fovea
8. _____ psychologists focus on the ways that we create a "whole" experience from the many and varied sensory inputs.   b) Gestalt
9. _____ is said to be the sensation of energy that cannot be measured or studied in replicable experiments. a) Extrasensory perception
10. Photoreceptors are activated by _____.a) electromagnetic energy
11. Chemoreceptors respond to _____.b) chemical substances
12. Mechanoreceptors respond to _____.c) mechanical energy
13. _____ refers to receptor cells' ability to detect subtle changes in stimulus strength.   d) Just noticeable difference (JND)
14. The relationship of sensation to change in stimulus strength is known as _____. Weber's Law
15. The olfactory system detects _____d) airborne chemicals
16. The gustatory system detects _____b) chemical substances
17. _____extend from the spinal cord to the body and are involved in the experience of pain. Nociceptors
18. The _____ provides the brain with information about body position and movement. kinesthetic system
19. The _____provides information about the position of our body relative to gravity and movement. vestibular system
20. _____are those characteristics of objects that affect our perception of the object. Personal factors
21. _____ include experience, values, expectations, context, and mental and emotional states that affect our perception.   b) Personal factors

Chapter 6 Motivation and Emotion

Chapter 6 Learning Objectives

Explain motivation, intrinsic motivation, and extrinsic motivation
Explain human motivation from an evolutionary perspective
Describe motivation in terms of needs, drives, and homeostasis
Describe motivation in terms of arousal
Explain Maslow's hierarch of motivation
Contrast Maslow's concept of self-actualization with a Christian perspective of the self
Describe lie detector tests
Describe the experience of emotions
Describe Sternberg triangle model of love
Describe the James-Lange theory of emotions
Describe the Cannon-Bard theory of emotions
Explain cognitive theories of emotions
Describe four situations in which motivations occur
Describe the type A and hardy personalities
Describe signs of stress
Explain the general adaptation syndrome

Key Concepts and People

Motivation	Drive reduction	Cannon-Bard theory
Yerkes-Dodson law	Arousal	Paul Eckman
Clark Hull	Self-actualization	Carl Lange
William McDougal	Emotion	Robert Plutchik
Instincts	Subjective experience	Robert Sternberg
Intrinsic motivation	Physiological response	Abraham Maslow
Extrinsic motivation	James-Lange theory	

Short Essay Questions

1. Describe human motivation and emotion from the biological, humanistic, social and evolutionary perspectives.
2. Describe the drive reduction theory of motivation.
3. Describe Maslow's five stages of motivation.
4. Define emotions and the three components of the experience of emotions.
5. Describe the James-Lange and Cannon-Bard theories of emotions.
6. Describe cognitive theories of emotions.
7. Describe psychological, emotional, physiological, and behavioral signs of stress.
8. Give examples of negative stress and of "good" stress.
9. Describe the type A personality.

For Further Study

1. Read: A Theory of Human Motivation http://psychclassics.yorku.ca/Maslow/motivation.htm By A. H. Maslow. Classics in the History of Psychology, an internet resource by Christopher D. Green, York University, Toronto, Ontario.
2. Read: What is an emotion? http://psychclassics.yorku.ca/James/emotion.htm by William James at Classics in the History of Psychology

Topics for Discussion

1. How are motivations and emotions similar and how are they different?
2. What emotions are described in the Bible?
3. During World War II Corrie ten Boom and her family risked death by hiding Jews from the Nazis. What motives and emotions were at play.
4. How do the behavioral, biological, and humanistic perspectives differ in terms of explaining human motivation and emotion?

Chapter 6 Worldview Issues

Free-will

We were made to glorify God and enjoy Him forever. That is our purpose – our reason for living, or, in the language of psychology, that is our motivation. Motivation is the force, or dynamic that initiates, directs, sustains, and terminates activity. From a Christian perspective, our highest motivation is to glorify and enjoy God. The Bible has lots to say about human motivation. It is a big part of the Christian worldview and of introductory psychology class.

Students learn about the behaviorist, Freudian, humanistic, and evolutionary perspectives on what motivates us – why we do what we do. Behaviorists say the environment motivates us – rewards and consequences. Freud thought that the urge for sensual pleasure – the libido – was the force that drove us. Humanists say it is the drive for self-actualization. Evolutionary psychology explains motivation in terms of survival and reproduction.

A Christian approach to psychology recognizes that humans are motivated to survive, we have biological drives and urges, and we seek pleasure and avoid punishment. As part of the natural order, human motivation is common. But there is more. As beings created in the image and likeness of God, human purpose – our motivation – is unique. We can exercise volition – the conscious ability to choose. A Christian approach to human motivation balances God's sovereignty and omniscience with Mankind's free-will in the context of the fall, redemption, and Christian maturity. When the Bible speaks of our heart it is speaking, in part, about our motivations.

The belief in free-will is a crucial part of the Biblical doctrine of Man. Free will exists in concert with God's sovereignty. A defining characteristic of what it means to be human, is to have free-will. Unlike the animals, we have freedom to choose, which brings with it responsibility for our choices. When one has God as one's ultimate authority, when one seeks the mind of Christ, we can be properly motivated.

The belief in free-will stands in stark contrast to naturalistic worldviews. Naturalism denies that we humans have real freedom. From a naturalistic perspective, we 'believe' that we have free-will, it 'feels' like we have free-will, but it is not real. Students will feel pressure to conform to a belief that fee-will is an illusion.

Humanism

Humanism, as psychology's "third force" appeared in psychology around the 1970s. Humanistic psychology to its credit, recognizes the importance of the individual. But humanism is a philosophy – a reaction to behaviorism and Freudian psychology, which seemed cold and unflattering. Behaviorism compared humans to animals. Freud said humans were motivated by libido-fueled psychic conflicts. Humanism describes humanity in noble terms.

Humanism, also known as secular humanism, describes principles for a fulfilling life. Humanism places human values, reason, and individual self-worth above all else. It specifically rejects God, sees Mankind as the culmination of evolution, and looks to reason and science to define morality. From a humanistic perspective, we're born good, and if left to our own devices, in accepting and nonjudgmental environments, we can be self-actualized – to achieve personal fulfillment and reach our full potential.

Students will feel pressure to conform to a belief that says sin, guilt, and the need for redemption are meaningless. A Christian perspective sees personal fulfillment and full potential differently. Paradoxically, we achieve fulfillment through self-renunciation and obedient service. A Christian worldview recognizes that despite being hungry, unsafe, and alone, we can be 'actualized' in our relationship with Jesus. Jesus is the measure of our actualization. We should first seek the kingdom of God and trust that our physical, safety, and other needs will be met. Contrition, self-denial, and humility are means by which we achieve spiritual growth, not group membership, achievement, or social status. Jesus, not knowledge or self-awareness, is the measure of Mankind's "actualization."

Humanism's emphasis on high self-esteem, self-expression, and reaching one's potential makes it appealing. Students will feel pressure to conform to the belief that high self-esteem is the foundation of sound mental health. Self-fulfillment, self-expression, self-love, and individualism are paramount. People should feel good about themselves, learn to love themselves, and rid themselves of shame and guilt. Guilt is to be avoided at all costs, and suffering is absurd.

Christians disagree about the importance of self-esteem. Some Christians equate high self-esteem with idolatrous pride. Others, like Dr. James Dobson, integrate self-esteem into their theology and balance our sinfulness with our special status in God's eyes. A Christian approach balances the fact that though pride is a form of idolatry, beings created in God's image do not exalt God by denigrating His Creation.

Emotions
In psychology class students learn the physiological, cognitive, and behavioral components of emotions. They learn that emotions involve regions of the cerebral cortex, the limbic system the amygdala, hippocampus, and thalamus. Emotions trigger changes in heart rate, blood pressure, respiration, perspiration, and even pupil dilation. Emotions are common – animals seem to have them, too. As we'll see, Darwin believed that emotions in animals were a proof of his theory.

But from a Christian perspective, human emotions are unique and God given. Human emotions are a proof that we were created in the likeness of God. God has emotions. Jesus was emotional. The Bible does not use the word emotion, but the heart is mentioned hundreds of times. When the Bible uses the word 'heart' it means, among other things, our emotional lives. Emotions are an expression of our hearts. The Bible is filled with instructions about emotions. We are commanded to experience certain emotions, avoid others, and not to let emotions control us.

God's emotions flow from His holy and righteous nature. Ours are marred by sin. A Christian worldview recognizes that sin corrupts the heart, and that includes emotions. By seeking the mind of Christ, with God as one's ultimate authority, our emotions are changed and renewed.

Study Guide Chapter 6

1. _____ is defined as an inner state and a process that arouses, directs, maintains, and terminates behavior.

2. Motivation is said to be_____, a force from within, or _____, a force from outside of us.

3. The biological perspective produced theories explaining motivation in term of
_____.

4. The behavioral perspective explained motivation in terms of
_____.

5. The humanistic perspective explained motivation in terms of
_____.

6. _____explain motivation in terms of adaptive functions that increased the chances of survival and reproduction.

7. According to drive reduction theory, _____are the primary motivator of human behavior.

8. _____ are unpleasant internal states of tension which arouse us to take action to meet a biologic need, to restore _____, and to reduce internal tension.

9. _____states that we are motivated achieve our individually optimal state of arousal.

10. _____describes the relationship between optimal arousal and performance on a task increases with physical and mental arousal, but when levels of arousal become too high, performance decreases,

11. Abraham Maslow is known as the _____.

12. Maslow proposed that Man is innately and naturally motivated to grow and progress through a _____, of physical and psychological steps or stages.

13. Maslow's idea was that people are born with a motivation to grow toward
_____.

14. In Maslow's theory, our primary motivations are _____– food, water, and shelter, and _____– security and protection from harm.

15. According to Maslow, when the most basic needs have been met, our motivational focus changes to _____, a feeling of belonging, love, family ties, and group membership.

16. According to Maslow, we are motivated by _____ the need to be recognized for our _____.

17. According to Maslow, _____is the drive to fulfill one's potential through self-awareness, knowledge, and creativity.

18. The Christian recognizes that despite being hungry, unsafe, and alone, one can be fully actualized in one's relationship with _____.

19. We should first seek the _____and trust that our physical, safety, and other needs will be met.

20. _____are means by which Christians achieve spiritual growth.

21. The _____describes a drive to meet high personal standards of excellence.

22. The _____is said to motivate forming friendships and associations.

23. The _____motivates forming intimate relationships.

24. The _____is said to motivate those who want to be in charge and to control others.

25. Emotions involve both _____processes.

26. The experience of emotions is characterized by at least two components: _____and _____.

27. Paul Ekman described six basic emotions _____.

28. _____describes our tendency to feel the same emotions being felt by those around us.

29. In the _____theory of emotions, the body responds automatically to environmental circumstances, and the brain interprets the body's response as emotion.

30. _____of emotions suggest that physiological responses and cognitive processes work together to produce the experience of emotions.

31. _____ is defined as a generalized (non-specific) response to a perceived threat.

32. The _____describes human reaction to prolonged stress.

Chapter 6 Quiz

1) _____ is defined as an inner state and a process that arouses, directs, maintains, and terminates behavior.
   a) Motivation
   b) Libido
   c) Drive
   d) Urge

2) Motivation coming from within is said to be _____.
   a) Extrinsic
   b) Intrinsic
   c) Personal
   d) Need for achievement

3) The _____ perspective produced theories explaining motivation in term of instincts, drives, and needs.
   a) behavioral
   b) biological
   c) humanistic
   d) psychodynamic

4) The _____ perspective explained motivation in terms of external forces, rewards, and consequences.
   a) behavioral
   b) biologic
   c) humanistic
   d) psychodynamic

5) The _____ perspective explains motivation in terms of an intrinsic human need to grow and achieve.
   a) behavioral
   b) biologic
   c) humanistic
   d) psychodynamic

6) The _____ psychologists explain motivation in terms of adaptive functions that increased the chances of survival and reproduction.
   a) behavioral
   b) biologic
   c) humanistic
   d) evolutionary

7) _____ are automatic, involuntary, and unlearned patterns of behavior that are triggered by particular stimuli
   a) Reflexes
   b) Instincts
   c) Memory traces
   d) conditioned responses

8) According to drive reduction theory, _____ needs are the primary motivator of human behavior.
   a) biological
   b) sensual
   c) unconscious
   d) selfish

9) According to the _____, biological needs are the primary motivator of human behavior.
   a) drive reduction theory
   b) psychosexual theory
   c) humanistic theory
   d) motivational theory

10) _____ are unpleasant internal states of tension which arouse us to take action to meet the need, restore homeostasis, and reduce internal tension.
   a) Needs
   b) Urges
   c) Temptations
   d) Drives

11) _____ is known as the father of humanistic psychology.
   a) Sigmund Freud
   b) Abraham Maslow
   c) Abraham Lincoln
   d) B. F. Skinner

12) Maslow's idea that people are born with a motivation to grow toward _____ is central to a humanistic worldview today.
   a) potentiation
   b) self-actualization
   c) maturation
   d) selflessness

13) _____ states that we are motivated achieve our individually optimal state of arousal.
   a) Arousal theory
   b) Individual potential theory
   c) Maslow's theory
   d) Freud's theory

14) The _____ describes the relationship between optimal arousal and performance on a task increases with physical and mental arousal, but when levels of arousal become too high, performance decreases.
   a) Yerkes–Dodson Law
   b) Weber's Law
   c) Immigration Law
   d) Maximization Law

15) The _____ describes a drive to meet high personal standards of excellence.
   a) need for achievement
   b) need for affiliation
   c) need for intimacy
   d) need for power

16) The _____ personality is characterized by a need to achieve, time-urgency, and aggression and is associated with an elevated risk of hypertension and heart attack.
   a) Type B
   b) Type A

17) According to Maslow, when the most basic needs have been met, our motivational focus changes to _____, a feeling of belonging, love, family ties, and group membership.
   a) affiliation
   b) esteem
   c) self- actualization
   d) video gaming

18) The need for _____ motivates forming intimate relationships.
   a) achievement
   b) affiliation
   c) intimacy
   d) power

19) The need for _____ is said to motivate those who want to be in charge and to control others.
   a) achievement
   b) affiliation
   c) intimacy
   d) power

20) In the _____ theory of emotions, the body responds automatically to environmental circumstances, and the brain interprets the body's response as emotion.
   a) James-Lang
   b) Paul Eckman
   c) Abraham Maslow
   d) Sigmund Freud

21) _____ is defined as a generalized (non-specific) response to a perceived threat.
   a) Fight or flight response
   b) Stress
   c) The general adaptation syndrome
   d) Angst

22) The _____ describes the human reaction to prolonged stress.
   a) general adaptation syndrome
   b) mental illness
   c) depression
   d) learned helplessness

Chapter 6 Study Guide (Answers)

1. **Motivation** is defined as an inner state and a process that arouses, directs, maintains, and terminates behavior.
2. Motivation is said to be **intrinsic,** a force from within, or **extrinsic,** a force from outside of us.
3. The biological perspective produced theories explaining motivation in term of **instincts, drives, and needs.**
4. The behavioral perspective explained motivation in terms of **external forces, rewards, and consequences.**
5. The humanistic perspective explained motivation in terms of an **intrinsic human need to grow and achieve.**
6. **Evolutionary psychologists** explain motivation in terms of adaptive functions that increased the chances of survival and reproduction.
7. According to drive reduction theory, biological needs are the primary motivator of human behavior.
8. Drives are unpleasant internal states of tension which arouse us to take action to meet a biologic need, to restore homeostasis, and to reduce internal tension.
9. **Arousal theory** states that we are motivated achieve our individually optimal state of arousal.
10. **The Yerkes–Dodson Law** describes the relationship between optimal arousal and performance on a task increases with physical and mental arousal, but when levels of arousal become too high, performance decreases
11. Abraham Maslow **is** known as the **father of humanistic psychology.**
12. Maslow proposed that Man is innately and naturally motivated to grow and progress through a **hierarchy,** of physical and psychological steps or stages.
13. Maslow's idea was that people are born with a motivation to grow toward **self-actualization.**
14. In Maslow's theory, our primary motivations are **physiological needs** – food, water, and shelter, and **safety needs** – security and protection from harm.
15. According to Maslow, when the most basic needs have been met, our motivational focus changes to **affiliation,** a feeling of belonging, love, family ties, and group membership.
16. According to Maslow, we are motivated by **esteem** the need to be recognized for our **achievement, for social status, and for respect.**
17. According to Maslow, **self-actualization** is the drive to fulfill one's potential through self-awareness, knowledge, and creativity.
18. The Christian recognizes that despite being hungry, unsafe, and alone, one can be fully actualized in one's relationship with Jesus.
19. We should first seek the kingdom of God and trust that our physical, safety, and other needs will be met.
20. Contrition, self- denial, and humility are means by which Christians achieve spiritual growth.
21. The **need for achievement** describes a drive to meet high personal standards of excellence.
22. The **need for affiliation** is said to motivate forming friendships and associations.
23. The **need for intimacy** motivates forming intimate relationships.
24. The **need for power** is said to motivate those who want to be in charge and to control others.
25. Emotions involve both **physiological and psychological** processes.
26. The experience of emotions is characterized by at least two components: **subjective feelings** and **physiological responses**.
27. Paul Ekman described six basic emotions -- anger, disgust, fear, happiness, sadness, and surprise.
28. **Emotional contagion** describes our tendency to feel the same emotions being felt by those around us.
29. In the James-Lang theory of emotions, the body responds automatically to environmental circumstances, and the brain interprets the body's response as emotion.
30. **Cognitive theories** of emotions suggest that physiological responses and cognitive processes work together to produce the experience of emotions.
31. **Stress** is defined as a generalized (non-specific) response to a perceived threat.
32. The **general adaptation syndrome** describes human reaction to prolonged stress.

Chapter 6 Short Essay Questions (Answers)

1. The biological perspective explained motivation in terms of needs, drives, homeostasis, and arousal. Humanism believes that Mankind is innately and naturally motivated to grow and progress toward self-actualization, as defined by humanist morals and values, is central to a humanistic worldview today. A number of theories that explain human motivation in terms of social needs. The need for achievement, the need for affiliation, the need for intimacy, and the need for power. Evolutionary psychologists explain motivation and emotion in terms of adaptive mental structures that have become progressively more complex over time. Every human motivation and emotion exists because it served an adaptive function that increased the chances of survival and reproduction.

2. According to drive reduction theory, biological needs are the primary motivator of human behavior. The psychological experience of biological needs is called a drive. Drives are unpleasant internal states of tension which arouse us to take action to meet a biologic need, to restore homeostasis, and to reduce internal tension.

3. In Maslow's theory, our primary motivations are physiological needs. When those most basic needs have been met, our motivational focus changes to affiliation. Next, according to Maslow and humanism, we are propelled to meet esteem needs – to be recognized for our achievement, for social status, and for respect. Once our need for affiliation and esteem are met, according to Maslow, we can then pursue "self-actualization," a distinctly human drive to fulfill one's potential through self-awareness, knowledge, and creativity.

4. Emotions involve both physiological and psychological processes. The experience of emotions is characterized by at least two components: subjective feelings and physiological responses. Emotions are subjective experiences accompanied with universal physiological changes. We understand that some emotions are positive, some negative, and some a mixture of both.

5. William James and Carl Lange proposed that the body triggers the experience of emotions. In the James-Lang theory, the body responds automatically to environmental circumstances, and the brain interprets the body's response as emotion. Using the scenario of meeting a bear in the woods, James theorized that seeing a bear triggers automatic physical reactions. According to James, we do not fear the bear; we react physically to the risk of death and we interpret the experience of the body's reactions to the bear (rapid pulse, increased respiration, and adrenaline rush) as fear.

6. Cognitive theories suggest that the experience of an emotion is a function of both the physiologic response and our interpretation of what is causing the response. Physiological responses and cognitive processes work together to produce the experience of emotions.

7. Psychological. Slowed thinking, poor judgment, difficulty making decisions, worrying, and inability to relax. Emotional. Depressed mood, anxiety, agitation, and irritability. Physiological. Aches and pains, diarrhea or constipation, nausea, dizziness, chest pain, and rapid heartbeat. Behavioral. Disruption to diet, sleep, social activity, and meeting responsibilities as well as possible drug and alcohol use.

8. Getting married, a promotion at work, and having children are examples of "good" stress.

9. The Type A personality is characterized by time-urgency, aggression, and a need to achieve. The Type A personality is associated with an elevated risk of hypertension and heart attack.

Chapter 6 Quiz Answers

1. _____is defined as an inner state and a process that arouses, directs, maintains, and terminates behavior. a) Motivation

2. Motivation coming from within is said to be _____.   b) Intrinsic

3. The _____ perspective produced theories explaining motivation in term of instincts, drives, and needs.   b) biological

4. The _____ perspective explained motivation in terms of external forces, rewards, and consequences.   b) biologic

5. The _____ perspective explains motivation in terms of an intrinsic human need to grow and achieve.   c) humanistic

6. The _____ psychologists explain motivation in terms of adaptive functions that increased the chances of survival and reproduction.   d) evolutionary

7. _____ are automatic, involuntary, and unlearned patterns of behavior that are triggered by particular stimuli   a) Reflexes

8. According to drive reduction theory, _____ needs are the primary motivator of human behavior.   a) biological

9. According to the _____, biological needs are the primary motivator of human behavior.   a) drive reduction theory

10. _____ are unpleasant internal states of tension which arouse us to take action to meet the need, restore homeostasis, and reduce internal tension.   d) Drives

11. _____is known as the father of humanistic psychology. b) Abraham Maslow

12. Maslow's idea that people are born with a motivation to grow toward _____ is central to a humanistic worldview today.   b) self-actualization

13. _____ states that we are motivated achieve our individually optimal state of arousal. a) Arousal theory

14. The _____ describes the relationship between optimal arousal and performance on a task increases with physical and mental arousal, but when levels of arousal become too high, performance decreases. a) Yerkes–Dodson Law

15. The _____ describes a drive to meet high personal standards of excellence.   a) need for achievement

16. The _____ personality is characterized by a need to achieve, time-urgency, and aggression and is associated with an elevated risk of hypertension and heart attack.   b) Type A

17. According to Maslow, when the most basic needs have been met, our motivational focus changes to _____, a feeling of belonging, love, family ties, and group membership.   a) affiliation
18. The need for _____motivates forming intimate relationships.   c) intimacy
19. The need for _____ is said to motivate those who want to be in charge and to control others.   c) intimacy
20. In the _____ theory of emotions, the body responds automatically to environmental circumstances, and the brain interprets the body's response as emotion.   a) James-Lang
21. _____ is defined as a generalized (non-specific) response to a perceived threat.   b) Stress
22. The _____ describes human reaction to prolonged stress.   a) general adaptation syndrome

Chapter 7 Learning and Memory

Chapter 7 Learning Objectives

Define Learning
Describe Classical Conditioning
Describe Ivan Pavlov's experiments
Name and define the key components of classical conditioning
Describe Operant Conditioning
Describe Thorndike's Law of Effect
Describe B.F. Skinner's experiments
Define key terms from operant conditioning
Describe reinforcement schedules
Describe Cognitive theories of learning
Describe latent learning
Describe Social Learning theories
Describe the three-box model of human memory
Describe factors that influence forming, storing, and retrieving memories
Describe and use mnemonic techniques

Key Concepts & People

Behaviorism	John Watson	B. F. Skinner
Classical Conditioning	Herman Ebbinghaus	Albert Bandura
Operant Conditioning	John Garcia	Wolfgang Kohler
Latent Learning	Little Albert	
Ivan Pavlov	Edward Thorndike	

Short Essay Questions

1. Define Learning
2. Describe classical conditioning and Ivan Pavlov's experiments
3. Name and define the key components of classical conditioning
4. Describe operant conditioning, Thorndike's law of effect, and B.F. Skinner's experiments
5. Describe conditioned taste aversion
6. Describe John Watson's Little Albert experiment
7. Describe reinforcement schedules
8. Describe cognitive theories of learning
9. Describe latent learning
10. Describe Albert Bandura's Bobo doll study
11. Describe social learning theories
12. Describe the three-box model of human memory
13. Describe factors that influence forming, storing, and retrieving memories
14. Describe the primacy and recency effects
15. Describe and explain mnemonic techniques

For Further Study

1. Video: John Watson's Little Albert experiment at
    http://www.youtube.com/watch?v=KxKfpKQzow8&feature=related

2. Video: B. F. Skinner: Shaping at http://www.youtube.com/watch?v=bXCdsHH6S7Q
3. Video: Bandura – bobo doll experiment at http://www.youtube.com/watch?v=hHHdovKHDNU
4. Video: Thorndike – Law of Effect
   http://www.youtube.com/watch?v=Vk6H7Ukp6To&feature=related
5. Video: Classical Conditioning - Dr. Zimbardo narrates historical footage of famous experiments.
   http://www.youtube.com/watch?v=hhqumfpxuzI
6. Read: Ivan Pavlov's Nobel Prize Biography at
   http://nobelprize.org/nobel_prizes/medicine/laureates/1904/pavlov-bio.html
7. Read: John Watson's Studying the Mind of Animals at
   http://psychclassics.yorku.ca/Watson/Animals/index.htm
8. Video: BF Skinner Foundation – Pigeon Ping Pong Clip at
   http://www.youtube.com/watch?v=vGazyH6fQQ4&feature=related
9. Read Albert Bandura's Transmission of Aggression Through Imitation of Aggressive Models at
   http://psychclassics.yorku.ca/Bandura/bobo.htm
10. Read: Behavioral Psychology in the Sunday School Classroom by Donald Ratcliff at
    http://www.asa3.org/ASA/PSCF/1982/JASA12-82Ratcliff.html
11. Read: Superstition in the Pigeon by B.F. Skinner at http://psychclassics.yorku.ca/Skinner/Pigeon/

Topics for Discussion

1. Which is more important, nature or nurture?
2. What were the ethical problems with John Watson's work with Little Albert?
3. The effectiveness and appropriateness of corporal punishment (spanking) is a hot-button topic among Christians and psychologists alike. Explain your position on spanking and support it with the Bible.

Chapter 7 Worldview Issues

Behaviorism

The scientific study of behavior has produced countless important discoveries about the factors that influence human behavior, techniques to change behavior, and the ways in which we learn. The science of behaviorism is one thing, but behaviorism is also a worldview. Behaviorism was modern psychology's first school-of-thought and it made bold and disturbing claims about human nature – namely, that there was no real human nature.

Behaviorism is deterministic. We do the things we do because of the natural laws of behavior, not because of any personal volition or free-will. B.F. Skinner said that free-will was an illusion. All behavior, animal and human, is determined by the environment in a closed cause and effect system. We're more complicated than animals, but there is no real difference between man and animal. Behaviorism is mechanistic – humans are living machines that operate by impersonal mechanistic processes. We go through life reacting to stimuli from the environment (inputs) in predictable ways (outputs). It is a depressing worldview that removes freedom, dignity, self-determination, and responsibility from what it means to be human. Similarly, behaviorism rejects God and the immaterial aspect of humanity.

Study Guide Chapter 7

1. _____ is generally defined as a mental process leading to relatively permanent changes in behavior, knowledge, or mental processes due to practice or experience.

2. _____ refers to a very simple type of learning in which behavior changes as a result of repeated exposure to a stimulus.

3. _____ describes a learning process that occurs when two stimuli are repeatedly paired.

4. The _____ is an organism's reflexive unlearned response to a stimulus.

5. The unconditioned stimulus (UCS) naturally elicits the organism's _____.

6. A _____ does not elicit a reflexive response.

7. The response to the conditioned stimulus is known as the _____.

8. B. F. Skinner's discoveries, which came to be known as _____, expanded on classical conditioning to include the ways organisms operate on the environment to gain rewards and avoid negative consequences.

9. _____ is a consequence of behavior that increases the likelihood that a response will occur.

10. _____ is a consequence that is usually pleasant and increases the likelihood of a response.

11. _____ is a consequence of behavior that increases the likelihood of a response by removing a negative stimulus.

12. _____ is a consequence of a behavior that decreases the likelihood that a response will occur.

13. _____ is a consequence of behavior that is usually unpleasant (e.g., pain) and decreases the likelihood of a response.

14. _____ _____ (sometimes known as time-out) is a consequence of behavior in which a positive stimulus is removed.

15. _____ refers to the gradual disappearance of a response when reinforcement ceases.

16. _____ guides behavior toward the desired response by reinforcing successive approximations of desired behaviors.

17. _____ refer to the frequency or pattern of reinforcement.

18. Continuous reinforcement schedules reinforce a behavior _____.

19. _____ schedules reinforce behavior some of the time.

20. In fixed ratio reinforcement schedules reinforcement happens after _____.

21. _____ schedules reinforce behavior after a fixed amount of time.

22. Variable ratio reinforcement schedules reinforce behavior after a

_____.

23. _____ schedules reinforce behavior after a variable period of time.

24. _____ of learning describe the cognitive processes by which we acquire knowledge and skills and the ways we create and manipulate mental representations of physical objects and events.

25. _____ is a type of learning that is not demonstrated in an immediate behavioral response and occurs without direct behavioral reinforcement.

26. _____ theory explains learning as the result of observation, imitation, and modeling in a reciprocal interaction between cognitive, behavioral, and environmental influences.

27. Memory is the process by which information is _____.

28. _____ is like a temporary buffer where information is held very briefly and evaluated for further processing.

Chapter 7 Quiz

1) _____ is generally defined as a mental process leading to relatively permanent changes in behavior, knowledge, or mental processes due to practice or experience.
   a) Learning
   b) Wisdom
   c) Thinking
   d) Maturation

2) The process by which a conditioned response ends after the conditioned stimulus is repeatedly not paired with the unconditioned stimulus is called:
   a) extinction
   b) punishment
   c) time-out
   d) regression

3) _____ refers to a very simple type of learning in which behavior changes as a result of repeated exposure to a stimulus.
   a) Habituation
   b) Classical education
   c) Nagging
   d) Shaping

4) _____ refers to the same conditioned response occurring to similar, but not identical, stimuli.
   a) Stimulus discrimination
   b) Stimulus generalization
   c) Stimulus overload
   d) Stimulus package

5) _____ explains learning in terms of the rewards, punishments, and negative consequences of behaviors in a two-way interaction with the environment.
   a) Shaping
   b) Association
   c) Classical conditioning
   d) Operant Conditioning

6) _____ describes a learning process that occurs when two stimuli are repeatedly paired.
   a) Classical conditioning
   b) Operant Conditioning
   c) Reinforced learning
   d) Reflexive learning

7) The _____ is an organism's reflexive unlearned response to a stimulus.
   a) unconditioned response (UCR)
   b) unconditioned stimulus (UCS)
   c) neutral stimulus (NS)
   d) conditioned response (CR)

8) The _____ naturally elicits the organism's reflexive response.
   a) unconditioned response (UCR)
   b) unconditioned stimulus (UCS)
   c) neutral stimulus (NS)
   d) conditioned response (CR)

9) A _____ does not elicit a reflexive response.
   a) unconditioned response (UCR)
   b) unconditioned stimulus (UCS)
   c) neutral stimulus (NS)
   d) conditioned response (CR)

10) The response to the conditioned stimulus is known as the:
   a) unconditioned response (UCR)
   b) unconditioned stimulus (UCS)
   c) neutral stimulus (NS)
   d) conditioned response (CR)

11) _____ describes reinforcing successive approximations of the desired behavior.
   a) Learning
   b) Reinforcement
   c) Shaping
   d) Parenting

12) In _____ reinforcement the behavior is reinforced after a fixed number of responses.
   a) fixed ratio
   b) fixed interval
   c) variable ratio
   d) variable interval

13) _____ is a consequence of behavior that increases the likelihood that a response will occur.
   a) Reinforcement
   b) Punishment
   c) Extinction
   d) Shaping

14) _____ is a consequence of a behavior that decreases the likelihood that a response will occur.
   a) Reinforcement
   b) Punishment
   c) Extinction
   d) Shaping

15) _____ refer to the frequency or pattern of reinforcement.
   a) Contingency plans
   b) Schedules of reinforcement
   c) Classical reinforcement
   d) Operant reinforcement

16) _____ schedules reinforce a behavior every time it occurs.
   a) Continuous reinforcement
   b) Intermittent reinforcement
   c) fixed ratio reinforcement
   d) Fixed interval reinforcement

17) _____ schedules reinforce behavior some of the time.
   a) Continuous reinforcement
   b) Intermittent reinforcement
   c) fixed ratio reinforcement
   d) Fixed interval reinforcement

18) _____ schedules reinforce behavior after a fixed amount of time.
   a) Continuous reinforcement
   b) Intermittent reinforcement
   c) Fixed ratio reinforcement
   d) Fixed interval reinforcement

19) _____ schedules reinforce behavior after a varying number of responses.
   a) Continuous reinforcement
   b) Intermittent reinforcement
   c) Fixed interval reinforcement
   d) Variable ratio reinforcement

20) _____ schedules reinforce behavior after a variable period of time.
   a) Continuous reinforcement
   b) Fixed interval reinforcement
   c) Variable ratio reinforcement
   d) Variable interval reinforcement

21) _____ is like a temporary buffer where information is held very briefly and evaluated for further processing.
   a) Sensory memory
   b) Short term memory
   c) Buffering
   d) Latent memory

22) _____ is a form of learning that is not demonstrated in an immediate behavioral response and occurs without direct behavioral reinforcement.
   a) Short-term memory
   b) Latent learning
   c) Generalization
   d) Deferred learning

23) _____ theory proposes that we learn from one another through observation, imitation, and modeling.
   a) Social learning
   b) Behavioral learning
   c) Cognitive learning
   d) Demonstrative learning

24) _____ is the process by which information is acquired, encoded, stored, retrieved, and possibly forgotten.
   a) Memory
   b) Priming
   c) Learning
   d) Attention

25) _____ is/are short-term memory strategy(ies) to organize and group memory items into larger units allowing for more information to be stored.
   a) Mnemonics
   b) Chunking
   c) Pegging
   d) Method of loci

26) _____ refers to the influence of mental states and emotions on memory formation.
   a) Recency effect
   b) Serial position effect
   c) State-dependent learning
   d) Cognitive learning

Answer Key Chapter 7

Chapter 7 Study Guide (Answers)

1. **Learning** is generally defined as a mental process leading to relatively permanent changes in behavior, knowledge, or mental processes due to practice or experience.
2. **Habituation** refers to a very simple type of learning in which behavior changes as a result of repeated exposure to a stimulus.
3. **Classical conditioning** describes a learning process that occurs when two stimuli are repeatedly paired.
4. The **unconditioned response (UCR)** is an organism's reflexive unlearned response to a stimulus.
5. The unconditioned stimulus (UCS) naturally elicits the organism's **reflexive response**.
6. A **neutral stimulus (NS)** does not elicit a reflexive response.
7. The response to the conditioned stimulus is known as the **conditioned response (CR)**.
8. B. F. Skinner's discoveries, which came to be known as **operant conditioning**, expanded on classical conditioning to include the ways organisms operate on the environment to gain rewards and avoid negative consequences.
9. **Reinforcement** is a consequence of behavior that increases the likelihood that a response will occur.
10. **Positive Reinforcement** is a consequence that is usually pleasant and increases the likelihood of a response.
11. **Negative reinforcement** is a consequence of behavior that increases the likelihood of a response by removing a negative stimulus.
12. **Punishment** is a consequence of a behavior that decreases the likelihood that a response will occur.
13. **Positive punishment** is a consequence of behavior that is usually unpleasant (e.g., pain) and decreases the likelihood of a response.
14. **Negative punishment** (sometimes known as time-out) is a consequence of behavior in which a positive stimulus is removed.
15. **Extinction** refers to the gradual disappearance of a response when reinforcement ceases.
16. **Shaping** guides behavior toward the desired response by reinforcing successive approximations of desired behaviors.
17. **Schedules of reinforcement** refer to the frequency or pattern of reinforcement.
18. Continuous reinforcement schedules reinforce a behavior **every time it occurs**.
19. **Intermittent reinforcement** schedules reinforce behavior some of the time.
20. In fixed ratio reinforcement schedules reinforcement happens after a **fixed number of responses**.
21. **Fixed interval reinforcement** schedules reinforce behavior after a fixed amount of time.
22. Variable ratio reinforcement schedules reinforce behavior after a varying number of responses.
23. Variable interval reinforcement schedules reinforce behavior after a **variable period of time**.
24. **Cognitive theories** of learning describe the cognitive processes by which we acquire knowledge and skills and the ways we create and manipulate mental representations of physical objects and events.
25. **Latent learning** is a type of learning that is not demonstrated in an immediate behavioral response and occurs without direct behavioral reinforcement.
26. **Social learning theory** explains learning as the result of observation, imitation, and modeling in a reciprocal interaction between cognitive, behavioral, and environmental influences.
27. Memory is the process by which information is **acquired, encoded, stored, and retrieved**.
28. **Sensory memory** is like a temporary buffer where information is held very briefly and evaluated for further processing.

Chapter 7 Short Essay Questions (Answers)

1. Learning is generally defined as a mental process leading to relatively permanent changes in behavior, knowledge, or mental processes due to practice or experience.
2. Pavlov secured a dog in a harness behind a one-way glass. Pavlov delivered meat powder by remote control, allowing him to pair the delivery of meat powder with other stimuli. For example, after the dog became accustomed to the harness, Pavlov turned on a light and then delivered the meat powder. Initially, the dog did not salivate until the food powder was delivered. The light did not elicit a salivation response. After a number of trails in which the light was always followed by meat powder, the dog began to salivate as soon as the light was turned on. The light began to elicit a response. Pavlov's discovery, which he called signalization, came to be known as classical conditioning. Conditioning is a learning process that occurs when an organism associates a natural stimulus with an environmental stimulus. It came to be known as "classical" conditioning because it was modern psychology's first major theory of learning. Pavlov noted that when a signal is paired with a natural reflex-producing stimulus, the signal alone begins to activate a learned response similar to the natural reflex.

3. The key components of classical conditioning are: A reflex. Classical conditioning always starts with a reflex. Reflexes are not learned. Dogs reflexively salivate when given meat powder. The unconditioned stimulus (UCS). The UCS is a stimulus that naturally elicits a biological reflex. Meat powder is an unconditioned stimulus for a dog. The unconditioned response (UCR). The UCR is a natural response to a natural stimulus. Salivation is a dog's unconditioned response to meat. A neutral stimulus (NS). The neutral stimulus does not elicit a reflexive response. The sound of a metronome (or a bell or light) is a neutral stimulus to a dog. A conditioned stimulus (CS). The CS is a previously neutral stimulus that, after being associated with the unconditioned stimulus, eventually elicits a conditioned response. The light begins to elicit a response after being paired with food powder. A conditioned response (CR). The conditioned response is the learned response to the previously neutral stimulus.

4. Operant conditioning describes a type of learning involving a stimulus and response connection. The law of effect states that any behavior followed by a pleasant consequence tends to be repeated, and any behavior followed by unpleasant consequences tends not to be repeated. Edward Thorndike suggested that learning depended less on reflexes and more on the organism's operations on the environment. Skinner expanded on classical conditioning to include the ways animals and humans "operate" on the environment in order to gain rewards and avoid negative consequences. Skinner is known for his work with rats, pigeons, and animal boxes (Skinner boxes). In a Skinner box, an animal receives a food reward for performing various behaviors.

5. Classical conditioning generally requires several parings of the conditioned and unconditioned stimuli. In some instances, however, conditioning occurs with a single paring. In the 1970s psychologist John Garcia conducted a series of experiments on rats in which he paired a taste with sickness. Garcia presented groups of rats with saccharin-flavored water and over the next 24 hours induced sickness by exposing the rats to radiation. Some rats became sick immediately after drinking the water, others did not become ill for as much as 24 hours, and the control group did not become sick. Garcia noted that a strong and persistent aversion to the flavored water appeared after only one pairing of the flavor and sickness, even with a six-hour delay between taste and the onset of sickness.

6. Watson's subject, 9-month-old "Little Albert," was first exposed to a white rat, rabbit, monkey, and to burning newspaper to observe that Little Albert did not fear those things. Watson then paired the white rat with a loud clanging noise that startled Little Albert and caused him to cry. Watson repeatedly paired the presentation of the rat with the loud clang. Each time Little Albert cried. Eventually, Little Albert cried and tried to crawl away at the presentation of the rat, even without the loud clang. After conditioning, Albert also feared other furry or white objects, demonstrating the principle of stimulus generalization.

7. Schedules of reinforcement refers to the frequency or pattern of reinforcement. A behavior does not have to be reinforced every time it occurs. Reinforcement schedules can be continuous or intermittent. In a continuous reinforcement schedule the desired behavior is reinforced every time it occurs. In an intermittent reinforcement schedule the desired behavior is reinforced some of the time. Intermittent reinforcement schedules are more resistant to extinction than continuous reinforcement. There are two categories of intermittent reinforcement schedules: ratio and interval. There are four types of intermittent reinforcement schedules: fixed ratio, variable ratio, fixed interval, and variable interval. In a fixed ratio reinforcement schedule reinforcement happens after a fixed number of responses. In a fixed interval reinforcement schedule. Reinforcement happens after a fixed amount of time. In a variable ratio reinforcement schedule reinforcement happens after a variable number of responses. In a variable interval reinforcement schedule reinforcement happens after a variable period of time.

8. Cognitive psychologists emphasize the mental processes that are a part of learning. Where behaviorists believe that learning occurs without thought, cognitive theories suggest that all learning (including conditioning) involves cognitive processes. Cognitive psychologists explore mental processes such as information processing, mental representations, and expectations as central to a cognitive perspective of learning. Cognitive learning theories refer to the mental processes by which we acquire knowledge and skills and the ways we create and manipulate mental representations of physical objects and events.

9. Latent learning is a form of learning that is not demonstrated in an immediate behavioral response and occurs without direct behavioral reinforcement. Latent learning is said to demonstrate the importance of cognition in learning, in addition to the principles of behavioral learning. Latent learning is comparable to acquiring new knowledge (e.g., how to change a tire) that is not yet needed.

10. Bandura studied 36 boys and 36 girls ranging from 3 to 6 years old. Half of his subjects were exposed to aggressive adult models and half were exposed to models that were subdued and nonaggressive in their behavior. The aggressive models punched, kicked, hit with a mallet, and made angry comments toward a Bobo doll. A Bobo doll is an inflatable doll with a weight in the bottom, so each time it is knocked down, it pops right back up. The nonaggressive models quietly assembled blocks, totally ignoring the Bobo doll. Later, Bandura secretly observed the children in a room with a Bobo doll and other toys. The children who had witnessed the adult striking the Bobo doll were far more likely to strike their own Bobo doll than the children who had not seen the adults' aggressive behavior.

11. Social learning theory proposes that we learn from one another through observation, imitation, and modeling. Social learning theory explains learning in terms of the reciprocal interaction between cognitive, behavioral, and environmental influences.

12. Psychologists divide memory into three types: sensory memory, short-term memory, and long-term memory, sometimes called the "three-box" model of memory.

13. The serial position effect describes the relationship between the position of an item in a list and the ability to recall it. Some memories are context dependent, meaning that the environmental context in which we store a memory influences its retrieval. Some students report better results studying for a test in the classroom in which the test will be administered. Our personal emotional state influences encoding and retrieving memories. State-dependent memories refers to the influence of mental states and emotions. Interference refers to thoughts or memories that interfere with what we are trying to recall.

Interference can occur either retroactively or proactively. Mis-attribution, or memory source confusion, refers to the phenomenon in which information learned after an event becomes part of the memory of the event.

14. The primacy effect explains that items near the beginning of a list are easier to recall than those in the middle. The recency effect explains that items near the end of a list are easier to recall than those in the middle.

15. Mnemonics are techniques for retrieving memories that are otherwise difficult to recall. The rhyme "30 days hath September" is a mnemonic tool for remembering the number of days in each month. Acronyms are made by taking the first letter from each item in a list to be remembered. The first letter from items in a list can be used to form acrostic sentences. Using keywords involves making a connection between the new word and an image involving a related word that serves as a "key" to the new word. Method of loci, or method of location, refers to mentally placing objects in a well-known location.

Chapter 7 Quiz Answers

1) _____ is generally defined as a mental process leading to relatively permanent changes in behavior, knowledge, or mental processes due to practice or experience. a) Learning

2) The process by which a conditioned response ends after the conditioned stimulus is repeatedly not paired with the unconditioned stimulus is called _____. a) extinction

3) _____ refers to a very simple type of learning in which behavior changes as a result of repeated exposure to a stimulus. a) Habituation

4) _____ refers to the same conditioned response occurring to similar, but not identical, stimuli. b) Stimulus generalization

5) _____ explains learning in terms of the rewards, punishments, and negative consequences of behaviors in a two-way interaction with the environment. d) Operant Conditioning

6) _____ describes a learning process that occurs when two stimuli are repeatedly paired. a) Classical conditioning

7) The _____ is an organism's reflexive unlearned response to a stimulus. a) unconditioned response (UCR)

8) The _____ naturally elicits the organism's reflexive response. b) unconditioned stimulus (UCS)

9) A _____ does not elicit a reflexive response. b) unconditioned stimulus (UCS)

10) The response to the conditioned stimulus is known as the: d) conditioned response (CR)

11) _____ describes reinforcing successive approximations of the desired behavior. c) Shaping

12) In _____ reinforcement the behavior is reinforced after a fixed number of responses. a) fixed ratio

13) _____ is a consequence of behavior that increases the likelihood that a response will occur. a) Reinforcement

14) _____ is a consequence of a behavior that decreases the likelihood that a response will occur. b) Punishment

15) _____ refer to the frequency or pattern of reinforcement. b) Schedules of reinforcement

16) _____ schedules reinforce a behavior every time it occurs. a) Continuous reinforcement

17) _____ schedules reinforce behavior some of the time. b) Intermittent reinforcement

18) _____ schedules reinforce behavior after a fixed amount of time. c) Fixed ratio reinforcement

19) _____ schedules reinforce behavior after a varying number of responses. d) Variable ratio reinforcement

20) _____ schedules reinforce behavior after a variable period of time. d) Variable interval reinforcement

21) _____ is like a temporary buffer where information is held very briefly and evaluated for further processing. a) Sensory memory

22) _____ is a form of learning that is not demonstrated in an immediate behavioral response and occurs without direct behavioral reinforcement. b) Latent learning

23) _____ theory proposes that we learn from one another through observation, imitation, and modeling. a) Social learning

24) _____ is the process by which information is acquired, encoded, stored, retrieved, and possibly forgotten. a) Memory

25) _____ is/are short-term memory strategy(ies) to organize and group memory items into larger units allowing for more information to be stored. b) Chunking

26) _____ refers to the influence of mental states and emotions on memory formation. c) State-dependent learning

Chapter 8 Development

Chapter 8 Learning Objectives

Describe the characteristics of the various developmental theories.
Describe development theories in terms of the philosophies of Locke, Rousseau, Kant, and Hall.
Describe recapitulation theory.
Define cognition and cognitive styles.
Describe Piaget's stages of cognitive development.
Describe criticisms of Piaget's theory of cognitive development.
Describe cross-section and longitudinal developments research.
Describe Freudian psycho-sexual development.

Key Concepts and People

Fetal alcohol syndrome	Erik Erikson	Daniel Levinson
John Locke	Ernst Haeckel	Raymond Cattell
Jean Piaget	Sigmund Freud	Elisabeth Kubler-Ross
Jean Rousseau	Lawrence Kohlberg	Object permanence
Immanuel Kant	Bolby and Ainsworth	Social Development
G. Stanley Hall	Harry Harlow	Theories
Lev Vygotsky	Diana Baumrind	Psychosexual Development

Short Essay Questions

1. Describe the uses of developmental theories.
2. In what ways is development continuous, and in what ways is it discontinuous?
3. Describe nervous system development in the embryonic stage and fetal stages of development.
4. Describe fetal alcohol syndrome and how to prevent it.
5. Name and describe four reflexive abilities children have at birth.
6. Describe cross-section and longitudinal developmental research.
7. Describe development theories in terms of the philosophies of Locke, Rousseau, Kant, and Hall.
8. Piaget described four stages of cognitive development. Name and describe each stage.
9. Describe assimilation and accommodation in terms of Piaget's developmental theory.
10. Describe criticisms of Piaget's theory of cognitive development.

For Further Study

1. Read: The Heritage of the Recapitulation Theory by Henry Morris. icr.org/article/287/
2. Video: Dr. Money And The Boy With No Penis at https://documentarystorm.com/dr-money-and-the-boy-with-no-penis/
3. Video: John Bowlby: Attachment Theory Across Generations
   http://www.youtube.com/watch?v=8ljZ4a8Uc8Q
4. Video: Piaget's Developmental Theory: An Overview
   http://www.youtube.com/watch?v=lEam9lpa6TQ
5. Video: Vygotsky's Developmental Theory: An Introduction
   https://www.youtube.com/watch?v=InzmZtHuZPY
6. Video: Using Twin and Adoption Studies – Twin Studies
   https://www.youtube.com/watch?v=Trc2dJgeyvc
7. Read: Some Developmental Ideas of Jean Piaget by Bonnidell Clouse
   https://asa3.org/ASA/PSCF/1971/JASA9-71Clouse.html

Topics for Discussion

1. Are there personal examples of moral reasoning at each of Kohlberg's levels of moral development?
2. The text stated that "the Christian worldview includes an assurance that Kubler-Ross did not understand." In your own words, explain what Kubler-Ross' theory is missing.

Chapter 8 Worldview Issues

Freud

Sigmund Freud was a tremendously important figure in the history of psychology. In most introductory psychology classes, students learn Sigmund Freud's theories of development, mental disorders, psychoanalysis, the family, dreams, and more. But Freud best known for his theory about the structure of the mind.

According to Freud, humans are motivated by two competing forces in the *unconscious* mind – id and superego. Id is an innate drive for food, sex, comfort, and pleasure. Id is selfish and aggressive. Id wants what it wants, and it wants it now. Freud thought that the superego was an opposite force -- a type of conscience that uses guilt and shame to restrain the id. Ego, our conscious self, 'thinks' it knows why we do what we do, but for Freud, our behavior was determined by the outcome of the struggle between id and superego.

Few psychologists have provoked the ire of Christians more than Sigmund Freud. He was a naturalist influenced by Darwin's theory. He said that religious beliefs were false and believing in gods was a way that the ego found balance. Freud attempted to define the human condition without reference to God. From a Christian perspective, Freud's theories are an interesting fiction, not unlike Greek and Roman mythologies. His theories were influential, but they were not good science. From a Christian perspective, Freud's worldview seems silly.

Study Guide Chapter 8

1. Developmental psychology is the study of the _____.

2. _____ refers to the gradual and ongoing unfolding, or maturation, of inborn characteristics.

3. Some theories suggest we develop discontinuously, through a progressive series of _____.

4. John Locke believed that children are born a "blank slate," or _____.

5. The _____ stated that the prenatal development of an embryo follows the same stages as the evolutionary development of the embryo's species.

6. _____ is serious result of drinking alcohol during pregnancy, characterized by a combination of mental retardation, birth defects, abnormal facial features, behavior problems, cognitive and memory problems, growth problems, and central nervous system damage.

7. Fetal alcohol syndrome has no cure, but it is 100% preventable by _____ during any stage of pregnancy.

8. The _____ is an estimate of the extent to which a trait is inherited.

9. _____ is the life-long process of development that unfolds according to age independently of the environment.

10. Teratogens are _____ that can pass through the placenta and harm the developing child.

11. _____ refers to individual personality traits that appear in infancy. They are thought to be inborn and are relatively stable through life.

12. _____ is famous in the history of psychology for his theories of intellectual development in children.

13. Piaget believed that children are active participants in "constructing" or building _____, or ways of organizing, representing, and understanding the world.

14. Children _____ or "fit" new information into existing schemas.

15. _____ is the process by which children change or "expand" their schemas to account for new information. When a child learns that not all equines are horses, their schema is said to have changed to accommodate that new information.

16. Piaget called the first stage (from birth to 18 months), when the developing child experiences the world through the senses and motor activity, the _____ stage.

17. During the sensorimotor stage, infants discover relationships between their bodies and the environment and begin to develop _____ of objects and relationships.

18. In the sensorimotor stage, infants discover _____ – an understanding of cause-and-effect and the fact that they can control their bodies and move objects.

19. Later in the sensorimotor stage, children understand _____ – that objects do not cease to exist when out of view.

20. The _____ stage, from around 18 months to 6 years, is characterized by the use of symbols to represent things (as in imaginary play), the ability to classify and categorize objects, and language skills development.

21. The pre-operational stage thinking tends to be _____, meaning that young children cannot conceive of someone else's perspective.

22. Piaget observed that around age six, children develop _____, the understanding that matter does not increase or decrease because of a change in form.

23. Conservation is one of many mental operations that characterize Piaget's 3rd stage of development, the _____ stage.

24. During the concrete-operational stage, children begin to use _____.

25. Piaget's final stage, from adolescence into adulthood, is called the _____ stage.

26. Piaget was a _____, meaning he was interested in how knowledge developed in humans in a type of cognitive recapitulation theory.

27. _____ involves studying a variety of ages at a single point in time.

28. In _____, psychologists study the same group of subjects for many years.

29. _____ emphasized unconscious sexual forces in psychological development.

30. Freud is famous in the history of modern psychology for his _____ theory.

31. According to Freud, the _____ seeks physical, especially sexual, gratification.

32. Freud thought that during the _____, the first year of life, gratification was mouth-oriented.

33. Freud though that during the _____ gratification centers on feces, parental expectations, and training and discipline techniques.

34. Freud thought that during the _____, ages two to six, children's libidinal energy is focused on sexuality and the genitals.

35. Freud thought during the _____, age six to twelve, sexual urges were dormant.

36. Freud thought that beginning at puberty, we spend the rest of our lives in the _____, in which we repress or redirect sexual libidinal energy.

37. Russian psychologist Lev Vygotsky proposed one of the first_____ theories.

38. Vygotsky described the role that social interaction, language, and culture play in _____.

39. _____ thought that development was driven by inborn forces and progressed through stages characterized by crises.

40. According to _____, children whose caregivers are available and responsive to infant's needs establish a sense of attachment and security.

41. Children who have _____ exhibit mild distress when separated from caregivers, are happy when the caregivers return, prefer parents to strangers, and seek comfort from parents when frightened.

42. Children who have _____ exhibit more severe distress when a parent leaves, may be wary of strangers, and are not comforted by the parent's return.

43. Children with _____, when offered a choice, show no preference between a caregiver and a complete stranger, and may avoid or not seek comfort or contact from parents.

44. _____ is a loss of brain function that occurs with certain diseases and brain injuries and affects memory, thinking, language, judgment, and behavior.

45. According to Cattell, _____ is made up of basic mental abilities like reasoning, abstract thinking, solving novel problems, and encoding short-term memories.

46. According to Cattell, _____ refers to the general knowledge, vocabulary, and ability accumulated over a lifetime.

47. _____ is famous in the history of psychology for her study of death and dying.

48. Kubler-Ross believed that when we are faced with impending death, we move back and forth through five stages or attitudes:

_____.

49. Kubler-Ross' first stage, _____, is characterized by shock, numbness, and refusal to accept the news.

50. The _____ is characterized by feelings of injustice and "why me?"

51. In the _____, many people facing death try to find a way around it. The dying may make promises of good behavior or other life change in an effort to postpone death.

52. During the fourth stage, _____, as the terminally ill begins to accept the reality of impending death, they may feel overwhelming grief, depression, and hopelessness.

53. Kubler-Ross' final stage of dying is _____. Acceptance means a quiet expectation – being neither depressed nor bitter while contemplating the end of one's life.

Chapter 8 Quiz

1) _____ stated that the prenatal development of an embryo followed the same stages as the evolutionary development of the embryo's species.
   a) Evolutionary Theory
   b) Recapitulation Theory
   c) Biologism
   d) Ontogeny paradigm

2) John Locke believed that children are born a blank slate or _____.
   a) Blanco Biographia
   b) in a state of natural goodness.
   c) tabula rasa
   d) humanistic bliss

3) _____ examines the role of genes in our thoughts, behaviors, and even our personality.
   a) Environmental determinism
   b) Genetic determinism
   c) Behavioral genetics
   d) Nature vs. nurture

4) The _____ is an estimate of the extent to which a trait is inherited.
   a) heritability index
   b) dominance or recession
   c) validity
   d) inheritance factor

5) _____ is the life-long process of development that unfolds according to age and independent of the environment.
   a) Genetic endowment
   b) Maturation
   c) Psychological aging
   d) Behaviorism

6) The embryonic stage is a critical period of human development during which exposure to _____ is especially damaging.
   a) refined sugar
   b) alcohol
   c) teratogens
   d) negative thoughts

7) A result of drinking alcohol during pregnancy characterized by combination of mental retardation, birth defects, abnormal facial features, behavior problems, cognitive and memory problems, growth problems, and central nervous system damage is called:
   a) Down's syndrome
   b) Attention deficit disorder
   c) failure to thrive
   d) fetal alcohol syndrome

8) Fetal alcohol syndrome has no cure, but it can be prevented by _____ during any stage of pregnancy.
   a) having a designated driver
   b) limiting consumption to a few drinks each week
   c) not drinking alcohol
   d) only drinking beer

9) Jean Piaget is famous in the history of psychology for his theories of _____.
   a) intellectual development in children
   b) the sensorimotor stage
   c) moral development in children
   d) cognitive epistemology

10) Piaget believed that children are active participants in constructing, or building _____, or ways of organizing, representing, and understanding the world.
   a) mental representations
   b) schemas
   c) Legos
   d) worldviews

11) _____ is the process by which children change or "expand" their schemas to account for new information.
   a) Development
   b) Assimilation
   c) Accommodation
   d) Maturation

12) In the sensorimotor stage, infants discover _____, an understanding of cause-and-effect and the fact that they can control their bodies and move objects.
   a) object permanence
   b) causality
   c) conservation
   d) logic

13) Later in the sensorimotor stage, children understand _____, that objects do not cease to exist when out of view.
   a) object permanence
   b) causality
   c) conservation
   d) logic

14) The _____, from around 18 months to 6 years, is characterized by the use of symbols to represent things (as in imaginary play), the ability to classify and categorize objects, and language skills development.
   a) sensorimotor stage
   b) pre-operational stage
   c) concrete-operational
   d) formal operational stage

15) Conservation is one of many mental operations that characterize Piaget's 3rd stage of development, _____ stage.
   a) sensorimotor stage
   b) pre-operational stage
   c) concrete-operational
   d) formal operational stage

16) During the _____, children begin to use logic, mental manipulations, and mathematics.
   a) sensorimotor stage
   b) pre-operational stage
   c) concrete-operational
   d) formal operational stage

17) Piaget's final stage, from adolescence into adulthood, is called the _____.
   a) sensorimotor stage
   b) pre-operational stage
   c) concrete-operational
   d) formal operational stage

18) The pre-operational stage thinking tends to be _____, meaning that young children cannot conceive of someone else's perspective.
   a) egocentric
   b) illogical
   c) causal
   d) relational

19) Piaget observed that around age six, children develop _____; understanding that matter does not increase or decrease because of a change in form.
   a) conservation
   b) object permanence
   c) causality
   d) logic

20) _____ involves studying a variety of ages at a single point in time.
   a) Cross-sectional research
   b) Longitudinal research

21) In _____, psychologists study the same group of subjects for many years.
   a) Cross-sectional research
   b) Longitudinal research

22) Freud is famous in the history of modern psychology for his _____.
   a) attachment theory
   b) psycho-sexual theory
   c) psycho-social theory
   d) humanistic theory

23) According to Freud, the _____ seeks physical, especially sexual, gratification.
   a) id
   b) ego
   c) libido
   d) unconscious

24) Freud thought that during the _____, the first year of life, gratification was mouth-oriented.
   a) oral stage
   b) anal stage
   c) phallic stage
   d) latency stage

25) Freud though that during the
_____ gratification
centers on feces, parental expectations, and
training and discipline techniques.
    a) oral stage
    b) anal stage
    c) phallic stage
    d) latency stage

26) Freud thought that during the
_____, ages two to six,
children's libidinal energy is focused on
sexuality and the genitals.
    a) oral stage
    b) anal stage
    c) phallic stage
    d) latency stage

27) Freud thought during the
_____, age six to twelve,
sexual urges were dormant.
    a) oral stage
    b) anal stage
    c) phallic stage
    d) latency stage

28) Freud thought that beginning at puberty, we
spend the rest of our lives in the
_____, in which we
repress or redirect sexual libidinal energy.
    a) oral stage
    b) anal stage
    c) phallic stage
    d) genital stage

29) Russian psychologist Lev Vygotsky
proposed one of the first
_____ theories.
    a) psycho-sexual development
    b) psycho-social development
    c) social learning
    d) attachment

30) According to attachment theory, children
who have _____ exhibit
mild distress when separated from
caregivers, are happy when the caregivers
return, prefer parents to strangers, and seek
comfort from parents when frightened.
    a) secure attachment
    b) ambivalent attachment
    c) avoidant attachment
    d) positive attachment

31) According to attachment theory, children
who have _____
exhibit more severe distress when a parent
leaves, may be wary of strangers, and are
not comforted by the parent's return.
    a) secure attachment
    b) ambivalent attachment
    c) avoidant attachment
    d) positive attachment

32) According to attachment theory, children
with_____,
when offered a choice, show no preference
between a caregiver and a complete
stranger, and may avoid or not seek comfort
or contact from parents.
    a) secure attachment
    b) ambivalent attachment
    c) avoidant attachment
    d) positive attachment

33) _____ is a loss of brain
function that occurs with certain diseases
and brain injuries and affects memory,
thinking, language, judgment, and behavior.
    a) dementia
    b) delirium
    c) senility
    d) insanity

34) According to Cattell, _____ is
made up of basic mental abilities like
reasoning, abstract thinking, solving novel
problems, and encoding short-term
memories.
    a) flexible intelligence
    b) crystallized intelligence

35) According to Cattell, _____
refers to the general knowledge, vocabulary,
and ability accumulated over a lifetime.
    a) flexible intelligence
    b) crystallized intelligence

36) Which is NOT one of Elisabeth Kubler-
Ross' 5 stages of grief when faced with
impending death?
    a) denial and isolation
    b) anger
    c) bargaining
    d) hope

Answer Key Chapter 8

Chapter 8 Study Guide (Answers)

1. Developmental psychology is the study of the **lifelong process of change**.
2. **Continuous development** refers to the gradual and ongoing unfolding, or maturation, of inborn characteristics.
3. Some theories suggest we develop discontinuously, through a progressive series of **distinct steps or stages**.
4. John Locke believed that children are born a "blank slate," or **tabula rasa**.
5. The **recapitulation theory** stated that the prenatal development of an embryo follows the same stages as the evolutionary development of the embryo's species.
6. **Fetal Alcohol Syndrome** is serious result of drinking alcohol during pregnancy, characterized by a combination of mental retardation, birth defects, abnormal facial features, behavior problems, cognitive and memory problems, growth problems, and central nervous system damage.
7. Fetal alcohol syndrome has no cure, but it is 100% preventable by **not drinking alcohol** during any stage of pregnancy.
8. The **heritability index** is an estimate of the extent to which a trait is inherited.
9. **Maturation** is the life-long process of development that unfolds according to age independently of the environment.
10. Teratogens are **environmental toxins** that can pass through the placenta and harm the developing child.
11. **Temperament** refers to individual personality traits that appear in infancy. They are thought to be inborn and are relatively stable through life.
12. **Jean Piaget** is famous in the history of psychology for his theories of intellectual development in children.
13. Piaget believed that children are active participants in "constructing" or building **schemas**, or ways of organizing, representing, and understanding the world.
14. Children **assimilate** or "fit" new information into existing schemas.
15. **Accommodation** is the process by which children change or "expand" their schemas to account for new information. When a child learns that not all equines are horses, their schema is said to have changed to accommodate that new information.
16. Piaget called the first stage (from birth 18 months), when the developing child experiences the world through the senses and motor activity, the **sensorimotor** stage.
17. During the sensorimotor stage, infants discover relationships between their bodies and the environment and begin to develop **mental representations** of objects and relationships.
18. In the sensorimotor stage, infants discover causality – an understanding of cause-and-effect and the fact that they can control their bodies and move objects.
19. Later in the sensorimotor stage, children understand object permanence – that objects do not cease to exist when out of view.
20. The **pre-operational** stage, from around 18 months to 6 years, is characterized by the use of symbols to represent things (as in imaginary play), the ability to classify and categorize objects, and language skills development.
21. The pre-operational stage thinking tends to be **egocentric**, meaning that young children cannot conceive of someone else's perspective.
22. Piaget observed that around age six, children develop **conservation**, the understanding that matter does not increase or decrease because of a change in form.
23. Conservation is one of many mental operations that characterize Piaget's 3rd stage of development, the **concrete-operational** stage.
24. During the concrete-operational stage, children begin to use **logic, mental manipulations, and mathematics**.
25. Piaget's final stage, from adolescence into adulthood, is called the **formal operational** stage.
26. Piaget was a **genetic epistemologist**, meaning he was interested in how knowledge developed in humans in a type of cognitive recapitulation theory.
27. **Cross-sectional research** involves studying a variety of ages at a single point in time.
28. In **longitudinal research**, psychologists study the same group of subjects for many years.
29. **Sigmund Freud** emphasized unconscious sexual forces in psychological development.

30. Freud is famous in the history of modern psychology for his **psycho-sexual** theory.
31. According to Freud, the **libido** seeks physical, especially sexual, gratification.
32. Freud thought that during the **oral stage**, the first year of life, gratification was mouth-oriented.
33. Freud though that during the **anal stage** gratification centers on feces, parental expectations, and training and discipline techniques.
34. Freud thought that during the **phallic stage**, ages two to six, children's libidinal energy is focused on sexuality and the genitals.
35. Freud thought during the **latency stage**, age six to twelve, sexual urges were dormant.
36. Freud thought that beginning at puberty, we spend the rest of our lives in the **genital stage**, in which we repress or redirect sexual libidinal energy.
37. Russian psychologist Lev Vygotsky proposed one of the first **psycho-social development** theories.
38. Vygotsky described the role that social interaction, language, and culture play in **cognitive development**.
39. **Erik Erikson** thought that development was driven by inborn forces and progressed through stages characterized by crises.
40. According to **attachment theory**, children whose caregivers are available and responsive to infant's needs establish a sense of attachment and security.
41. Children who have **secure attachment** exhibit mild distress when separated from caregivers, are happy when the caregivers return, prefer parents to strangers, and seek comfort from parents when frightened.
42. Children who have **ambivalent attachment** exhibit more severe distress when a parent leaves, may be wary of strangers, and are not comforted by the parent's return.
43. Children with **avoidant attachment**, when offered a choice, show no preference between a caregiver and a complete stranger, and may avoid or not seek comfort or contact from parents.
44. **Dementia** is a loss of brain function that occurs with certain diseases and brain injuries and affects memory, thinking, language, judgment, and behavior.
45. According to Cattell, **flexible intelligence** is made up of basic mental abilities like reasoning, abstract thinking, solving novel problems, and encoding short-term memories.
46. According to Cattell, **crystallized intelligence** refers to the general knowledge, vocabulary, and ability accumulated over a lifetime.
47. **Elisabeth Kubler-Ross** is famous in the history of psychology for her study of death and dying.
48. Kubler-Ross believed that when we are faced with impending death, we move back and forth through five stages or attitudes: **denial and isolation, anger, bargaining, depression, and acceptance**.
49. Kubler-Ross' first stage, **denial and isolation**, is characterized by shock, numbness, and refusal to accept the news.
50. The **anger stage** is characterized by feelings of injustice and "why me?"
51. In the **bargaining phase**, many people facing death try to find a way around it. The dying may make promises of good behavior or other life change in an effort to postpone death.
52. During the fourth stage, **depression**, as the terminally ill begins to accept the reality of impending death, they may feel overwhelming grief, depression, and hopelessness.
53. Kubler-Ross' final stage of dying is **acceptance**. Acceptance means a quiet expectation – being neither depressed nor bitter while contemplating the end of one's life.

Chapter 8 Short Essay Questions (Answers)

1. Theories of human development provide psychologists with an organizing framework for describing, explaining, and predicting developmental changes. Developmental theories describe our physical, sexual, cognitive, emotional, moral, and social growth and change. Developmental theories also provide guidance for appropriately interacting with people at different developmental levels.
2. Development is continuous in that it is gradual, linear, and similar across the life-span. Behavioral and social learning theories (e.g. Skinner and Bandura) hold this view. Development is discontinuous in that is like a series of stair steps, and each step is dependent on the previous step.
3. After about two or three weeks of rapid cell division, the zygote forms an embryo and implants in the mother's uterus. At this point some cells begin to differentiate and form the neural groove – the beginning of the brain and nervous system. By the 7th week the brain stem develops, and by the 9th week the child begins displaying spontaneous movement. Throughout the fetal period, from eight weeks until birth, the brain and nervous system develop at a tremendous rate; adding as many as 250,000 new neurons every minute and making countless new synaptic connections. The unborn child feels touch and pain and can taste, hear, smell, and see.
4. A serious result of drinking alcohol during pregnancy is fetal alcohol syndrome. Fetal alcohol syndrome is characterized by a combination of mental retardation, birth defects, abnormal facial features, behavior problems, cognitive and memory

problems, growth problems, and central nervous system damage. Fetal alcohol syndrome has no cure, but it is 100% preventable by not drinking alcohol, especially during any stage of pregnancy. Alcohol often does its most serious damage before the mother knows she is pregnant.

5. The swallowing reflex enables neonates to swallow liquids without choking. The rooting reflex causes a newborn to turn its head toward something touching its cheek and search around with its mouth for the nipple. The grasping reflex causes infants to close their fists around anything that is put in their hands. The stepping reflex causes newborn babies to make little stepping motions if they are held upright with their feet just touching a surface.

6. Cross-sectional research involves studying a variety of ages at a single point in time. A cross-sectional research design might study a group of 8, 9, and 10-year-old children to learn how they differ in some characteristic. In longitudinal research, psychologists study the same group of subjects for many years.

7. Locke believed that children are born a blank slate. From this perspective, nurturing, learning, and the environment are the primary developmental influences. Development is driven primarily by interaction with the environment. Rousseau believed that the natural unfolding of inborn characteristics drives development. Kant believed that the interaction between inborn characteristics (genetic influences) and the external world (environmental influences) drives development. From this perspective, children are active agents in their own development.

8. The sensorimotor stage. From birth to 18 months the developing child experiences the world solely through the senses and motor activity. Pre-operational Stage. From around 18 months to 6 years the child develops logical mental operations and the use of symbols to represent things. Concrete-operational Stage. At around age 6, children begin to use logic, mental manipulations, and mathematics. Formal-operations Stage. From adolescence into adulthood the ability for abstract thinking, to think about hypothetical situations, plan complex behavior, imagine the consequences of an action, and use formal logic.

9. Assimilation and accommodation are the mental processes by which children develop and modify their schema. Children assimilate new information into existing schemas. Children accommodate, or change, or expand their schema to fit new information.

10. Piaget underestimated childhood cognitive ability and over-stated the consistency of the four stages. Piaget was a genetic epistemologist, meaning he was interested in how knowledge developed in humans in a type of cognitive recapitulation theory. By understanding how cognitive development progresses in children, he hoped to discover how cognitive abilities evolved in Mankind.

Chapter 8 Quiz Answers

1) _____ stated that the prenatal development of an embryo followed the same stages as the evolutionary development of the embryo's species. b) Recapitulation Theory

2) John Locke believed that children are born a blank slate or _____. c) tabula rasa

3) _____ examines the role of genes in our thoughts, behaviors, and even our personality. c) behavioral genetics

4) The _____ is an estimate of the extent to which a trait is inherited. a) heritability index

5) _____ is the life-long process of development that unfolds according to age and independent of the environment. b) Maturation

6) The embryonic stage is a critical period of human development during which exposure to _____ is especially damaging. c) teratogens

7) A result of drinking alcohol during pregnancy characterized by combination of mental retardation, birth defects, abnormal facial features, behavior problems, cognitive and memory problems, growth problems, and central nervous system damage is called _____. d) fetal alcohol syndrome

8) Fetal alcohol syndrome has no cure, but it can be prevented by _____ during any stage of pregnancy. c) not drinking alcohol

9) Jean Piaget is famous in the history of psychology for his theories of _____.
a) intellectual development in children

10) Piaget believed that children are active participants in constructing, or building _____, or ways of organizing, representing, and understanding the world. b) schemas

11) _____ is the process by which children change or "expand" their schemas to account for new information. c) Accommodation

12) In the sensorimotor stage, infants discover _____, an understanding of cause-and-effect and the fact that they can control their bodies and move objects. b) causality

13) Later in the sensorimotor stage, children understand _____, that objects do not cease to exist when out of view. a) object permanence

14) The _____, from around 18 months to 6 years, is characterized by the use of symbols to represent things (as in imaginary play), the ability to classify and categorize objects, and language skills development. b) pre-operational stage

15) Conservation is one of many mental operations that characterize Piaget's 3rd stage of development, _____ stage. c) concrete-operational

16) During the _____, children begin to use logic, mental manipulations, and mathematics. c) concrete-operational

17) Piaget's final stage, from adolescence into adulthood, is called the _____. d) formal operational stage

18) The pre-operational stage thinking tends to be _____, meaning that young children cannot conceive of someone else's perspective.   a) egocentric

19) Piaget observed that around age six, children develop _____; understanding that matter does not increase or decrease because of a change in form.   a) conservation

20) _____ involves studying a variety of ages at a single point in time. a) Cross-sectional research

21) In _____, psychologists study the same group of subjects for many years. b) Longitudinal research

22) Freud is famous in the history of modern psychology for his _____.   b) psycho-sexual theory

23) According to Freud, the _____ seeks physical, especially sexual, gratification.   a) id

24) Freud thought that during the _____, the first year of life, gratification was mouth-oriented.   a) oral stage

25) Freud though that during the _____ gratification centers on feces, parental expectations, and training and discipline techniques.   b) anal stage

26) Freud thought that during the _____, ages two to six, children's libidinal energy is focused on sexuality and the genitals. c) phallic stage

27) Freud thought during the _____, age six to twelve, sexual urges were dormant.   d) latency stage

28) Freud thought that beginning at puberty, we spend the rest of our lives in the _____, in which we repress or redirect sexual libidinal energy.   d) genital stage

29) Russian psychologist Lev Vygotsky proposed one of the first _____ theories. b) psycho-social development

30) According to attachment theory, children who have _____ exhibit mild distress when separated from caregivers, are happy when the caregivers return, prefer parents to strangers, and seek comfort from parents when frightened.   a) secure attachment

31) According to attachment theory, children who have _____ exhibit more severe distress when a parent leaves, may be wary of strangers, and are not comforted by the parent's return.   b) ambivalent attachment

32) According to attachment theory, children with_____, when offered a choice, show no preference between a caregiver and a complete stranger, and may avoid or not seek comfort or contact from parents.   c) avoidant attachment

33) _____ is a loss of brain function that occurs with certain diseases and brain injuries and affects memory, thinking, language, judgment, and behavior.   a) dementia

34) According to Cattell, _____ is made up of basic mental abilities like reasoning, abstract thinking, solving novel problems, and encoding short-term memories.   a) flexible intelligence

35) According to Cattell, _____ refers to the general knowledge, vocabulary, and ability accumulated over a lifetime.   b) crystallized intelligence

36) Which is NOT one of Elisabeth Kubler-Ross' 5 stages of grief when faced with impending death? d) hope

Chapter 9 Consciousness

Chapter 9 Learning Objectives

Discuss various definitions of human consciousness.

Describe a Christian perspective of human consciousness.

Describe various states of consciousness.

Describe sleep, REM sleep, stages of sleep, sleep deprivation, and disorders of sleep.

Describe dreams and discuss the meaning of dreams from various worldview perspectives, including a Christian worldview.

Describe hypnosis, its history, and worldview issues related to hypnosis.

Discuss meditation from various worldview perspectives.

Define psychoactive drugs and describe how they generally work.

Describe tolerance, dependence, and withdrawal.

Describe the four major categories of psychoactive drugs.

Key Concepts and People

Consciousness	Information consolidation theory of sleep	Hypnosis
God-likeness		Meditation
Sleep	Adaptive theories of sleep	Psychoactive drugs
REM sleep	Circadian rhythm	Psychopharmacology
Alpha, Beta, Theta, and	Sleep deprivation	Tolerance
Delta waves	Dreams	Dependence
Repair and restoration theory of sleep	Psychoanalytic theory of dreams	

Short Essay Questions

1. Describe a Christian perspective of human consciousness.
2. Describe various states of consciousness.
3. Describe sleep, REM sleep, stages of sleep, sleep deprivation, and disorders of sleep.
4. Describe dreams and discuss the meaning of dreams from various worldview perspectives, including a Christian worldview.
5. Describe hypnosis, its history, and worldview issues related to hypnosis.
6. Define psychoactive drugs and describe how they generally work.
7. Describe tolerance, dependence, and withdrawal.

For Further Study

1. Read: Biblical references to dreams and dreaming in: Read Matt. 1:20, 2:12-13, 7:19, Gen. 40:8, Gen. 41:1-25, Joel 2:28, and Jer. 23:25-28.
2. Read Meditation: A Requirement by Helen E. Martin in Science in the Christian Perspective https://asa3.org/ASA/PSCF/1979/JASA6-79Martin.html
3. Web: Teens: The Science Behind Drug Abuse The National Institute on Drug Abuse https://teens.drugabuse.gov/drug-facts
4. Read: Drugs: Shatter the Myths at the National Institute on Drug Abuse https://teens.drugabuse.gov/national-drug-facts-week
5. Read: InfoFacts: Understanding Drug Abuse and Addiction at the National Institute on Drug Abuse https://www.drugabuse.gov/publications/drugfacts/understanding-drug-use-addiction
6. Video: The Meth Epidemic FRONTLINE, in association with The Oregonian, investigates the meth rampage in America: the appalling impact on individuals, families and communities. https://www.pbs.org/wgbh/frontline/film/meth/

7. Web: DEA Fact Sheets at the U. S. Drug Enforcement Administration
   http://www.justice.gov/dea/druginfo/factsheets.shtml
8. Web: InfoFacts: Science-based Facts on Drug Abuse and Addiction at the National Inst. on Drug Abuse https://www.drugabuse.gov/publications/finder/t/160/DrugFacts
9. Read: Defining Consciousness: Christian and Psychological Perspectives, by Willaim M. Struthers https://asa3.org/ASA/PSCF/2001/PSCF6-01Struthers.html

Topics for Discussion

1. Is there a difference between drug use and drug abuse? Is there a difference between alcohol use and alcohol abuse? Is there a difference between caffeine use and caffeine abuse? If so, what is the difference?
2. Debate it. Should Christians submit to hypnosis?

Chapter 9 Worldview Issues

Consciousness

In every psychology and philosophy class, students learn about the problem of consciousness. A major difference between Christian and naturalist psychology has to do with consciousness.

A Christian approach to consciousness also begins with a sense of awe and wonder. Consciousness is the defining characteristic of being human. It is part of what it means to be made in the image and likeness of God. The word 'consciousness' is really a misnomer. Consciousness is you. Consciousness is supernatural. Consciousness is the Mind. Consciousness is our Heart. Consciousness is our Soul. You are conscious in this life and you will be in the next.

Naturalistic psychologists today talk about consciousness on two levels – the easy and the hard problems of consciousness. The easy problem is about proximate cause, the hard problem is about ultimate cause. Psychology textbooks often focus on the easy problem and ignore the hard.

The easy problem of consciousness is differentiating states of consciousness. Advances in neuroscience have provided exciting glimpses into the mechanics of consciousness. The easy problem is using technology to 'see' the physical neural processes associated with consciousness. The hard problem is to explain how and why physical neural processes give rise to the subjective experience of consciousness. It is in the context of human consciousness that naturalism seems silly. Naturalism presumes that consciousness MUST be solely the product of brain activity.

Dreams

It psychology class, students learn that dreams evolved to rehearse strategies to survive in a hostile environment, or that dreams are the interpretation of random neural activity. Sigmund Freud is famous in the history of psychology for his psychosexual libido-driven interpretations of dreams. Throughout history mystics of every tradition believed that dreams held special meaning. Many people today see dreams as evidence of a mystical spiritual realm or an alternate reality which we can only glimpse in dreams. Some people use dreams to diagnose illness or to foretell the future. Popular literature contains countless interpretive guides promising to reveal the hidden meaning of dreams.

What do dreams really mean? From a naturalistic perspective, the idea of God communicating through dreams seems silly, but the Bible is rich with examples of God speaking through dreams. In the Old Testament, God chose to communicate to the people of Israel through dreams and He continued to communicate through dreams as told in the New Testament. Many believe that He continues to communicate through dreams today – that dreams contain special revelation.

Does God communicate through dreams today? He can if he wants to. If He does, how do we to interpret the content? A Christian approach to dreams begins with discernment. In all areas of life, we must distinguish Gods voice from meaningless chatter. We must be cautious, skeptical, and wise when prophets claim that their dreams contain special revelation and be wary of those who claim to have a special ability to interpret dreams.

Hypnosis

In every psychology class students learn that hypnosis is an altered state of consciousness in which one is very susceptible to suggestion. Hypnosis, once performed on stage for entertainment, is now widely accepted as an effective therapeutic tool to get rid of bad habits, establish good habits, build confidence, lose weight, or eliminate phobias.

But from a Christian perspective, the question 'what about hypnosis?' is about appropriateness, not effectiveness. Many Christians, including those in the Christian Hypnosis Association, practice hypno-therapy and many Christians attest to its benefits. But others believe that hypnotism is an occult practice condemned by the Bible. To submit to hypnosis surrenders control of the mind to the hypnotist or perhaps to demons. If that's the case, the Christian should to avoid submitting to hypnosis.

Students will feel pressure to conform to a belief that worldviews do not matter when it comes to hypnosis. Naturalism presumes that the hypnotic trance is a natural phenomenon. The concept of 'occult practices' is meaningless. A Christian approach to hypnosis begins with a belief in a supernatural realm. The study and practice of hypnosis is not to be trifled with and requires wisdom and discernment. Worldviews matter.

Meditation

In psychology class students learn that meditation is simply a form of deep concentration. It's the described as the practice of calming the brain and focusing attention. Students learn that mediation improves physical and mental health and reduces stress and in some psychology classes students are taught various meditation techniques.

Student will feel pressure to conform to a belief that meditation is only about the benefits – that religious beliefs and worldviews are not important. Once again, do not believe it. Worldviews matter. The Bible tells us to meditate. Mediation means concentrating on God, focusing on scripture, listening for God's voice, and reflecting on His works and His will. It is not surprising that mediation is associated with physical, psychological, and spiritual well-being.

Study Guide Chapter 9

1. The _____is a concept developed by Francis Crick, co-discoverer of DNA, that every mental experience of sentient beings is nothing more than the result of electrical-chemical reactions in the brain.

2. The study of consciousness is made more difficult by the fact that it is not a _____.

3. Different patterns of brain waves are associated with different _____.

4. The 1950s and the discovery of _____ began a time of intensive research into the nature of sleep.

5. REM sleep is sometimes called _____because the brain wave pattern during REM sleep is similar to patterns while awake.

6. There are four patterns or types of brain waves: _____, _____, _____, and _____.

7. _____are slower and characteristic of rest, decreased attention to the environment, and the beginning of sleep.

8. _____are characteristic of alertness, thought, and concentration (an engaged mind). Beta waves have low amplitude and high frequency.

9. _____have even greater amplitude and slower frequency and are characteristic of the transition from wakefulness to sleep (i.e., when we are falling asleep).

10. _____have a very slow frequency and are characteristic of deep dreamless sleep.

11. _____suggests that the purpose of sleep is to allow the body and the brain to repair themselves. In the repair and restoration theory, REM sleep and dreams are essential to restoring mental functions.

12. The _____theory of sleep suggests that the purpose of sleep is to allow the brain to consolidate and process the events and experiences of the day.

13. _____, also known as adaptive theories, suggest that sleep evolved to serve some adaptive survival purpose.

14. Our pattern of sleep is part of a set of daily physiological cycles or _____.

15. _____refers to the fatigue and disorientation air travelers feel after a long flight when environmental cues do not match the circadian rhythm.

16. _____is the difference between the amount time spent sleeping and the amount of sleep needed.

17. _____refers to the chronic and severe lack of adequate sleep.

18. _____are two of a group of conditions in which there is a disturbance in sleep patterns.

19. _____ is a sleep disorder in which activities normally done while awake are done while asleep.

20. _____, or sleep talking, is another normally harmless sleep disorder.

21. _____ is a very serious sleep disorder in which people fall asleep suddenly and without warning while performing ordinary activities.

22. Narcolepsy is particularly dangerous because it is frequently accompanied by _____, the complete loss of voluntary muscle control.

23. _____is a sleep disorder in which, during sleep, breathing stops (as often as 20 to 30 times each hour), the sufferer briefly wakens to gasp for air.

24. _____describes the experience of being awake but temporarily unable to move or speak that occurs as we are just falling asleep or as we are just becoming fully awake.

25. _____is a sleep disorder that involves acting-out vivid, intense, and sometimes violent dreams.

26. _____of dreams suggests that dreams evolved as a way to rehearse strategies to survive in a hostile environment.

27. In the _____of dreams, the brain generates dreams to "explain" the random neural impulses (brain sparks) that occur during sleep.

28. Some theories state that dreams are part of the process by which the brain eliminates, strengthens, and _____.

29. Some use _____metaphors to explain dreams. The brain is like a computer and dreams are the way the brain defragments and re-organizes its data.

30. Another model proposes that dreams are a safe means for experiencing powerful emotions, _____ and solving difficult problems.

31. Sigmund Freud's _____of dreams suggested that dreams were a representation of unconscious thoughts and desires.

32. Freud believed that dreams contain _____ or hidden meanings.

33. Carl Jung saw dreams as _____of memories and instincts shared by all people.

34. _____ an altered, trance-like state of consciousness in which a person is hyper-suggestible or easily influenced.

35. _____ is usually credited with the discovery of hypnosis.

36. Mesmer's technique was focused on healing illnesses by manipulating the _____, a mysterious energy field thought to surround living creatures.

37. In the early 19th century, James Braid developed a form of _____ using eye fatigue to induce a _____.

38. Psychologists describe _____ as a form of deep concentration in which the mind is focused on a single thing or emptied of thought.

39. _____ is the study of the relationship between drugs and mental processes. Psychopharmacology addresses illicit (illegal) and licit (legal) drugs.

40. _____ drugs work by crossing the blood-brain barrier and altering the way neurotransmitters work.

41. _____ may cause more or less of a neurotransmitter to be released, block the reception of a neurotransmitter, or block re-absorption of a neurotransmitter.

42. _____ refers to decreased susceptibility to the same quantity of a drug.

43. _____, commonly known as addiction is characterized by unpleasant physical and/or emotional symptoms called withdrawal symptoms when not using the drug.

44. _____ symptoms are so unpleasant that the user compulsively seeks and uses the drug despite obvious and serious consequences.

45. In _____ the user experiences mental or emotional discomfort when not using the drug.

46. In _____ the user experiences physical symptoms when not using the drug (i.e., seizures, diarrhea, pain).

47. Psychologists classify psychoactive drugs into four categories:

_____, _____,

_____, _____.

48. _____ are a class of drugs that depress neural activity in the brain.

49. _____ is the most familiar and most widely abused drug in our society.

50. Alcohol is a _____, not a stimulant.

51. _____ mimic adrenaline, a hormone produced in high-stress situation,

52. _____ is the most widely used psychoactive drug in the world.

53. Methamphetamine's _____, or the percentage of users who develop dependence, is very high.

54. Opiates, also called _____ are some of the oldest drugs used by humans.

55. _____ (a long-acting opiate) allowed many opiate-dependent people to avoid withdrawal symptoms and resume some normal social behavior.

56. _____ are a class of psychoactive drugs that produce hallucinations, depersonalization, thought disturbances, and mood changes.

57. The active ingredient in marijuana is _____.

Chapter 9 Quiz

1) Different patterns of _____ are associated with different states of consciousness.
   a) neuro-transmission
   b) affects, behaviors, and cognitions (ABCs)
   c) sensation and perception
   d) brain waves

2) The 1950s and the discovery of _____ began a time of intensive research into the nature of sleep.
   a) electroencephalography (EEG)
   b) rapid eye movement
   c) magnetic resonance imaging
   d) hypnotic induction

3) The _____ of sleep suggests that the purpose of sleep is to allow the body and the mind to repair and restore.
   a) repair and restoration theory
   b) Christian perspective
   c) information consolidation theory
   d) adaptive theories of sleep

4) The _____ of sleep suggests that the purpose of sleep is to allow the brain to consolidate and process the events and experiences of the day.
   a) Christian perspective
   b) repair and restoration theory
   c) information consolidation theory
   d) adaptive theories

5) In the _____ theory of dreams, the brain generates dreams to explain random neural impulses.
   a) adaptive
   b) repair and restoration theory
   c) information consolidation
   d) activation-synthesis

6) _____ suggests that dreams evolved as a way to rehearse strategies to survive in a hostile environment.
   a) Evolutionary theory
   b) Information consolidation theory
   c) Christian perspective
   d) Repair and restoration theory

7) A _____ is a 24-hour physiological cycle.
   a) diurnal cycle
   b) biorhythm
   c) circadian rhythm
   d) lunar rhythm

8) _____ is the difference between the amount time spent sleeping and the amount of sleep needed.
   a) Sleep deprivation
   b) College life
   c) Fatigue
   d) Sleep debt

9) _____ refers to the chronic and severe lack of adequate sleep.
   a) Sleep deprivation
   b) Sleep apnea
   c) Sleep debt
   d) Narcolepsy

10) _____ is a very serious sleep disorder in which people fall asleep suddenly and without warning, while performing ordinary activities.
    a) Rapid eye movement behavior disorder (RBD)
    b) Sleep apnea
    c) Hypersomnia
    d) Narcolepsy

11) Which is NOT one of the four patterns or types of brain waves?
    a) alpha
    b) beta
    c) gamma
    d) delta

12) _____ waves are slower and characteristic of rest, decreased attention to the environment, and the beginning of sleep.
    a) Alpha
    b) Beta
    c) Theta
    d) Delta

13) _____ waves are characteristic of alertness, thought, and concentration (an engaged mind).
    a) Alpha
    b) Beta
    c) Theta
    d) Delta

14) _____ waves have even greater amplitude and slower frequency and are characteristic of the transition from wakefulness to sleep (i.e., when falling asleep).
   a) Alpha
   b) Beta
   c) Theta
   d) Delta

15) _____ waves have a very slow frequency and are characteristic of deep dreamless sleep.
   a) Alpha
   b) Beta
   c) Theta
   d) Delta

16) _____ is a sleep disorder in which, during sleep, breathing stops (as often as 20 to 30 times each hour), the sufferer briefly wakens to gasp for air.
   a) Sleep deprivation
   b) Sleep apnea
   c) Narcolepsy
   d) Somniloquy

17) _____ is a sleep disorder that involves acting-out vivid, intense, and sometimes violent dreams.
   a) Sleep paralysis
   b) Narcolepsy
   c) Somniloquy
   d) REM behavior disorder

18) _____ psycho-analytic theory of dreams suggested that dreams were a representation of unconscious thoughts and desires.
   a) Sigmund Freud's
   b) Carl Jung's
   c) Franz Mesmer's
   d) James Braid's

19) Psychologists describe _____ as a form of deep concentration in which the mind is focused on a single thing or emptied of thought.
   a) hypnosis
   b) meditation
   c) attention
   d) hallucinations

20) _____ refers to decreased susceptibility to the same quantity of a drug.
   a) Tolerance
   b) Dependence
   c) Habituation
   d) Withdrawal

21) _____ is characterized by unpleasant physical and/or emotional symptoms when not using a drug.
   a) Tolerance
   b) Dependence
   c) Habituation
   d) Withdrawal

22) _____ symptoms are so unpleasant that the user compulsively seeks and uses the drug despite obvious and serious consequences.
   a) Tolerance
   b) Dependence
   c) Habituation
   d) Withdrawal

23) Which is NOT a classification/category of psychoactive drug"
   a) Depressants
   b) Anti-hypertensives
   c) Stimulants
   d) Opiates

24) _____ are a class of drugs that depress neural activity in the brain.
   a) Depressants
   b) Stimulants
   c) Opiates
   d) Hallucinogens

25) Alcohol is a:
   a) depressant
   b) stimulant.

26) _____ mimic adrenaline, a hormone produced in high-stress situation.
   a) Depressants
   b) Stimulants
   c) Opiates
   d) Hallucinogens

Answer Key Chapter 9

Chapter 9 Study Guide (Answers)

1. The **astonishing hypothesis** is a concept developed by Francis Crick, co-discoverer of DNA, that every mental experience of sentient beings is nothing more than the result of electrical-chemical reactions in the brain.

2. The study of consciousness is made more difficult by the fact that it is not a **single constant mental state.**

3. Different patterns of brain waves are associated with different **states of consciousness.**

4. The 1950s and the discovery of **rapid eye movement** (REM) began a time of intensive research into the nature of sleep.

5. REM sleep is sometimes called **paradoxical sleep** because the brain wave pattern during REM sleep is similar to patterns while awake.

6. There are four patterns or types of brain waves: **alpha, beta, theta, and delta.**

7. **Alpha waves** are slower and characteristic of rest, decreased attention to the environment, and the beginning of sleep.

8. **Beta waves** are characteristic of alertness, thought, and concentration (an engaged mind). Beta waves have low amplitude and high frequency.

9. **Theta waves** have even greater amplitude and slower frequency and are characteristic of the transition from wakefulness to sleep (i.e., when we are falling asleep).

10. **Delta waves** have a very slow frequency and are characteristic of deep dreamless sleep.

11. **The repair and restoration theory of sleep** suggests that the purpose of sleep is to allow the body and the brain to repair themselves. In the repair and restoration theory, REM sleep and dreams are essential to restoring mental functions.

12. The **information consolidation** theory of sleep suggests that the purpose of sleep is to allow the brain to consolidate and process the events and experiences of the day.

13. **Evolutionary theories of sleep**, also known as adaptive theories, suggest that sleep evolved to serve some adaptive survival purpose.

14. Our pattern of sleep is part of a set of daily physiological cycles or **circadian rhythm.**

15. **Jet lag** refers to the fatigue and disorientation air travelers feel after a long flight when environmental cues do not match the circadian rhythm.

16. **Sleep debt** is the difference between the amount time spent sleeping and the amount of sleep needed.

17. **Sleep deprivation** refers to the chronic and severe lack of adequate sleep.

18. **Insomnia** and **hypersomnia** are two of a group of conditions in which there is a disturbance in sleep patterns.

19. **Somnambulism** is a sleep disorder in which activities normally done while awake are done while asleep.

20. Somniloquy, or sleep talking, is another normally harmless sleep disorder.

21. **Narcolepsy** is a very serious sleep disorder in which people fall asleep suddenly and without warning while performing ordinary activities.

22. Narcolepsy is particularly dangerous because it is frequently accompanied by **cataplexy**, the complete loss of voluntary muscle control.

23. **Sleep apnea** is a sleep disorder in which, during sleep, breathing stops (as often as 20 to 30 times each hour), the sufferer briefly wakens to gasp for air.

24. **Sleep paralysis** describes the experience of being awake but temporarily unable to move or speak that occurs as we are just falling asleep or as we are just becoming fully awake.

25. **REM behavior disorder** (RBD) is a sleep disorder that involves acting-out vivid, intense, and sometimes violent dreams.

26. **Evolutionary theory** of dreams suggests that dreams evolved as a way to rehearse strategies to survive in a hostile environment.

27. In the **activation-synthesis theory** of dreams, the brain generates dreams to "explain" the random neural impulses (brain sparks) that occur during sleep.

28. Some theories state that dreams are part of the process by which the brain eliminates, strengthens, and **re-organizes neural connections.**

29. Some use **information-processing** metaphors to explain dreams. The brain is like a computer and dreams are the way the brain defragments and re-organizes its data.

30. Another model proposes that dreams are a safe means for experiencing powerful emotions, **resolving psychic conflict**, and solving difficult problems.

31. Sigmund Freud's **psycho-analytic theory** of dreams suggested that dreams were a representation of unconscious thoughts and desires.

32. Freud believed that dreams contain **latent** or hidden meanings.

33. Carl Jung saw dreams as **symbolic representations** of memories and instincts shared by all people.

34. **Hypnosis** is an altered, trance-like state of consciousness in which a person is hyper-suggestible or easily influenced.

35. **Franz Anton Mesmer** is usually credited with the discovery of hypnosis.

36. Mesmer's technique was focused on healing illnesses by manipulating the **animal magnetism**, a mysterious energy field thought to surround living creatures.

37. In the early 19th century, James Braid developed a form of **hypnotic induction** using eye fatigue to induce a **hypnotic trance**.

38. Psychologists describe **meditation** as a form of deep concentration in which the mind is focused on a single thing or emptied of thought.

39. **Psychopharmacology** is the study of the relationship between drugs and mental processes. Psychopharmacology addresses illicit (illegal) and licit (legal) drugs.

40. **Psychoactive** drugs work by crossing the blood-brain barrier and altering the way neurotransmitters work.

41. **Psychoactive drugs** may cause more or less of a neurotransmitter to be released, block the reception of a neurotransmitter, or block re-absorption of a neurotransmitter.

42. **Tolerance** refers to decreased susceptibility to the same quantity of a drug.

43. **Dependence**, commonly known as addiction is characterized by unpleasant physical and/or emotional symptoms called withdrawal symptoms when not using the drug.

44. **Withdrawal** symptoms are so unpleasant that the user compulsively seeks and uses the drug despite obvious and serious consequences.

45. In **psychological dependence** the user experiences mental or emotional discomfort when not using the drug.

46. In **physiological dependence** the user experiences physical symptoms when not using the drug (i.e., seizures, diarrhea, pain).

47. Psychologists classify psychoactive drugs into four categories: **Depressants or Sedative-hypnotics, Stimulants, Opiates or Narcotics, Hallucinogens or Psychedelics**.

48. **Depressants** are a class of drugs that depress neural activity in the brain.

49. **Alcohol** is the most familiar and most widely abused drug in our society.

50. Alcohol is a **depressant**, not a stimulant.

51. **Stimulants** mimic adrenaline, a hormone produced in high-stress situation.

52. **Caffeine** is the most widely used psychoactive drug in the world.

53. Methamphetamine's **capture ratio**, or the percentage of users who develop dependence, is very high.

54. Opiates, also called **narcotics** are some of the oldest drugs used by humans.

55. **Methadone** (a long-acting opiate) allowed many opiate-dependent people to avoid withdrawal symptoms and resume some normal social behavior.

56. **Hallucinogens** are a class of psychoactive drugs that produce hallucinations, depersonalization, thought disturbances, and mood changes.

57. The active ingredient in marijuana is **delta-4-tetrahydrocannabinol (THC)**.

Chapter 9 Short Essay Questions (Answers)

1. Christian worldview sees consciousness as part of our God-likeness and the vehicle of our relationships with God and others. Consciousness is a pre-requisite to free-will, and free-will is a pre-requisite to moral accountability. The principles of free-will and moral accountability are central to the Christian worldview. Without moral accountability, sin and salvation are meaningless. Without consciousness, humans are nothing more than very complex machine-like animals. Theories of consciousness that deny the "specialness" of human consciousness are incompatible with a Christian view of Mankind.

2. Consciousness is not a single constant mental state. Dreams, daydreams, hypnosis, meditation, and hallucinations are states of consciousness. Psychoactive drugs alter consciousness, as do extremes of heat, fatigue, exhaustion, dehydration, and malnutrition. Different patterns of brain waves are associated with different states of consciousness.

3. REM sleep is similar to patterns while awake. During REM sleep we dream, breathing fluctuates, heart rate varies, traces of muscle activity appear across the body, and our eyes move rapidly back and forth up to eight times each second. Sleep begins with the transition from wakefulness to sleep as brain waves change from predominately Beta waves to predominately Alpha waves. In stage 1 sleep there are mostly theta waves. In stage 1 sleep, we lose conscious awareness of the environment, heart and breathing rates drop, body temperature drops, and muscles relax. Stage 2 is characterized by

short bursts of distinctive brain wave patterns called sleep spindles, short bursts of brain activity that represent the brain's effort to keep us relaxed. In stages 3 and 4, brain waves slow even more and we pass into deep sleep. In stage 4, body functions decline to the deepest state of rest, we move little, and we are oblivious to our surroundings. Sleep deprivation refers to the chronic and severe lack of adequate sleep. Extreme sleep deprivation, however, can have serious effects on mental and physical health. Sleep disorders involve any difficulties related to sleeping, including difficulty falling or staying asleep, falling asleep at inappropriate times, excessive total sleep time, or abnormal behaviors associated with sleep.

4. The Bible is rich with examples of God speaking through dreams. Achieving a Christian view of dreams is made more difficult by the biblical cautions of false dreams and warnings about lies in the form of dreams. The Bible is clear that the Gospel message is complete. If dreams have no role in further "revelation," do they have a role as a means of "illumination" for the individual dreamer? If our dream life is part of our God-likeness, if God still speaks through dreams, the Christian student of psychology must, as is the case in most of psychology's content, guard against exclusively naturalistic explanations of dreams. We should not simply dismiss dreams as meaningless unconscious imagery. If we seek meaning in our dreams, we should not accept completely secular interpretations and, as a prelude to this text's discussion of psychotherapies, the Christian student must also be cautious, skeptical, and wise when Christian dreamers claim special revelation.

5. Hypnosis is an altered, trance-like state of consciousness in which a person is hyper-suggestible or easily influenced. Christians disagree with other Christians over whether hypnotism is acceptable for Christians. Some say that hypnosis is a type of idolatry or the practice of a false religion. They equate hypnosis with Buddhism and other Eastern religions. Christian critics of hypnosis compare the hypnotic trance with the yogic trance. Some believe that hypnosis is an occult practice (see Leviticus 19:31) and that hypnosis leaves one open to satanic attack. They see hypnosis as a religious activity in which one surrenders control of the mind to the hypnotist or perhaps to Satan. Hypnotists who claim to be able to contact the dead, lead us to past or future lives, or divine the future are, according to a Christian worldview, practicing the occult. Some compare hypnosis, especially self-hypnosis, with deep Christian meditation and intense prayer. They compare the hypnotic trance with the examples of trances and visionary states in the Bible (see Acts 10:10). Some claim that to equate hypnosis with false religions and demon possession is to confuse the practice of hypnosis with the purpose of hypnosis. Some see hypnosis as a powerful tool to help get rid of bad habits, establish good habits, build confidence, lose weight, or have pain-free dental work. Others note that instead of looking inward for our help that we should look to God. The spiritual dimension of hypnosis will likely cause introductory psychology courses to dismiss hypnosis as an interesting phenomenon or a cool parlor trick.

6. Psychoactive or psychotropic drugs alter consciousness, behavior, cognition, and emotions. Psychoactive drugs work by crossing the blood-brain barrier and altering the way neurotransmitters work. Psychoactive drugs may cause more or less of a neurotransmitter to be released, block the reception of a neurotransmitter, or block re-absorption of a neurotransmitter. Several factors impact the effect of a drug. Drug effects vary according to the amount of the drug ingested; the drug's potency; the route of administration; the user's previous experience and expectation; the user's age, body weight, and mood; and the environment in which the drug is used.

7. Tolerance refers to decreased susceptibility to the same quantity of a drug. A drug user who over time requires more of a drug to achieve the same effect is developing a tolerance to the drug. With continued use, drug users may develop dependence, commonly known as addiction. Someone who is drug dependent experiences very unpleasant physical and/or emotional symptoms called withdrawal symptoms when not using the drug. Withdrawal symptoms are so unpleasant that the user compulsively seeks and uses the drug despite obvious and serious consequences.

Chapter 9 Quiz Answers

1) Different patterns of _____ are associated with different states of consciousness.   d) brain waves

2) The 1950s and the discovery of _____ began a time of intensive research into the nature of sleep.   b) rapid eye movement

3) The _____ of sleep suggests that the purpose of sleep is to allow the body and the mind to repair and restore.   a) repair and restoration theory

4) The _____ of sleep suggests that the purpose of sleep is to allow the brain to consolidate and process the events and experiences of the day.   c) information consolidation theory

5) In the _____ theory of dreams, the brain generates dreams to explain random neural impulses.   d) activation-synthesis

6) _____ suggests that dreams evolved as a way to rehearse strategies to survive in a hostile environment.   a) Evolutionary theory

7) A _____ is a 24-hour physiological cycle.   c) circadian rhythm

8) _____ is the difference between the amount time spent sleeping and the amount of sleep needed.   d) Sleep debt

9) _____ refers to the chronic and severe lack of adequate sleep.   a) Sleep deprivation

10) _____ is a very serious sleep disorder in which people fall asleep suddenly and without warning, while performing ordinary activities. d) Narcolepsy

11) Which is NOT one of the four patterns or types of brain waves? c) gamma

12) _____ waves are slower and characteristic of rest, decreased attention to the environment, and the beginning of sleep. a) Alpha

13) _____ waves are characteristic of alertness, thought, and concentration (an engaged mind). b) Beta

14) _____ waves have even greater amplitude and slower frequency and are characteristic of the transition from wakefulness to sleep. c) Theta

15) _____ waves have a very slow frequency and are characteristic of deep dreamless sleep. d) Delta

16) _____ is a sleep disorder in which, during sleep, breathing stops (as often as 20 to 30 times each hour), the sufferer briefly wakens to gasp for air. b) Sleep apnea

17) _____ is a sleep disorder that involves acting-out vivid, intense, and sometimes violent dreams. d) REM behavior disorder

18) _____ psycho-analytic theory of dreams suggested that dreams were a representation of unconscious thoughts and desires. a) Sigmund Freud's

19) Psychologists describe _____ as a form of deep concentration in which the mind is focused on a single thing or emptied of thought. b) meditation

20) _____ refers to decreased susceptibility to the same quantity of a drug. a) Tolerance

21) _____ is characterized by unpleasant physical and/or emotional symptoms when not using a drug. d) Withdrawal

22) _____ symptoms are so unpleasant that the user compulsively seeks and uses the drug despite obvious and serious consequences. d) Withdrawal

23) Which is NOT a classification/category of psychoactive drug b) Anti-hypertensives

24) _____ are a class of drugs that depress neural activity in the brain. a) Depressants

25) Alcohol is a: a) depressant

26) _____ mimic adrenaline, a hormone produced in high-stress situation. b) Stimulants

Chapter 10 Thinking, Language, and Intelligence

Chapter 10 Learning Objectives

Define cognition
Define concepts including conjunctive concepts, disjunctive concepts, and relational concepts
Describe cognitive maps
Define schemas and cognitive scripts
Identify effective decision-making and problem-solving techniques
Identify barriers to problem-solving and decision-making
Define language
Describe the stages of language development
Describe Noam Chomsky's Nativist theory of language development
Describe the difficulties defining intelligence

Key Concepts and People

Concepts
Conjunctive and Disjunctive concepts
Cognitive maps
Schemas
Cognitive scripts and styles
Field-dependent and field-independent thinking
Metacognition
Deductive reasoning, algorithms, logic, and heuristics
Perceptual barriers
Fixations, mental set, belief bias, confirmation bias, and

belief bias
Convergent and divergent thinking
Semantics
Kanzi
Psycho linguistics
Phonemes, morphemes
Nativist theory
Noam Chomsky
Language acquisition device and universal grammar
Differential psychology
Sir Francis Galton
Franz Gall
Psychometrics

Eugenics
Robert Sternberg
L. L. Thurstone
Artificial intelligence
Charles Spearman and Spearman's g
Alfred Binet
David Wechsler
Raymond Cattell
Howard Gardner
Intelligence quotient
Fluid and crystallized intelligence

Short Essay Questions

1. Describe cognition.
2. Describe simple, conjunctive, disjunctive, and relational concepts.
3. Describe the concept of cognitive style.
4. Compare the processes of decision-making and problem-solving.
5. Describe barriers to decision-making and problem-solving.
6. What is language?
7. Describe semantics and syntax.
8. Describe language development in children.
9. Describe Noam Chomsky's nativist theory of language development.

For Further Study

1. Web: Human Intelligence, by Dr. Jonathan Plucker Indiana University
   http://www.intelltheory.com/
2. Read: Speaking Bonobo, an article about Kanzi, the speaking Bonobo, at Smithsonian.com
   https://www.smithsonianmag.com/science-nature/speaking-bonobo-134931541/
3. Web: Savant Syndrome, a web site maintained by the Wisconsin Medical Society
   https://www.wisconsinmedicalsociety.org/professional/savant-syndrome/

4. Web: Language Development in Children, a site maintained by the Child Development Institute. https://childdevelopmentinfo.com/child-development/language_development/#.WvM8fYgvxhE

Topics for Discussion

1. What biases do you have?
2. What thinking errors do you see in yourself?
3. In what ways do Christians experience prejudice?
4. In which of the types of intelligence do you excel?

Chapter 10 Worldview Issues

Critical Thinking

Christians studying psychology need to be critical thinkers. Faith requires skeptical curiosity. Students should always ask:

- What is the claim?
- What is the evidence?
- What are you being asked to believe?
- Are there other ways to interpret the evidence?
- What worldview assumptions underlie the claim?
- What does the Bible have to say?
- What conclusions are most reasonable?

Study Guide Chapter 10

1. _____ is the mental processes of thinking, feeling, perceiving, problem-solving, and remembering.

2. _____ refers to thinking about thinking.

3. _____ are categories by which we describe the physical world that the brain cannot directly experience.

4. _____ are the basic components of thought.

5. Simple, or formal, concepts have a _____ in common.

6. A _____ is an ideal example of a concept.

7. _____ are classified by the presence of two or more common features

8. _____ have "either-or" characteristics.

9. _____ are classified by the relationship between features.

10. _____ are mental representations of a given place or situation.

11. The individual way we create and organize concepts is called a _____.

12. _____ is the term psychologists use to describe our usual way of organizing concepts – a type of cognitive autopilot.

13. The term _____ refers to the way in which one usually processes information.

14. _____, also called analytic thinkers, generally break down thinking into component parts and process information in a detailed step-by-step approach.

15. _____, also called holistic or global thinkers, tend to look at the "big picture" and process information with focus on meaning, connections, and purpose.

16. Formal or _____ involves using algorithms and formal rules of logic.

17. _____ are simple "rules-of-thumb" that serve as cognitive shortcuts to solving complex problems.

18. _____ refers to our ability to concentrate on one thing while ignoring others.

19. _____ refers the ways to we perceive and process certain pieces of information but exclude others.

20. _____ is a focused form of attention in which we ignore anything that is not related to a particular cognitive task.

21. _____ is the term for the study of the mental activity involved in acquiring, using, and understanding language.

22. _____ is defined as a set of symbols (i.e., sounds, gestures, or written characters) used to represent objects (i.e., actions, events, and ideas) according to a set of rules.

23. Semantics is the study of the _____.

24. _____ are the smallest distinguishable sounds in a language.

25. _____ are the smallest meaningful units in a language.

26. _____ describe the system of rules that govern how words form phrases and sentences.

27. Humans in all cultures go through the same stages of _____.

28. Between about 9 and 13 months, children begin to produce simple single word sentences called _____ to express feelings or desires.

29. We learn to comprehend language (_____) faster than we learn to produce it (_____).

30. Noam Chomsky suggested that humans have an inborn mental structure, a type of "organ," called the _____.

31. Chomsky theorized that children are born pre-programmed with a set of rules about language known as _____.

32. _____ is interested in the psychological differences between people and not in psychological similarities.

33. _____ is the study of measuring psychological characteristics, knowledge, abilities, attitudes, and personality traits.

34. Francis Galton coined the term _____, which means from good stock and hereditarily endowed with noble qualities.

35. _____ is famous in the history of psychology for creating the first test of intelligence.

36. The _____ was calculated as the ratio of mental age to chronological age times 100.

37. _____ is the ability to define and understand words.

Chapter 10 Quiz

1) When we think, we use mental categories, representations, images, and symbols for objects, actions, events, words, and ideas called _____.
   a) concepts
   b) cognitions
   c) ideas
   d) worldviews

2) The individual way we create and organize concepts is called a _____.
   a) heuristics
   b) cognitive script
   c) cognitive style
   d) schema

3) The term _____ refers to the way in which one usually processes information.
   a) semantics
   b) schema
   c) cognitive style
   d) worldview

4) _____ are simple "rules-of-thumb" that serve as cognitive shortcuts to solving complex problems.
   a) Heuristics
   b) Fixations
   c) Biases
   d) Logic

5) Psychologists define creative thinking, also called _____, as the ability to generate new ideas or concepts, to make new associations, and the ability to act or think in novel ways.
   a) convergent thinking
   b) divergent thinking
   c) meta-cognition
   d) heuristics

6) _____ is the term for the study of the mental activity involved in acquiring, using, and understanding language.
   a) Deductive reasoning
   b) Phonemes
   c) Psycholinguistics
   d) Morphemes

7) Chomsky theorized that children are born pre-programmed with a set of rules about language known as _____.
   a) universal grammar
   b) language acquisition device
   c) syntax
   d) semantics

8) _____ is interested in the psychological differences between people and not on psychological similarities.
   a) Eugenics
   b) Comparative psychology
   c) Personality psychology
   d) Differential psychology

9) _____, also called analytic thinkers, generally break down thinking into component parts and process information in a detailed step-by-step approach.
   a) Field-independent thinkers
   b) Field-dependent thinkers
   c) Deductive thinkers
   d) Inductive thinkers

10) _____, also called holistic or global thinkers, tend to look at the "big picture" and process information with focus on meaning, connections, and purpose.
   a) Field-independent thinkers
   b) Field-dependent thinkers
   c) Deductive thinkers
   d) Inductive thinkers

11) _____ refers the ways to we perceive and process certain pieces of information but exclude others.
   a) Concentration
   b) Selective attention
   c) Ignorance
   d) Bias

12) _____ is the study of the meaning of language.
   a) Grammar
   b) Semantics
   c) Psycholinguistics
   d) Syntax

13) _____ are the smallest distinguishable sounds in a language.
   a) Morphemes
   b) Phonemes
   c) Holophrases
   d) Pheromones

14) _____ are the smallest meaningful units in a language.
   a) Morphemes
   b) Phonemes
   c) Holophrases
   d) Pheromones

15) Francis Galton coined the term _____, which means from good stock and hereditarily endowed with noble qualities.
   a) reproductive fitness
   b) eugenics
   c) survival of the fittest
   d) evolution

Chapter 10 Study Guide (Answers)

1. **Cognition** is the mental processes of thinking, feeling, perceiving, problem-solving, and remembering.
2. **Metacognition** refers to thinking about thinking.
3. **Concepts** are categories by which we describe the physical world that the brain cannot directly experience.
4. **Simple and formal concepts** are the basic components of thought.
5. Simple, or formal, concepts have a **single feature** in common.
6. A **prototype** is an ideal example of a concept.
7. **Conjunctive concepts** are classified by the presence of two or more common features
8. **Disjunctive concepts** have "either-or" characteristics.
9. **Relational concepts** are classified by the relationship between features.
10. **Cognitive maps** are mental representations of a given place or situation.
11. The individual way we create and organize concepts is called a **schema**.
12. **Cognitive script** is the term psychologists use to describe our usual way of organizing concepts – a type of cognitive autopilot.
13. The term **cognitive style** refers to the way in which one usually processes information.
14. **Field-independent thinkers**, also called *analytic thinkers*, *generally* break down thinking into component parts and process information in a detailed step-by-step approach.
15. **Field-dependent thinkers**, also called holistic or global thinkers, tend to look at the "big picture" and process information with focus on meaning, connections, and purpose.
16. Formal or **deductive reasoning** involves using algorithms and formal rules of logic.
17. **Heuristics** are simple "rules-of-thumb" that serve as cognitive shortcuts to solving complex problems.
18. **Attention** refers to our ability to concentrate on one thing while ignoring others.
19. **Selective attention** refers the ways to we perceive and process certain pieces of information but exclude others.
20. **Concentration** is a focused form of attention in which we ignore anything that is not related to a particular cognitive task.
21. **Psycho linguistics** is the term for the study of the mental activity involved in acquiring, using, and understanding language.
22. **Language** is defined as a set of symbols (i.e., sounds, gestures, or written characters) used to represent objects (i.e., actions, events, and ideas) according to a set of rules.
23. Semantics is the study of the **meaning of language**.
24. **Phonemes** are the smallest distinguishable sounds in a language.
25. **Morphemes** are the smallest meaningful units in a language.
26. **Grammar** and **syntax** describe the system of rules that govern how words form phrases and sentences.
27. Humans in all cultures go through the same stages of **language development**.
28. Between about 9 and 13 months, children begin to produce simple single word sentences called **holophrases** to express feelings or desires.
29. We learn to comprehend language (**receptive language**) faster than we learn to produce it (**expressive language**).
30. Noam Chomsky suggested that humans have an inborn mental structure, a type of "organ," called the **language acquisition device**.
31. Chomsky theorized that children are born pre-programmed with a set of rules about language known as **universal grammar**.
32. **Differential Psychology** is interested in the psychological differences between people and not in psychological similarities.
33. **Psychometrics** is the study of measuring psychological characteristics, knowledge, abilities, attitudes, and personality traits.
34. Francis Galton coined the term **eugenics**, which means from good stock and hereditarily endowed with noble qualities.
35. **Alfred Binet** is famous in the history of psychology for creating the first test of intelligence.
36. The **intelligence quotient** was calculated as the ratio of mental age to chronological age times 100.
37. **Verbal Intelligence** is the ability to define and understand words.

Chapter 10 Short Essay Questions (Answers)

1. Cognition is the mental processes of thinking, feeling, perceiving, problem-solving, and remembering. Cognition is the way we manipulate and understand information. Cognitions are our thoughts.
2. Simple concepts have a single feature in common. For example, "square" is a simple concept; all squares have four sides and four equal angles. Conjunctive concepts are classified by the presence of two or more common features. For example, cotton balls and clouds are both fluffy and white. We also build conceptual categories based on differences. Disjunctive concepts have "either-or" characteristics. The concept of "strike" may mean a work stoppage, a baseball player's swing and miss, or knocking down all ten pins with the first ball in a frame in bowling; but it cannot mean different things at the same time. Relational concepts are classified by the relationship between features.
3. The term "cognitive style" refers to the way in which one usually processes information. Though your specific cognitive style is unique to you, psychologists categorize cognitive styles as field-independent or field-dependent. Field-independent thinkers, also called analytic thinkers, generally break down thinking into component parts and process information in a detailed step-by-step approach. Field-dependent thinkers, also called holistic or global thinkers, tend to look at the "big picture" and process information with focus on meaning, connections, and purpose.
4. Decision-making and problem-solving are closely related cognitive processes. They are some of the most complex of all human mental activities. Both involve perception, memories, emotions, attitudes, and reasoning. We spend tremendous mental energy solving problems and making decisions. Some psychologists suggest that all thought is, at some level, problem solving.
5. Perceptual barriers refer to the ways we perceive circumstances. If we perceive a situation incorrectly, the solution/decision may be faulty. Fixations refer to the tendencies to repeat wrong solutions and bad decisions and to fixate on them to the exclusion of alternatives. Mental set refers to approaching all decisions and problems in similar ways or not using novel approaches. Belief bias, also called confirmation bias, refers to our tendency to favor information that confirms existing assumptions. Believe perseverance refers to our tendency to stick with a decision once we have made it, even in the face of disconfirming evidence. Availability bias refers to our tendency to make decisions based on available examples that we can remember and to not look for new solutions. Functional fixedness refers to the inability to see new uses for a familiar object outside of its traditional use.
6. Language is defined as a set of symbols (i.e., sounds, gestures, or written characters) used to represent objects (i.e. actions, events, and ideas) according to a set of rules. Language allows us to describe abstract concepts, objects that are in another place, and events that occurred at a different time.
7. Semantics is the study of the meaning of language. Grammar and syntax describe the system of rules that govern how words form phrases and sentences.
8. Babies respond to spoken language at birth, but from 0 to 4 months, babies communicate by crying. At around 3 months, babies begin to produce vocal sounds and at around 6 months, they babble and make sounds that resemble the phonemes of the language they hear. Between about 9 and 13 months, children begin to produce simple single word sentences called holophrases to express feelings or desires. At about two years old, children begin to combine two or three words to make short sentences.
9. Chomsky's theory suggested that humans have an inborn mental structure, a type of "organ," called the language acquisition device. Chomsky theorized that children are born pre-programmed with a set of rules about language known as universal grammar. The pre-programming makes us receptive to the commonalities of all languages allowing us to easily learn any language if it is consistent with the universal grammar. Chomsky believed that language has an evolutionary explanation.

Chapter 10 Quiz Answers

1) When we think, we use mental categories, representations, images, and symbols for objects, actions, events, words, and ideas called _____.   a) concepts

2) The individual way we create and organize concepts is called a _____.   d) schema

3) The term _____ refers to the way in which one usually processes information.   c) cognitive style

4) _____ are simple "rules-of-thumb" that serve as cognitive shortcuts to solving complex problems.   a) Heuristics

5) Psychologists define creative thinking, also called _____, as the ability to generate new ideas or concepts, to make new associations, and the ability to act or think in novel ways.   b) divergent thinking

6) _____ is the term for the study of the mental activity involved in acquiring, using, and understanding language.   c) Psycholinguistics

7) Chomsky theorized that children are born pre-programmed with a set of rules about language known as _____.   a) universal grammar

8) _____ is interested in the psychological differences between people and not on psychological similarities.   d) Differential psychology

9) _____, also called analytic thinkers, generally break down thinking into component parts and process information in a detailed step-by-step approach. a) Field-independent thinkers

10) _____, also called holistic or global thinkers, tend to look at the "big picture" and process information with focus on meaning, connections, and purpose.   b) Field-dependent thinkers

11) _____ refers the ways to we perceive and process certain pieces of information but exclude others.   b) Selective attention

12) _____ is the study of the meaning of language.   b) Semantics

13) _____ are the smallest distinguishable sounds in a language. b) Phonemes

14) _____ are the smallest meaningful units in a language. a) Morphemes

15) Francis Galton coined the term _____, which means from good stock and hereditarily endowed with noble qualities.   b) eugenics

Chapter 11 Personality

Chapter 11 Learning Objectives

Describe the Holy Spirit's supernatural influence on a believer's personality.
Describe personality traits.
Describe Hippocrates' four humors.
Describe Sigmund Freud's personality theory.
Describe Jung's concept of archetypes.
Describe Alfred Adler's concept of individual psychology.
Describe the Big Five personality traits.
Explain how personality psychologist use twin studies.
Explain why humanistic psychology was known as psychology's "third force."
Describe projective personality assessments.

Key Concepts and People

Traits and states
Hippocrates
Sanguine, phlegmatic,
melancholic, and
choleric temperaments
Somatotype theory
Sigmund Freud
Libido
Id, ego, and superego
Ego defense mechanisms

Psycho-sexual stages
Carl Jung
Neo-Freudian
Analytic psychology
Archetypes
Alfred Adler
Individual Psychology
Trait theories of personality
Gordon Allport
Central and cardinal traits

Big Five personality traits
Albert Bandura
External and internal locus
of control
Minnesota Multiphasic
Personality Inventory
Myers-Briggs Type Indicator
Projective personality
assessments

Short Essay Questions

1. Define personality, traits, and personality types.
2. Describe tests that psychologists use to assess personality.
3. Describe the personality theory of Sigmund Freud.
4. Describe the personality theory of Carl Jung.
5. Describe the personality theory of Alfred Adler.
6. Describe the personality theory of Albert Bandura.
7. Describe the personality theory of Carl Rogers.
8. Describe personality development from a behaviorist's perspective.
9. Describe the "Big Five" factors of personality.
10. Describe the MMPI and Myers-Briggs Type Indicator.

For Further Study

1. Read: Wanted: A Christian Theory of Personality by Gary Collins at
   http://www.asa3.org/ASA/PSCF/1967/JASA6-67Collins.html
2. Read: Personality Traits: Their Classification and Measurement, by Floyd H. and Gordon W. Allport
   at http://psychclassics.yorku.ca/Allport/Traits/

Topics for Discussion

1. In what ways are you "like" your friends and family?
2. How are your moods, preferences, sensitivities, and emotions similar to those of the people
   around you?
3. How are they different?

4.   What are your attitudes, what do you think about, and how do you relate to other people?

Chapter 11 Worldview Issues

Personality

Personality is a big part of psychology class. Personality psychology is interested in describing and measuring of personality traits – our individual differences. It describes ways to assess personality, predicts the relationship between personality and behavior, and proposes ways to change personality.

The scientific study of personality is young, but interest in personality is old. Philosophers and theologians debated whether our personality is shaped by experience or determined at birth – by nature or nurture. Some Each of psychology's major schools-of-thought developed theories of personality

Behaviorists explain personality in terms of learned patterns of behavior. Freud believed personality was shaped in the unconscious in a series of psychosexual stages. Humanists believe that the need for self-actualization shapes personality. Evolutionists explain it in terms of evolved patterns of behavior.

But from a Christian perspective, there is a bigger issue. Few topics come closer to the core of the Bible's message of, "what is Man?' than personality psychology. Who are you, really? What are you like, in your heart. Your personality is a gift of God, mysterious, intricate, and complex.

A Christian approach to psychology distinguishes between personality and personhood. Personality is about traits we can measure. Personhood is bigger. We can speak about our pets' personalities, but personhood is a reflection of God – it transcends personality. A Christian approach to psychology recognizes that of our personhood comes directly from God and reflects His image. He knew us before we were born. The value of the unborn, the very old, and the disabled is their personhood, not personality.

A Christian approach recognizes the effect of sin on personality. The new birth of a believer and the work of the Spirit includes personality changes. Conforming to the mind of Christ – growing toward Christian maturity – is an ongoing process of personality change.

Study Guide Chapter 11

1. _____ is generally defined as a relatively stable pattern of psychological characteristics called traits.

2. _____ are enduring and consistent patterns of thoughts, feelings, attitudes and behaviors.

3. One of the more revolutionary aspects of Freud's personality theory was his belief that much of our personality operates at the level of the _____.

4. According to Freud, the mind operates on three interacting levels of awareness: _____.

5. The _____ contains mental events of which we are actively aware at the moment.

6. The _____ contains aspects of mental life which are not conscious at any moment, but can be easily brought to awareness.

7. The _____ contains thoughts, feelings, and motives which are not available either at the conscious or pre-conscious level.

8. Freud's theory is known as the _____ personality theory.

9. According to Freud, all mental activity is driven by two competing, universal, and inborn life forces or instincts – the sexual life force called _____ and the death force called _____.

10. Freud believed there are three parts of personality. He named them _____ _____.

11. _____ was said to be an instinctive and unconscious aspect of the personality that seeks immediate gratification.

12. Id operates on the _____ – libido's drive to find sexual gratification.

13. Freud described ego as our _____, the public and private expression of our personality.

14. _____ operates like a judge or supervisor of personality.

15. _____ are the means by which Freud thought we avoid consciously confronting troublesome thoughts, memories, and impulses.

16. _____ is refusing to admit something has happened. Teens who think it ok to use drugs and alcohol are "in denial" about the dangers.

17. _____ is making up good-sounding or over-stated, but wrong, explanations for one's behavior.

18. _____ describes taking a detached, rational, and logical approach to emotionally uncomfortable issues.

19. _____ refers to seeing our own unpleasant/unacceptable impulses in others.

20. _____ describes focusing unpleasant emotions somewhere other than where they belong.

21. _____ refers to pushing uncomfortable memories into the subconscious.

22. _____ refers to channeling primitive sexual and aggressive impulses into socially acceptable activities.

23. _____ describes an unconscious effort to defend ego from stress by reverting to behavior characteristics of a younger age.

24. Carl Jung called his personality theory _____.

25. Jung believed that the mind existed in three levels: the _____ _____, _____.

26. _____ are universal images and universal ways that people behave and interpret experiences.

27. Alfred Adler is famous in the history of psychology for his approach to personality that he called _____.

28. Adler was an early supporter of the importance of _____ on personality development.

29. According to the _____ perspective, personality is nothing more than learned patterns of behavior.

30. _____ are the mental characteristics that make up our personalities.

31. _____ are collections of traits that occur together in some individuals.

32. Today, most psychologists believe that personality can be well-described in terms of the _____ personality traits.

33. The Big Five personality traits are: _____, _____, _____, _____, _____.

34. _____ refers to the extent to which individuals perceive they have control over the events in life.

35. An _____ refers to the perception that chance or outside forces determine one's "fate."

36. An _____ refers to the perception that one controls one's own fate.

37. _____ is the most popular self-report personality inventory in use today.

38. The four dichotomies in the MBTI are: _____, _____, and _____.

39. _____ ask subjects to interpret ambiguous images or scenes.

Chapter 11 Quiz

1) _____ is generally defined as the relatively stable pattern of psychological characteristics called traits.
   a) Personality
   b) Temperament
   c) Archetype
   d) The Big Five

2) Four hundred years before Christ, the Greek physician Hippocrates characterized personality in terms of four _____.
   a) humors
   b) temperaments
   c) somatotypes
   d) elements

3) _____ are the mental characteristics that make up our personalities.
   a) Traits
   b) temperaments
   c) somatotypes
   d) elements

4) One of the more revolutionary aspects of Freud's personality theory was his belief that much of our personality operated at the level of the _____.
   a) id and ego
   b) destrudo
   c) sensual pleasure
   d) unconscious

5) The _____ contains mental events of which we are actively aware at the moment.
   a) conscious mind
   b) pre-conscious
   c) unconscious
   d) mostly conscious

6) The _____ contains aspects of mental life which are not conscious at any moment but can be easily brought to awareness.
   a) conscious mind
   b) pre-conscious
   c) unconscious
   d) mostly conscious

7) The _____ contains thoughts, feelings, and motives which are not available either at the conscious or pre-conscious level.
   a) conscious mind
   b) pre-conscious
   c) unconscious
   d) mostly conscious

8) _____ operates on the pleasure principle; libido's drive to find sensual gratification.
   a) Id
   b) Ego
   c) Superego
   d) Consciousness

9) _____ operates on the reality principle which serves to consciously and unconsciously restrain Id.
   a) Ego
   b) Id
   c) Superego
   d) Libido

10) _____ operates like a judge or supervisor of personality and insists that we behave according to the highest ideals taught by society, religion, and most importantly, our parents.
   a) Ego
   b) Id
   c) Superego

11) _____ is refusing to admit something has happened.
   a) Denial
   b) Rationalization
   c) Projection
   d) Displacement

12) _____ is making up good-sounding or over-stated, but wrong, explanations for one's behavior.
   a) Denial
   b) Rationalization
   c) Projection
   d) Displacement

13) _____ refers to seeing our own unpleasant/unacceptable impulses in others.
   a) Denial
   b) Rationalization
   c) Projection
   d) Displacement

14) _____ describes focusing unpleasant emotions somewhere other than where they belong.
   a) Denial
   b) Rationalization
   c) Projection
   d) Displacement

15) Freud believed that personality develops through _____.
   a) conscious, preconscious, and unconscious
   b) continuous development
   c) discontinuous development
   d) psychosexual stages

16) Jung is known as a _____ or "new" Freudian.
   a) neo-Freudian
   b) pseudo-Freudian
   c) reformed-Freudian
   d) analytic-Freudian

17) Jung identified dream themes said to be common to all cultures. Those themes are called _____.
   a) the collective unconscious
   b) complexes
   c) archetypes
   d) latency

18) Alfred Adler was an early supporter of the importance of _____ on personality development.
   a) birth order
   b) early life experiences
   c) attachment
   d) genetics

19) The _____ is the most popular self-report personality inventory in use today.
   a) MMPI
   b) Myers-Briggs Type Indicator
   c) Big Five
   d) Rorschach test

Answer Key Chapter 11

Chapter 11 Study Guide (Answers)

1. **Personality** is generally defined as a relatively stable pattern of psychological characteristics called traits.
2. **Traits** are enduring and consistent patterns of thoughts, feelings, attitudes and behaviors.
3. One of the more revolutionary aspects of Freud's personality theory was his belief that much of our personality operates at the level of the **unconscious**.
4. According to Freud, the mind operates on three interacting levels of awareness: **the conscious, pre-conscious, and unconscious.**
5. The **conscious mind** contains mental events of which we are actively aware at the moment.
6. The **pre-conscious** contains aspects of mental life which are not conscious at any moment, but can be easily brought to awareness.
7. The **unconscious** contains thoughts, feelings, and motives which are not available either at the conscious or pre-conscious level.
8. Freud's theory is known as the **psycho-dynamic**, **psycho-analytic**, or **psycho-sexual** personality theory.
9. According to Freud, all mental activity is driven by two competing, universal, and inborn life forces or instincts – the sexual life force called **eros** and the death force called **thantos**.
10. Freud believed there are three parts of personality. He named them **id, ego, and superego.**
11. **Id** was said to be an instinctive and unconscious aspect of the personality that seeks immediate gratification.
12. Id operates on the **pleasure principle** – libido's drive to find sexual gratification.
13. Freud described ego as our **sense of self**, the public and private expression of our personality.
14. **Superego** operates like a judge or supervisor of personality.
15. **Defense mechanisms** are the means by which Freud thought we avoid consciously confronting troublesome thoughts, memories, and impulses.
16. **Denial** is refusing to admit something has happened. Teens who think it ok to use drugs and alcohol are "in denial" about the dangers.
17. **Rationalization** is making up good-sounding or over-stated, but wrong, explanations for one's behavior.
18. **Intellectualization** describes taking a detached, rational, and logical approach to emotionally uncomfortable issues.
19. **Projection** refers to seeing our own unpleasant/unacceptable impulses in others.
20. **Displacement** describes focusing unpleasant emotions somewhere other than where they belong.
21. **Repression** refers to pushing uncomfortable memories into the subconscious.
22. **Sublimation** refers to channeling primitive sexual and aggressive impulses into socially acceptable activities.
23. **Regression** describes an unconscious effort to defend ego from stress by reverting to behavior characteristics of a younger age.
24. Carl Jung called his personality theory **analytic psychology**.
25. Jung believed that the mind existed in three levels: the **conscious. the personal unconscious (comparable to id), and the collective unconscious**.
26. **Archetypes** are universal images and universal ways that people behave and interpret experiences.
27. Alfred Adler is famous in the history of psychology for his approach to personality that he called **individual psychology**.
28. Adler was an early supporter of the importance of **birth order** on personality development.
29. According to the **behaviorist** perspective, personality is nothing more than learned patterns of behavior.
30. **Traits** are the mental characteristics that make up our personalities.
31. **Personality types** are collections of traits that occur together in some individuals.
32. Today, most psychologists believe that personality can be well-described in terms of the **Big Five** personality traits.
33. The Big Five personality traits are: **extroverted or introverted, agreeable or antagonistic, conscientious or negligent, emotionally stable or emotionally unstable, open to new experiences/ideas or closed to new experiences/ideas.**
34. **Locus of Control** refers to the extent to which individuals perceive they have control over the events in life.
35. An **external locus of control** refers to the perception that chance or outside forces determine one's "fate."
36. An **internal locus of control** refers to the perception that one controls one's own fate.
37. **The Myers-Briggs Type Indicator** is the most popular self-report personality inventory in use today.
38. The four dichotomies in the MBTI are: **extraversion vs. introversion, sensing vs. intuition, thinking vs. feeling, and judging vs. perceiving.**
39. **Projective personality assessments** ask subjects to interpret ambiguous images or scenes.

Chapter 11 Short Essay Questions (Answers)

1. There is no universally accepted definition of personality. It is generally defined as a relatively stable pattern of psychological characteristics called traits. Traits are enduring and consistent patterns of thoughts, feelings, attitudes and behaviors. By grouping a number of personality traits, we can describe different personality types. Personality types are collections of traits that occur together in some individuals.

2. Self-report inventories are a type of questionnaire in which people provide information about themselves by answering questions. Projective tests ask subjects to interpret ambiguous images or scenes. Psychologists believe that because the images are ambiguous, people "project" unconscious thoughts into their interpretations.

3. According to Freud, all mental activity is driven by two competing, universal, and inborn life forces or instincts – the sexual life force called Eros and the death force called Thanatos. Eros produces a drive for sensual and sexual gratification called libido. Thanatos produces a drive for aggression, death, and destruction called destrudo. Personality, according to Freud, is formed through the psychic warring of libido vs. destrudo.

4. Carl Jung called his personality theory analytic psychology. Jung believed that the psyche (mind) existed in three levels: the conscious (comparable to Freud's concept of the ego), the personal unconscious (comparable to id), and the collective unconscious. Like Freud, Jung thought the most important factors influencing personality were unconscious. The personal unconscious contains all of one's life experiences and memories – influential, but inaccessible by the conscious mind. Jung thought that the collective unconscious was a storehouse of the collective experiences of all Mankind – a type of genetic memory containing the primitive stories and symbols passed down from our ancestors. Jung believed that we unconsciously experience emotions about the content of our personal and the collective unconscious. The experience of those memories cluster in emotion-laden themes or associations, called complexes, that affect our personality and behavior.

5. Alfred Adler believed that a driving force in personality is striving for perfection in the context of early relationships. Failing to achieve perfection produces feelings of inferiority that provide the impetus for personality development. According to Adler, compensating for feelings of inferiority shapes our personality.

6. Albert Bandura believed that personality develops through an interaction of behavior, the environment, and cognitive processes. Bandura suggested that we learn our personality by observing and modeling. Bandura believed that we consciously regulate our behavior and develop personality through a number of cognitive processes including self-observation, judgment, attention, memory, motivation, self-regulation, expectation, and self-concept in a reciprocal relationship with our environment. He labeled this concept reciprocal determinism.

7. Humanistic personality theories suggest that a tendency toward personal fulfillment and self-actualization is the primary force driving personality development.

8. To behavioral psychologists like B. F. Skinner and John Watson, what we call personality is nothing more than learned patterns of behavior. If we are outgoing, it is because outgoing behavior was reinforced. If we are shy and reserved, it is because outgoing behavior was punished or extinguished. Personality, according to behaviorism, is determined solely by external environmental forces – the result of learning, reinforcement, shaping, and modeling.

9. Extroverted or introverted, Agreeable or antagonistic, Conscientious or negligent, emotionally stable or emotionally unstable, Open to new experiences/ideas or closed to new experiences/ideas

10. The MMPI was designed to make predictions about mental disorders. People with known mental conditions were given a large battery of true/false questions. Their responses were compared to "normal" people. The Myers-Briggs Type Indicator describes ways of thinking and acting in terms of 16 possible combinations of four dichotomous preferences.

Chapter 11 Quiz Answers

1) _____ is generally defined as the relatively stable pattern of psychological characteristics called traits.   a) Personality

2) Four hundred years before Christ, the Greek physician Hippocrates characterized personality in terms of four _____.   b) temperaments

3) _____ are the mental characteristics that make up our personalities. a) Traits

4) One of the more revolutionary aspects of Freud's personality theory was his belief that much of our personality operated at the level of the _____.   d) unconscious

5) The _____ contains mental events of which we are actively aware at the moment.   a) conscious mind

6) The _____ contains aspects of mental life which are not conscious at any moment but can be easily brought to awareness.   b) pre-conscious

7) The _____ contains thoughts, feelings, and motives which are not available either at the conscious or pre-conscious level. c) unconscious

8) _____ operates on the pleasure principle; libido's drive to find sensual gratification.   a) Id

9) _____ operates on the reality principle which serves to consciously and unconsciously restrain Id.   a) Ego

10) _____ operates like a judge or supervisor of personality and insists that we behave according to the highest ideals taught by society, religion, and most importantly, our parents. c) Superego

11) _____ is refusing to admit something has happened. a) Denial

12) _____ is making up good-sounding or over-stated, but wrong, explanations for one's behavior.   b) Rationalization

13) _____ refers to seeing our own unpleasant/unacceptable impulses in others.   c) Projection

14) _____ describes focusing unpleasant emotions somewhere other than where they belong.   d) Displacement

15) Freud believed that personality develops through _____.   d) psychosexual stages

16) Jung is known as a _____ or "new" Freudian.   a) Neo-Freudian

17) Jung identified dream themes said to be common to all cultures. Those themes are called _____.   c) archetypes

18) Alfred Adler was an early supporter of the importance of _____ on personality development.   a) birth order

19) The _____ is the most popular self-report personality inventory in use today.   b) Myers-Briggs Type Indicator

Chapter 12 Abnormal Psychology

Chapter 12 Learning Objectives

Describe "abnormal." Describe difficulties differentiating normal from abnormal.
Describe mental illness and explain worldview perspectives of the causes of mental illness.
Describe historical perspectives of the causes of mental illness.
Describe the classes of mental illness and key characteristics of major disorders.

Key Concepts and People

Abnormal thoughts, feelings, and behavior
Mental illness
Rosenhan experiment
Insanity

The Diagnostic and Statistical Manual of Mental Disorders
Cognitive disorders
Substance use disorders

Psychotic disorders
Mood disorders
Anxiety disorders

Short Essay Questions

1. How does worldview impact one's beliefs about the causes of mental illness?
2. Describe supernatural explanations of mental illness.
3. Describe various approaches toward defining what is abnormal.
4. Describe the causes of mental illness from the behaviorist perspective.
5. Describe the causes of mental illness from the Freudian psychodynamic perspective.
6. Describe the causes of mental illness from the humanistic perspective.
7. Describe the causes of mental illness from the cognitive perspective.
8. Describe the causes of mental illness from the evolutionary perspective.
9. Describe the Diagnostic and Statistical Manual of Mental Disorders (DSM).

For Further Study

1. Video: When medicine got it wrong. http://whenmedicine.org/MedW/Home.html
2. Web: National Down Syndrome Society. http://ndss.org/
3. Web: The World's Leading Website on Learning Disabilities http://ldonline.org/
4. Web: National Autism Association http://nationalautismassociation.org/
5. For Alzheimer's Association at http://alz.org/index.asp
6. Video: Medicating Kids. FRONTLINE examines the dramatic increase in the prescription of behavior-modifying drugs for children, at
   http://pbs.org/wgbh/pages/frontline/shows/medicating/watch/
7. Video: Schizophrenia: Gerald, Part 1 http://youtube.com/watch?v=gGnl8dqEoPQ
8. Video: Schizophrenia: Gerald, Part 2 http://youtube.com/watch?v=i6h8Ic-I7R0&feature=related
9. Web: National Center on Birth Defects and Developmental Disabilities
   http://cdc.gov/ncbddd/index.html
10. Web: National Institute of Mental Health at http://nimh.nih.gov/health/topics/index.shtml

Topics for Discussion

1. Give examples from the Christian life of thoughts, behaviors, and emotions that are abnormal according to the world's standards.
2. Rates of depression reportedly have increased 10-20 times what they were 50 years ago. Why?
3. Does abnormal mean dangerous? Does abnormal mean "bad?"
4. Are people with antisocial personality disorder (sociopaths) evil or sick?

Chapter 12 Worldview Issues

Mental Pain and Suffering

Sometimes something goes wrong. Sometimes people think, feel, and behave in ways that are abnormal. Sometimes people get depressed. Sometimes people hear voices, believe crazy things, act in bizarre ways and sometimes people kill themselves or kill other people. Part of what it means to be human in a fallen world is the experience of mental pain and suffering. Abnormal and treatment psychology are interesting, important, difficult, and sometimes personal topics. If it hasn't happened already, you or someone you love will experience mental pain and suffering.

But few topics in psychology are more worldview-laden and controversial among Christians than abnormal and treatment psychology. The worldview questions surrounding the causes of and cures for mental pain and suffering are complex and multi-faceted.

Topics like the nervous system, sensation and perception, memory, and others are clearly not the focus of the Bible's message. The causes of and cures for mental pain and suffering, however, are close to the core of our humanity and clearly a focus of the Bible's message. Sin, salvation, restoration, and sanctification are at the heart of the Gospel message and are foundational to a Christian understanding of the causes of and cures for mental pain and suffering. A Christian approach to the causes and cures of mental pain and suffering requires wrestling with difficult questions like:

- Is the experience of mental pain and suffering a mental 'illness' or is it the result of sin and disunity with God?
- Are mental disorders caused by chemical imbalances, trauma and life experiences, genetics, or some combination?
- Are mental disorders best treated from a spiritual or a medical perspective?
- Can Christians safely borrow techniques from modern psychology to help those in mental pain?

Causes and Cures

Throughout history, worldviews influenced beliefs about the causes of and cures for mental pain and suffering. For much of human history, understanding of mental wellness and pain went hand-in-hand with spiritual and religious beliefs. 'Mental disorders' were caused by gods, demons, witches, sorcerers, and spirits supernaturally monkeying around with humans. The 'treatment,' casting spells, offering sacrifices, and performing rituals to appease the spirits, flowed logically from the diagnosis.

If mental disorders were understood in terms of an individual's moral weaknesses, it followed logically that treatment meant punishment – starvation, fetters, and flogging in hopes of that 'patients' would repent and change their evil ways. Throughout the 17th and 18th centuries, when the mentally ill were thought of as zombie-like soulless animals, it made sense to cage and chain them like animals.

Today, mental pain and suffering is understood in terms of illness and disease known as the 'medical model.' The discovery of Thorazine in 1952 started a revolution that continues today – the pharmacological revolution. Thorazine was called a miracle drug. Patients who had to be restrained because of violent behavior, could be unchained. Patients who once stood without moving or speaking, began to walk and talk normally. Since the discovery of Thorazine, many new drugs have been developed for the varieties of mental pain and suffering. Americans spend tens of billions of dollars annually on psychiatric drugs.

The medical model reflects a belief that psychological disorders are biological problems. Good psychological health and bad psychological health are reducible to electro-chemical determinants. Critics of the medical model suggest that the emphasis on medications provides a false hope that a 'magic pill' will fix all our problems. Critics suggest that the emphasis on alleviating symptoms with medications ignores underlying spiritual and social problems.

Each of psychology's major schools-of-thought made claims about the causes of mental pain and suffering. Each suggested a model for treating mental pain and suffering that flowed from the assumptions about causes.

Behaviorists suggested that what we call abnormal was conditioned by association, punishment, and reinforcement. Behavior therapy (also called behavior modification) applies the laws of behavior to treatment of psychological disorders. Behavior therapy doesn't focus on internal mental states and does not address or unconscious issues or conflicts.

The cognitive perspective suggests that irrational beliefs and distorted thinking lead to psychological problems. Cognitive therapy seeks to change the way we think. It is based on the premise that the way we think about a situation is more important than the situation itself. Cognitive-behavioral therapy (CBT) combines a cognitive and behavioral approach to change distorted thoughts and unwanted behaviors. CBT is one of the most commonly used approaches to therapy today.

Freudian psychodynamic theories explained mental illness in terms of unconscious psychic conflicts. Freud's techniques were created to access the unconscious mind, so he could discover and treat the source of psychological problems.

Humanists believe that mental pain and suffering happens when circumstances block one's progress toward self-actualization. Humanistic therapies help patients achieve self-actualization and high self-esteem. In accepting and nonjudgmental environments of unconditional positive regard, the goodness in us will propel us toward our full potential.

The biological, or medical model, approaches mental illness as diseases of the mind that, like ordinary physical diseases, have discrete physical causes. The biological perspective is seen in Hippocrates' idea that mental disorders were caused by imbalances in four body fluids. From this perspective, though more sophisticated today, mental illnesses are caused by chemical imbalances in the brain.

Self-help
In addition to the theories from 'mainstream' academic psychology, there are hundreds, perhaps thousands, of popular 'self-help' psychologies in books, magazines, TV, talk radio, and on the internet. Popular psychology offers advice for living, mental health, child-rearing, relationships, and many other topics, often not supported by sound research. And popular psychology is not limited to the secular perspective. Christians spend millions of dollars annually on self-help books, and some Christians uncritically accept good-sounding advice – thinly veiled in Christian terms, that are inconsistent with a Christian worldview. Christian popular psychology is often

based on bad science and bad theology. We should recognize when someone disguises anti-Christian ideas by sprinkling in Jesus' name and a few verses of the New Testament.

What About Sin?

From a naturalistic perspective, it is ridiculous to suggest that sin and salvation have anything to do with mental pain and suffering. From a naturalistic perspective, guilt and suffering are meaningless and are harmful emotions to be avoided. But a Christian approach to understanding mental pain and suffering must deal with the problem of sin. Sin, as part of the human condition, is the ultimate cause for all pain and suffering – mental and otherwise. But to what extent is mental pain and suffering the result of genetics, brain-based disorders, trauma, chemical imbalances, bad parenting, red dye #7, and too much screen time? To what extents is mental pain and suffering the result of individual sin and disunity with God?

A Christian approach to understanding and caring for mental pain and suffering begins with the Bible's message of God's love, the dignity of all life, sin and sinfulness, and redemption and grace. Christians believe that sin and disunity from God effects mental health and that real healing involves salvation, restoration, and sanctification.

A Christian approach to mental pain and suffering is complicated by the nature of suffering. Consider Job, whose considerable mental anguish was not a result of his sin but was part of God's divine purpose. Guilt, pain, and suffering are tools at God's disposal as He conforms us to Christ's image. Jesus was a man of sorrows. Though many Christians share modern psychology's belief that emotional pain must be avoided at all costs, a Christian perspective recognizes that through suffering we are refined and made more Christ-like. We recognize that redemption and restoration make us whole and that the Christian life does not necessarily mean ease and comfort.

Study Guide Chapter 12

1. Statistically, something is _____ if it varies sufficiently from the average, the usual, or the customary.

2. Many people define abnormal in terms of _____.

3. Thoughts, emotions, and behaviors are generally considered abnormal if they are:

    _____.

4. Mental illness literally means _____.

5. _____ is any pattern of emotions, behavior, or thoughts inappropriate to the situation and leading to personal distress or the inability to achieve important goals.

6. _____ suggested that abnormal thoughts and behaviors are learned by association, punishment, and reinforcement.

7. The _____ suggested that distorted patterns of understanding and interpreting experiences and relationships are responsible.

8. _____ theories explained psychological disorders in terms of unconscious psychic conflicts.

9. The _____ explained that mental illness developed when circumstances blocked one's progress toward self-actualization.

10. The _____ suggested that patterns of thought and behavior that today are detrimental must have served an adaptive survival purpose for ancient humans.

11. This _____, also called the medical model view mental illness like every other physical disease, with discrete physical causes.

12. _____ categorizes various mental conditions and describes the characteristic symptoms of each condition.

13. _____ are disorders of the growth and development of the brain or nervous system.

14. _____ – previously called Mental Retardation -- impact both cognitive ability (IQ) and adaptive functioning.

15. _____ describe deficits in verbal and nonverbal communication.

16. _____ describes deficits in reading, mathematics, and written expression.

17. _____are characterized by significant impairment in the normal development of motor abilities.

18. _____is a new diagnosis for a group of neurodevelopmental disorders that can cause significant social, communication and behavioral challenges.

19. _____ is the single most common problem that brings children to the attention of psychologists and psychiatrists.

20. The word _____ stems from the Greek "psyche," meaning soul or mind, and "osis," meaning diseased or abnormal condition.

21. _____are perceptual experiences of stimuli that do not exist. A hallucination may be a sound, sight, touch, taste, or smell.

22. _____, once the accepted term for mental illness, is a legal concept based one's ability to know or understand right from wrong, to control their actions, and to participate in a legal defense

23. _____ are beliefs that are clearly false but that are firmly and persistently believed to be true.

24. _____are a type of delusion in which one believes that common events, remarks, or objects in the environment have special and personal meaning.

25. _____are exaggerated beliefs in one's importance or a belief that one has special powers, talents, or abilities.

26. _____ refers to a stereotype that having a mental illness is a reflect ion of one's character.

27. _____are characterized by symptoms of both depression and mania.

28. A _____is characterized by a depressed mood most of the day nearly every day, decreased interest in activities, significant weight change, too much or too little sleep, fatigue, feelings of worthlessness or guilt, poor concentration or indecisiveness, and thoughts of death and suicide.

29. A _____is described as an abnormally and persistently elevated, expansive, or irritable mood. Manic episodes are characterized by inflated self-esteem or grandiosity; decreased need for sleep; pressured, loud, and rapid speech; flight of ideas; distractibility; increased goal-directed activities; restlessness; and excessive involvement in pleasurable activities with a high potential for painful consequences.

30. _____was formerly known as manic-depressive disorder,

31. _____ is extreme anxiety and intense fear with severe physiological reactions. Panic is the essential feature of most anxiety disorders.

32. A _____ describes the sudden onset of intense fear, apprehension, an urge to escape, and a sense of impending danger, doom, or death. Palpitations, sweating, trembling, shortness of breath, chest pain, nausea, dizziness, numbness, or chills accompany the feeling of panic.

33. A _____ – or "morbid fear" -- is a persistent and irrational fear of an object or situation that is disproportional to the actual danger with causing distress and impairment in social or occupational activities.

34. _____ characterized by anxiety due to an environment's openness or crowdedness.

35. _____ is characterized by intense fear, distress, and impaired functioning in social situations.

36. _____ are recurrent, unwanted, and intrusive thoughts.

37. _____ are unwanted and irrational urges to repeat certain behaviors.

38. _____ is a severe disorder resulting from exposure to an extremely traumatic event that involved, or could have caused, death or serious injury.

39. _____ describes disturbed and inappropriate social behavior in most contexts and is characterized by serious problems in emotional attachments.

40. _____ are characterized by changes in personality or consciousness.

41. _____, formerly known as multiple personality disorder, is said to be the existence of two or more distinct identities or personality states that take control of an individual's behavior.

42. _____ is characterized by a refusal to maintain a minimally normal body weight, an intense fear of gaining weight, and a disturbance in the perception of body size or shape.

43. _____ is characterized by binge eating followed by inappropriate compensatory behavior (e.g., vomiting and using laxatives).

44. _____ are characterized by a severe and persistent disturbance of sexual desire or in the sexual response cycle.

45. _____ is a new diagnostic category in DSM-5 that reflects a change in beliefs about gender and sexuality, characterized by cross-gender identification, aversion toward one's gender, and a strong desire to be the other gender.

46. _____ are characterized by problems in the self-control of emotions and behaviors that violate the rights of others or that conflict with societal norms or authority figures.

47. _____ describes children with a pattern of negativistic, hostile, and defiant behavior, who often lose their temper, argue with adults, defy or refuse to comply with requests or rules, deliberately annoy people, blame others for own mistakes, or who are irritable, angry; resentful, spiteful, or vindictive.

48. _____describes repetitive and persistent patterns of behavior in which the basic rights of others or societal norms or rules are violated.

49. _____ is characterized by a recurrent failure to resist impulses to steal objects that are not needed for personal use or for their monetary value.

50. _____ is characterized by deliberate and purposeful fire setting to relieve tension and for self-gratification.

51. _____ refers to a decreased reaction to a substance so that larger doses are required to achieve the same effect.

52. _____ refers to distressing physical and/or psychological symptoms when no longer using the substance.

53. _____are a category of conditions that involve disturbances in thinking, memory, language, and awareness of surroundings.

54. _____ describes a disorder of consciousness that develops over a short period of time, characterized by rambling and incoherent speech, disorientation, hallucinations, and memory impairment.

55. _____is a slow, gradual, and persistent decline in mental functioning.

56. _____ is characterized by an impaired ability to create new memories or to retrieve past memories.

57. _____describe enduring, pervasive, and inflexible patterns of thinking, feeling, and behaving that deviate substantially from the expectations of the culture.

58. _____ is characterized by disregard for and violation of the rights of others.

59. _____ is characterized by pervasive instability in interpersonal relationships, self-image, mood, and extreme impulsivity.

60. The _____ is characterized by a grandiose self-image, exaggerated sense of self-worth, and lack of empathy for others.

61. A _____, also called a fetish, is an atypical sexual urge, fantasy, or behavior that involves unusual objects, activities, or situations.

Chapter 12 Quiz

1) Statistically, something is _____ if it varies sufficiently from the average, the usual, or the customary.
   a) abnormal
   b) unusual
   c) a variance
   d) insignificant

2) _____ is a legal concept based on a person's ability to know or understand right from wrong, to control their actions, and to participate in a legal defense.
   a) Insanity
   b) Mental illness
   c) Mental retardation
   d) Lunacy

3) The _____ perspective suggests that abnormal thoughts and behaviors are learned by association, punishment, and reinforcement.
   a) cognitive
   b) behavioral
   c) psychodynamic
   d) humanist

4) _____ is any pattern of emotions, behavior, or thoughts inappropriate to the situation and leading to personal distress or the inability to achieve important goals.
   a) Schizophrenia
   b) Psychopathology
   c) Psychosis
   d) Panic attack

5) The _____ perspective suggested that distorted patterns of understanding and interpreting experiences and relationships are responsible.
   a) behavioral
   b) psychodynamic
   c) cognitive
   d) humanist

6) _____ theories explained mental illness in terms of unconscious psychic conflicts
   a) Evolutionary
   b) Humanist
   c) Behavioral
   d) Psychodynamic

7) The _____ perspective explains that mental illnesses in terms of circumstances blocking one's progress toward self-actualization.
   a) humanist
   b) psychodynamic
   c) cognitive
   d) behavioral

8) According to an _____ perspective, mental disorders must have served an adaptive survival purpose for ancient humans.
   a) psychodynamic
   b) psychodynamic
   c) evolutionary
   d) humanist

9) From the _____ perspective of mental illness, mental illnesses are diseases of the mind that, like ordinary physical diseases, with have discrete physical causes.
   a) biological
   b) psychodynamic
   c) cognitive
   d) humanist

10) _____ is a diagnosis for a group of neurodevelopmental disorders that can cause significant social, communication and behavioral challenges.
   a) Mental retardation
   b) Autism spectrum disorder
   c) Attention-deficit disorder
   d) Schizophrenia

Chapter 12 Study Guide (Answers)

1. Statistically, something is **abnormal** if it varies sufficiently from the average, the usual, or the customary.
2. Many people define abnormal in terms of **variance from culturally accepted standards.**
3. Thoughts, emotions, and behaviors are generally considered abnormal if they are: **maladaptive, disturbing, unusual, and irrational**.
4. Mental illness literally means **disease of the mind**.
5. **Psychopathology** is any pattern of emotions, behavior, or thoughts inappropriate to the situation and leading to personal distress or the inability to achieve important goals.
6. **Behaviorists** suggested that abnormal thoughts and behaviors are learned by association, punishment, and reinforcement.
7. The **cognitive perspective** suggested that distorted patterns of understanding and interpreting experiences and relationships are responsible.
8. **Freudian psycho-dynamic** theories explained psychological disorders in terms of unconscious psychic conflicts.
9. The **humanist perspective** explained that mental illness developed when circumstances blocked one's progress toward self-actualization.
10. The **evolutionary perspective** suggested that patterns of thought and behavior that today are detrimental must have served an adaptive survival purpose for ancient humans.
11. This **disease view**, also called the medical model view mental illness like every other physical disease, with discrete physical causes.
12. **The Diagnostic and Statistical Manual of Mental Disorders (DSM)** categorizes various mental conditions and describes the characteristic symptoms of each condition.
13. **Neurodevelopmental Disorders** are disorders of the growth and development of the brain or nervous system.
14. **Intellectual Developmental Disorders** – previously called Mental Retardation -- impact both cognitive ability (IQ) and adaptive functioning.
15. **Language and Speech Disorders** describe deficits in verbal and nonverbal communication.
16. **Specific Learning Disorder** describes deficits in reading, mathematics, and written expression.
17. **Motor Disorders** are characterized by significant impairment in the normal development of motor abilities.
18. **Autism Spectrum Disorder** is a new diagnosis for a group of neurodevelopmental disorders that can cause significant social, communication and behavioral challenges.
19. **Attention-deficit/hyperactivity disorder (ADHD)** is the single most common problem that brings children to the attention of psychologists and psychiatrists.
20. The word **psychosis** stems from the Greek "psyche," meaning soul or mind, and "osis," meaning diseased or abnormal condition.
21. **Hallucinations** are perceptual experiences of stimuli that do not exist. A hallucination may be a sound, sight, touch, taste, or smell.
22. **Insanity**, once the accepted term for mental illness, is a legal concept based one's ability to know or understand right from wrong, to control their actions, and to participate in a legal defense
23. **Delusions** are beliefs that are clearly false but that are firmly and persistently believed to be true.
24. **Ideas of reference** are a type of delusion in which one believes that common events, remarks, or objects in the environment have special and personal meaning.
25. **Delusions of grandeur** are exaggerated beliefs in one's importance or a belief that one has special powers, talents, or abilities.
26. **Stigma** refers to a stereotype that having a mental illness is a reflect ion of one's character.
27. **Bipolar disorders** are characterized by symptoms of both depression and mania.
28. A **Major Depressive Episode** is characterized by a depressed mood most of the day nearly every day, decreased interest in activities, significant weight change, too much or too little sleep, fatigue, feelings of worthlessness or guilt, poor concentration or indecisiveness, and thoughts of death and suicide.
29. **Manic Episode** is described as an abnormally and persistently elevated, expansive, or irritable mood. Manic episodes are characterized by inflated self-esteem or grandiosity; decreased need for sleep; pressured, loud, and rapid speech; flight of ideas; distractibility; increased goal-directed activities; restlessness; and excessive involvement in pleasurable activities with a high potential for painful consequences.
30. **Bipolar disorder** was formerly known as manic-depressive disorder,

31. **Panic** is extreme anxiety and intense fear with severe physiological reactions. Panic is the essential feature of most anxiety disorders.
32. A **panic attack** describes the sudden onset of intense fear, apprehension, an urge to escape, and a sense of impending danger, doom, or death. Palpitations, sweating, trembling, shortness of breath, chest pain, nausea, dizziness, numbness, or chills accompany the feeling of panic.
33. A **phobia** – or "morbid fear" -- is a persistent and irrational fear of an object or situation that is disproportional to the actual danger with causing distress and impairment in social or occupational activities.
34. **Agoraphobia** characterized by anxiety due to an environment's openness or crowdedness.
35. **Social Anxiety Disorder** is characterized by intense fear, distress, and impaired functioning in social situations.
36. **Obsessions** are recurrent, unwanted, and intrusive thoughts.
37. **Compulsions** are unwanted and irrational urges to repeat certain behaviors.
38. **Post-traumatic stress disorder (PTSD)** is a severe disorder resulting from exposure to an extremely traumatic event that involved, or could have caused, death or serious injury.
39. **Reactive-attachment disorder (RAD)** describes disturbed and inappropriate social behavior in most contexts and is characterized by serious problems in emotional attachments.
40. **Dissociative Disorders** are characterized by changes in personality or consciousness.
41. **Dissociative identity disorder**, formerly known as multiple personality disorder, is said to be the existence of two or more distinct identities or personality states that take control of an individual's behavior.
42. **Anorexia Nervosa** is characterized by a refusal to maintain a minimally normal body weight, an intense fear of gaining weight, and a disturbance in the perception of body size or shape.
43. **Bulimia Nervosa** is characterized by binge eating followed by inappropriate compensatory behavior (e.g., vomiting and using laxatives).
44. **Sexual dysfunctions** are characterized by a severe and persistent disturbance of sexual desire or in the sexual response cycle.
45. **Gender Dysphoria** is a new diagnostic category in DSM-5 that reflects a change in beliefs about gender and sexuality, characterized by cross-gender identification, aversion toward one's gender, and a strong desire to be the other gender.
46. **Disruptive, Impulse-control, and Conduct Disorders** are characterized by problems in the self-control of emotions and behaviors that violate the rights of others or that conflict with societal norms or authority figures.
47. **Oppositional Defiant Disorder (ODD)** describes children with a pattern of negativistic, hostile, and defiant behavior, who often lose their temper, argue with adults, defy or refuse to comply with requests or rules, deliberately annoy people, blame others for own mistakes, or who are irritable, angry; resentful, spiteful, or vindictive.
48. **Conduct Disorder** describes repetitive and persistent patterns of behavior in which the basic rights of others or societal norms or rules are violated.
49. **Kleptomania** is characterized by a recurrent failure to resist impulses to steal objects that are not needed for personal use or for their monetary value.
50. **Pyromania** is characterized by deliberate and purposeful fire setting to relieve tension and for self-gratification.
51. **Tolerance** refers to a decreased reaction to a substance so that larger doses are required to achieve the same effect.
52. **Withdrawal** refers to distressing physical and/or psychological symptoms when no longer using the substance.
53. **Neurocognitive disorders** are a category of conditions that involve disturbances in thinking, memory, language, and awareness of surroundings.
54. **Delirium** describes a disorder of consciousness that develops over a short period of time, characterized by rambling and incoherent speech, disorientation, hallucinations, and memory impairment.
55. **Dementia** is a slow, gradual, and persistent decline in mental functioning.
56. **Amnesia** is characterized by an impaired ability to create new memories or to retrieve past memories.
57. **Personality Disorders** describe enduring, pervasive, and inflexible patterns of thinking, feeling, and behaving that deviate substantially from the expectations of the culture.
58. **Anti-social personality disorder** is characterized by disregard for and violation of the rights of others.
59. **Borderline Personality Disorder** (BPD) is characterized by pervasive instability in interpersonal relationships, self-image, mood, and extreme impulsivity.
60. The **Narcissistic Personality Disorder** is characterized by a grandiose self-image, exaggerated sense of self-worth, and lack of empathy for others.
61. A **paraphilia**, also called a fetish, is an atypical sexual urge, fantasy, or behavior that involves unusual objects, activities, or situations.

Chapter 12 Short Essay Question (Answers)

1. Some topics that psychologists study are more worldview-dependent than others. Topics like the nervous system and sensory processes are far from the "core" of our humanity and are not the focus of the Bible's message. Others, like personality, development, and consciousness define us. Few topics in psychology come closer to the "core" aspects of the human condition – our sin nature, salvation, restoration, and sanctification, than "abnormal" psychology. One's perspective on sin, personal responsibility, and moral absolutes has huge implications on one's view of the causes of abnormal thoughts, feelings, and behaviors. As you might predict, the gravity of the subject matter contributes to disagreements among Christians about the nature and causes of abnormal thoughts, feelings, and behaviors. For the Christian studying psychology, the nature and importance of these issues require great caution. For the Christian who plans to serve God in a career in mental health care, an in-depth and Holy Spirit-informed Christian worldview is crucial.

2. As has been the case for centuries, many people explain abnormal thoughts, feelings, and behaviors in terms of the supernatural influences of gods, demons, witchcraft, sorcery, and "spirits." In ancient cultures, abnormal thoughts and behavior were believed to be the result of supernatural beings taking possession of a person's mind and body. Performing rituals and offering sacrifices to placate the supernatural beings was part of one's daily routine.

3. Statistically, something is abnormal if it varies sufficiently from the average, the usual, or the customary. Many people define abnormal in terms of variance from culturally accepted standards (i.e., political correctness). Some define abnormal subjectively (i.e., "If I believe that my feelings are abnormal, they are abnormal"). Some people believe that normal and abnormal are no more than value judgments, and that to label another's thoughts and behaviors as abnormal is to exercise power inappropriately. Some people define abnormal in terms of dysfunctions in biological processes, some in terms of sin and disunity with God, and others describe abnormality as a failure to live according to moral rules.

4. Behaviorists suggested that abnormal thoughts and behaviors are learned by association, punishment, and reinforcement.

5. Freudian psycho-dynamic theories explained psychological disorders in terms of unconscious psychic conflicts.

6. The humanist perspective explained that mental illness developed when circumstances blocked one's progress toward self-actualization.

7. The cognitive perspective suggested that distorted patterns of understanding and interpreting experiences and relationships are responsible.

8. The evolutionary perspective suggested that mental disorders can be explained using the same evolutionary principles that have been applied to other aspects of psychology and physiology. From this perspective, patterns of thought and behavior that today are detrimental must have served an adaptive survival purpose for ancient humans.

9. The DSM categorizes various mental conditions and describes the characteristic symptoms of each condition. The DSM provides checklists of symptoms serving as diagnostic rules, and it provides a standard vocabulary for describing mental disorders. There are no laboratory tests for most mental illness, so the DSM provides a standard language, diagnostic criteria, and nomenclature for psychiatrists, insurance companies, and pharmaceutical companies.

Chapter 12 Quiz Answers

1) Statistically, something is _____ if it varies sufficiently from the average, the usual, or the customary.   a) abnormal

2) _____ is a legal concept based on a person's ability to know or understand right from wrong, to control their actions, and to participate in a legal defense.   a) Insanity

3) The _____ perspective suggests that abnormal thoughts and behaviors are learned by association, punishment, and reinforcement.   b) behavioral

4) ___ is any pattern of emotions, behavior, or thoughts inappropriate to the situation and leading to personal distress or the inability to achieve important goals. b) Psychopathology

5) The _____ perspective suggested that distorted patterns of understanding and interpreting experiences and relationships are responsible.   c) cognitive

6) _____ theories explained mental illness in terms of unconscious psychic conflicts   d) Psychodynamic

7) The _____ perspective explains that mental illnesses in terms of circumstances blocking one's progress toward self-actualization.   a) humanist

8) According to an _____ perspective, mental disorders must have served an adaptive survival purpose for ancient humans.   c) evolutionary

9) From the _____ perspective of mental illness, mental illnesses are diseases of the mind that, like ordinary physical diseases, with have discrete physical causes.   a) biological

10) ___ is a diagnosis for a group of neurodevelopmental disorders that can cause significant social, communication and behavioral challenges.   b) Autism spectrum disorder

Chapter 13 Treatment

Chapter 13 Learning Objectives

Describe some of the historical approaches to treating mental illness, including the worldview assumptions underlying the approach.

Describe treatments for mental illness from the Middle Ages through the Renaissance.

Describe treatments for mental illness in colonial America and the 17th and 18th century.

Describe how attitudes toward the mentally ill changed in the 19th century.

Describe the history of lobotomy and electroconvulsive therapy.

Describe the discovery of Thorazine and the pharmacological revolution.

Describe the classification of psychiatric medications.

Explain the phrase "chemical imbalance of the brain.

Describe worldview issues underlying psychopharmacology.

Describe the deinstitutionalization of the mentally ill.

Describe the unintended consequences of deinstitutionalization.

Define therapy.

Describe Freudian psychotherapy.

Describe behavior therapy.

Describe cognitive therapies.

Describe humanistic therapy.

Describe family therapy.

Describe "spiritual" treatments.

Describe Christian anti-psychology.

Describe "integration."

Describe Biblical counseling.

Describe popular psychology.

Key Concepts and People

Trephination	Thorazine	Behavior therapy
Abnormal	Psychotropic	Cognitive-behavioral therapy
Moral management	Anti-depressant	Humanistic therapy
Dorothea Dix	Anxiolytic	Family therapy
Benjamin Rush	Mood stabilizer	Anti-psychology
Lobotomy	The Community Mental	Biblical counseling
Walter Freeman	Health Act of 1963	Nouthetic counseling
Convulsive therapies	Deinstitutionalization	Integration
Psychopharmacology	Therapy	Popular psychology
Pharmacological revolution	Freudian psycho-therapy	

Short Essay Questions

1. Describe some of the historical approaches to treating abnormal thoughts, feelings, and behaviors, including the worldview assumptions underlying the approach.
2. Describe how attitudes toward the mentally ill changed in the 19th century.
3. Describe the history of lobotomy and electroconvulsive therapy.
4. Describe the discovery of Thorazine and the pharmacological revolution.
5. Describe the classification of psychiatric medications.
6. Explain the phrase "chemical imbalance of the brain.
7. Describe psychopharmacology.
8. Describe the de-institutionalization of the mentally ill.
9. Describe the unintended consequences of de-institutionalization.
10. Define therapy.
11. Describe Freudian psycho-therapy.

12. Describe behavior therapy.
13. Describe cognitive therapies.
14. Describe humanistic therapy.
15. Describe family therapy.
16. Describe "spiritual" treatments.
17. Describe Christian anti-psychology.
18. Describe "integration."
19. Describe biblical counseling.

For Further Study

1. Read: The Myth of Mental Illness by Dr. Thomas Szasz at Classics in the History of Psychology http://psychclassics.yorku.ca/Szasz/myth.htm
2. Read: Biography of Anton Boisen, by Rev. Robert Leas, The Association for Clinical Pastoral Education https://www.acpe.edu/pdf/History/ACPE%20Brief%20History.pdf
3. Read: Psychology and the Doctrines of Devils, by T. A. McMahon http://thebereancall.org/node/2431
4. Read: The History of Lobotomy, by Renato M.E. Sabbatini http://cerebromente.org.br/n02/historia/lobotomy.htm
5. Read: Bedlam from New Advent http://newadvent.org/cathen/02387b.htm
6. Web: International Association of Biblical Counselors http://iabc.net/
7. Web: The Institute for Nouthetic Studies http://nouthetic.org/
8. Web: Mental Health Medications. National Institute of Mental Health. http://nimh.nih.gov/health/publications/mental-health-medications/complete-index.shtml
9. Web: The Society for Christian Psychology's mission is to promote the development of a distinctly Christian psychology (including theory, research, and practice) that is based on a Christian understanding of human nature http://christianpsych.org/wp_scp/
10. Web: The History of Psychosurgery, by Renato M.E. Sabbatini, PhD
11. http://edumed.org.br/cursos/neurociencia/01/Artigos/aula09/psicocirg_i.htm
12. Video: The New Asylums. FRONTLINE goes inside Ohio's state prison system to explore the issue of mentally ill prisoners http://pbs.org/wgbh/pages/frontline/shows/asylums/view/

Topics for Discussion

1. Jay Adams wrote, "A good seminary education rather than medical school or a degree in clinical psychology, is the most fitting background for a counselor." Discuss that statement.
2. Read 2 Corinthians 1:4. Look up Strong's # 3870 (parakaleo). Discuss biblical usage of parakaleo and verses containing parakaleo.
3. Are psychiatric medications a gift from God? If so, how might they be used and misused?
4. When should a Christian seek help from a pastor, and when should a Christian seek help from a professional counselor?

Chapter 13 Worldview Issues

Abnormal thoughts, feelings, and behaviors are the result of chemical imbalances in the brain, biological malfunctioning, sin, unconscious psychic conflict, trauma and abuse, the demonic, moral weakness, bad parenting, learning, blocked self-actualization, or the result of a combination of causes. Each model of treatment reflects underlying beliefs about the causes of the conditions.

Anti-psychology

Anti-psychology refers to beliefs among some Christians about the causes of and cures for mental pain and suffering. Anti-psychology is not against scientific psychology, it is 'anti' modern psychology's major theories and their application to the causes of and cures for mental pain and suffering. According to this position, by definition, modern psychology's underlying naturalism makes it wholly irreconcilable with a Christian worldview. From this perspective, psychology is spiritually dangerous, because it relies on knowledge derived from sources other than the Bible. Christians holding the anti-psychology position believe that there is nothing that psychology can contribute to our understanding about the human nature or about the nature of mental pain and suffering and what we can do about it.

From this perspective, it is inappropriate to use of any extra-biblical technique to care for mental pain and suffering. The only appropriate treatment is Biblical Counseling. While many Christians consider their approach to counseling 'biblical,' the biblical counseling movement, also known as nouthetic counseling, uses the bible exclusively. It emphasizes the redemptive and healing aspects of biblical admonition and instruction. Psychological problems are caused by personal sinfulness, wrong patterns of thinking and living, and disunity with God. The Bible is sufficient for dealing with all problems of living, even mental illnesses. From this perspective, using a technique, theory, or method from modern psychology is compromise (at best) or heresy (at worst). Biblical counselors discern sin and use the Bible to admonish, confront, motivate, and provide spiritual direction. The goals of Biblical counseling include confession, repentance, reconciliation and restoration, and supporting the counselee's walk with God to produce maturity and Godly living in their life.

The relationship between the Christian worldview and treatment psychology is known as 'integration,' the extent to which the Bible and scientific psychology can each contribute, in their own way, to a comprehensive approach to caring for mental pain and suffering.

What Works?

When it comes to treatment for mental pain and suffering, what works? Have psychology's schools of thought produced treatments that are effective? Does one approach work best?

In 1936, at a time when many new counseling techniques were being developed, Dr. Saul Rosenzweig suggested the answer was 'no.' Rosenzweig used an illustration from Lewis Carrol's Alice in Wonderland. In the novel, the characters get wet. The Dodo Bird suggests that they run a race – a caucus race – to dry. When asked who won the race, the Dodo Bird issued its famous verdict, "Everybody has won, and all must have prizes." The Dodo Bird's verdict has become a metaphor for the debate over the effectiveness of treatment psychology. The Dodo Bird verdict is a symbol for the idea that all approaches to counseling are equally effective.

The Dodo Bird verdict inspired a new sort of race – thousands of research studies, designed to demonstrate that treatment models are effective and to compare treatment models in hopes of discovering which works best. Is Freudian psychotherapy effective? Is it more effective than behavioral therapy? Are cognitive therapies more effective than humanistic? Is medication more effective than counseling? Is Biblical counseling more effective than the rest? The stakes were high. The most effective treatment should be the one grounded in the right worldview – the right perspective on the causes and cures for mental pain and suffering.

But by the mid-1990s, there were thousands of studies which seemed to suggest that the Dodo Bird was right. Therapy is effective, but each approach to therapies is about as effective as any other. Therapies based in very different worldviews using very different techniques seem to be equally effective. There must be, as Dr. Rosenzweig suggested, 'common factors' present in all approaches to counseling. The common factors, not the distinctive techniques, are what make that most difference.

The least potent of the factors, accounting for only 15% of therapies' effectiveness, are the therapeutic techniques. The placebo effect also accounts for 15% of the effectiveness. The most potent factors that work in counseling are the 'therapeutic relationship' and 'extra-therapeutic factors.

The quality of the relationship between the hurting person and caregiver accounts for 30% of what works in counseling. The extent to which the hurting person feels compassion – empathy, warmth, hope, encouragement, and genuine interest is powerful in counseling.

The research suggests that extra-therapeutic, or client factors are the most potent forces in counseling – accounting for 40% of effectiveness. Extra-therapeutic factors are internal characteristics like knowledge, faith, and motivation that the hurting person brings with them to counseling. It is also external strengths like family, friends, and church support. The evidence for a common factors approach is changing counselor education programs – de-emphasizing techniques and emphasizing relationship and extra-therapeutic factors.

As noted earlier, Christians disagree about anti-psychology and integration. The evidence for common factors makes the disagreement seem dated and irrelevant. What's timeless and relevant is compassion and support for people with mental pain and suffering. The Church has a long history of that.

Will you help?

In Luke 10:30-37 Jesus tells the story of the Good Samaritan. In the parable, Jesus tells us of one man's social interactions with a robber, a priest, a Levite, and a Samaritan. It is a story about helping. In 1973 social psychologists from Princeton Theological Seminary examined helping behavior in a re-creation of the parable of the Good Samaritan.

The researchers created a scenario in which subjects encountered a man; slumped over, coughing, and groaning in obvious distress. Would the subjects, seminary students, some of whom were on their way to deliver a sermon on the Good Samaritan, offer help? Not many did.

In 1964, 28-year-old Kitty Genovese was returning home from work late one night when she was attacked in front of her apartment building. At least 38 people, heard her screams, but no one called the police. Miss Genovese is famous in the history of psychology as an example of diffusion of responsibility. Everyone thought someone else would help.

It is one thing to study what works in helping people with mental pain and suffering. But it is something else to do something. Humans are selfish and tend to not help. Without the mind of Christ, we won't be very helpful, either.

Study Guide Chapter 13

1. Your _____ about what causes abnormal thoughts, feelings, and behaviors greatly influences your beliefs about treatment.

2. Every approach to caring for people with abnormal thoughts, feelings, and behaviors brings with it underlying beliefs about the _____.

3. _____, a Roman physician who lived around the time of Christ, recorded that treatment for mental illness consisted of starvation, chains, and flogging.

4. _____known, saw patients not as immoral possessed animals, but as people who were "sick" and in need of treatment.

5. _____is famous in the history of psychology for her work as an advocate for the humane treatment of the mentally ill.

6. Walter Freeman developed a quick and easy ten-minute procedure using an ice pick to sever neural connections in the frontal lobe of the brain known as _____.

7. _____used insulin overdose, chemicals, microwaves, oxygen deprivation, and electric currents to induce brain seizures.

8. The most commonly used convulsive therapy was called _____.

9. When tested on patients in psychiatric hospitals, _____ had a powerful calming and sedating effect.

10. The discovery of Thorazine started what has been called the _____, a search for new psychoactive drugs to treat a variety of psychological disorders.

11. _____are designed to alter the way neurotransmitters work.

12. From a worldview perspective, psychiatric drugs reflect the belief that psychological disorders are _____.

13. _____, also called neuroleptics, are used to treat psychotic symptoms.

14. _____treat depression.

15. _____ are used to treat anxiety symptoms and sleep difficulties.

16. _____have anti-mania qualities and anti-depressant effects and are often used in the treatment of bipolar disorder.

17. The discovery of psychotropic medications allowed many patients to leave psychiatric institutions to live at home in the community in a social movement that came to be called _____.

18. Today people with mental illness cannot be hospitalized against their will unless they are an obvious _____.

19. Freud's approach to treating was known as _____.

20. _____refers to the systematic application of behavioral techniques to the treatment of psychological disorders.

21. Behavior therapy presumes that psychological disorders are collections of

_____.

22. _____is a form of behavior therapy in which one is deliberately exposed to disturbing situations in order to learn to cope with them effectively.

23. _____is a form of behavior therapy for people with fears of specific objects or situations.

24. _____seeks to correct distorted thinking patterns that lead to unwanted feelings, and behaviors.

25. _____combines a cognitive and behavioral approach to recognize and change distorted thought patterns and unwanted behaviors.

26. _____, also called person-centered therapy, seeks to help patients achieve self-actualization and high self-esteem.

27. _____, also called systemic therapy and family systems therapy, focuses on relationships between people.

28. Where other therapies focus on individuals, family therapists deal with

_____.

29. _____, in a broad sense, are treatments that rely on spiritual or religious means to treat psychological disorders.

30. The word _____ refers to reasoning with someone through instruction and admonition; to admonish through instruction.

31. Many Christians denounce counseling psychology as _____, _____,

_____.

32. The _____rejects the use of any extra-biblical sources to understand or to care for abnormal thoughts, feelings, and behaviors.

33. Biblical counseling, also known as _____, emphasizes the redemptive and healing aspects of biblical admonition and instruction.

34. A key characteristic of biblical counseling is the belief that an individual's psychological problems are caused by that _____

_____.

35. The goals of _____ are confession, repentance, reconciliation and restoration, and support for the counselee's walk with God to produce maturity and Godly living in their life.

Chapter 13 Quiz

1) _____ refers to the systematic application of behavioral techniques to the treatment of psychological disorders.
   a) Behavior therapy
   b) Cognitive therapy
   c) Cognitive-behavioral therapy
   d) Humanistic therapies

2) _____ seeks to correct distorted thinking patterns that lead to unwanted thoughts, feelings and behaviors.
   a) Behavior therapy
   b) Cognitive therapy
   c) Cognitive-behavioral therapy
   d) Humanistic therapies

3) _____ combines a cognitive and behavioral approach to recognize and change distorted thought patterns and unwanted behaviors.
   a) Cognitive therapy
   b) Humanistic therapies
   c) Cognitive-behavioral therapy
   d) Family therapy

4) _____ help patients achieve self-actualization and high self-esteem.
   a) Family therapy
   b) Cognitive-behavioral therapy
   c) Cognitive therapy
   d) Humanistic therapies

5) _____, also called systemic therapy, focuses on relationships between people.
   a) Family therapy
   b) Cognitive-behavioral therapy
   c) Humanistic therapies
   d) Spiritual treatment

6) Beginning in the 19th century, a movement known as _____ saw the mentally ill not as immoral possessed animals, but as people who were "sick" and in need of treatment.
   a) pharmacological revolution
   b) humanism
   c) deinstitutionalization
   d) moral management

7) The surgical procedure called _____ involves cutting neural connections between the frontal lobe and the rest of the brain.
   a) lobotomy
   b) electro-convulsive therapy
   c) hemispherectomy
   d) neurosurgery

8) _____ is famous in the history of psychology for work as an advocate for the humane treatment of the mentally ill in the 19th century.
   a) Dorothea Dix
   b) Phineas Gage
   c) Carl Rogers
   d) Sigmund Freud

9) The pharmacological revolution started in 1954 with the approval of _____.
   a) anti-depressants
   b) Thorazine
   c) anxiolytics
   d) anti-psychotics

10) _____ therapies used insulin overdose, chemicals, microwaves, oxygen deprivation, and electric currents to induce brain seizures.
   a) Convulsive
   b) Ice bath
   c) Talk
   d) Dance

11) _____ is the study of drug-induced changes in perception, emotion, thinking, and behavior.
   a) Psycho-kinetics
   b) Psychopharmacology
   c) Family therapy
   d) Addiction

12) _____, also called neuroleptics, are used to treat psychotic symptoms.
   a) Anti-psychotics
   b) Anti-depressants
   c) Anxiolytics
   d) Mood stabilizers

13) _____ treat depression.
   a) Anti-psychotics
   b) Anti-depressants
   c) Anxiolytics
   d) Mood stabilizers

14) _____ are used to treat anxiety symptoms and sleep difficulties.
   a) Anti-psychotics
   b) Anti-depressants
   c) Anxiolytics
   d) Mood stabilizers

15) _____ have anti-mania qualities and anti-depressant effects and are often used in the treatment of bipolar disorder.
   a) Anti-psychotics
   b) Anti-depressants
   c) Anxiolytics
   d) Mood stabilizers

16) In Biblical counseling, which is NOT a key belief about the causes of psychological problems?
   a) sinfulness
   b) wrong patterns of thinking and living
   c) disunity with God
   d) low self-esteem

17) The goals of _____ are confession, repentance, reconciliation and restoration, and support for the counselee's walk with God to produce maturity and Godly living in their life.
   a) Christian counseling
   b) nouthetic counseling
   c) dance therapy
   d) psycho-analysis

Answer Key Chapter 13

Chapter 13 Study Guide (Answers)

1. Your **worldview** about what causes abnormal thoughts, feelings, and behaviors greatly influences your beliefs about treatment.
2. Every approach to caring for people with abnormal thoughts, feelings, and behaviors brings with it underlying beliefs about the **cause of the conditions**.
3. **Cornelius Celsus**, a Roman physician who lived around the time of Christ, recorded that treatment for mental illness consisted of starvation, chains, and flogging.
4. **Moral management** known, saw patients not as immoral possessed animals, but as people who were "sick" and in need of treatment.
5. **Dorothea Dix** is famous in the history of psychology for her work as an advocate for the humane treatment of the mentally ill.
6. Walter Freeman developed a quick and easy ten-minute procedure using an ice pick to sever neural connections in the frontal lobe of the brain known as **lobotomy**.
7. **Convulsive Therapies** used insulin overdose, chemicals, microwaves, oxygen deprivation, and electric currents to induce brain seizures.
8. The most commonly used convulsive therapy was called **electroconvulsive therapy** (ECT).
9. When tested on patients in psychiatric hospitals, **Thorazine** had a powerful calming and sedating effect.
10. The discovery of Thorazine started what has been called the **pharmacological revolution**, a search for new psychoactive drugs to treat a variety of psychological disorders.
11. **Psychiatric drugs** are designed to alter the way neurotransmitters work.
12. From a worldview perspective, psychiatric drugs reflect the belief that psychological disorders are **biological problems**.
13. **Anti-psychotics**, also called neuroleptics, are used to treat psychotic symptoms.
14. **Anti-depressants** treat depression.
15. **Anxiolytics** are used to treat anxiety symptoms and sleep difficulties.
16. **Mood stabilizers** have anti-mania qualities and anti-depressant effects and are often used in the treatment of bipolar disorder.
17. The discovery of psychotropic medications allowed many patients to leave psychiatric institutions to live at home in the community in a social movement that came to be called **de-institutionalization**.
18. Today people with mental illness cannot be hospitalized against their will unless they are an obvious **threat to themselves or others**.
19. Freud's approach to treating was known as **the talking cure**.
20. **Behavior therapy** refers to the systematic application of behavioral techniques to the treatment of psychological disorders.
21. Behavior therapy presumes that psychological disorders are collections of **learned responses**.
22. **Exposure therapy** is a form of behavior therapy in which one is deliberately exposed to disturbing situations in order to learn to cope with them effectively.
23. **Systematic desensitization** is a form of behavior therapy for people with fears of specific objects or situations.
24. **Cognitive therapy** seeks to correct distorted thinking patterns that lead to unwanted feelings, and behaviors.
25. **Cognitive-behavioral therapy** combines a cognitive and behavioral approach to recognize and change distorted thought patterns and unwanted behaviors.
26. **Humanistic therapy**, also called person-centered therapy, seeks to help patients achieve self-actualization and high self-esteem.
27. **Family therapy**, also called systemic therapy and family systems therapy, focuses on relationships between people.
28. Where other therapies focus on individuals, family therapists deal with **interaction patterns within a family system**.
29. **Spiritual treatments**, in a broad sense, are treatments that rely on spiritual or religious means to treat psychological disorders.

30. The word **nouthetic** refers to reasoning with someone through instruction and admonition; to admonish through instruction.
31. Many Christians denounce counseling psychology as **idolatrous, heretical, and ungodly**.
32. The **biblical counseling movement** rejects the use of any extra-biblical sources to understand or to care for abnormal thoughts, feelings, and behaviors.
33. Biblical counseling, also known as **nouthetic counseling**, emphasizes the redemptive and healing aspects of biblical admonition and instruction.
34. A key characteristic of biblical counseling is the belief that an individual's psychological problems are caused by that **individual's sinfulness, wrong patterns of thinking and living, and disunity with God**.
35. The goals of **nouthetic counseling** are confession, repentance, reconciliation and restoration, and support for the counselee's walk with God to produce maturity and Godly living in their life.

Chapter 13 Short Essay Questions (Answers)

1. Shamans cast healing spells, offered sacrifices, and cast out evil spirits. Some cultures practiced trephination, a primitive type of brain surgery, which may have been a spiritual approach to treatment. Cornelius Celsus recorded that treatment for mental illness consisted of starvation, chains, and flogging, reflecting a view that the mentally ill were morally responsible for their condition. Lobotomies and convulsive therapies reflected a biologic perspective. Freudian psychotherapy reflects a psychodynamic approach. The mentally ill were viewed as less than human and were locked away like animals, caged, chained, and beaten, and put on display. Behavior modification reflected behavioral assumptions.
2. Beginning in the 19th century, public attitudes about the care of the mentally ill began to change. Moral management, as it was known, saw patients not as immoral possessed animals, but as people who were "sick" and in need of treatment. The mentally ill were unchained and treated in more home-like facilities, they were given structured work activities, and punishment was eliminated as a treatment.
3. A lobotomy was first performed on humans in the 1890s. Early procedures were time-consuming and delicate and involved drilling holes in patients' skulls to allow surgeons to destroy brain tissue. In 1945, Walter Freeman developed a quick and easy ten-minute procedure using an ice pick to sever neural connections in the frontal lobe of the brain. Freeman later replaced the ice pick with a flat cutting tool that he inserted into the brain through the eye socket. Sweeping the tool from side to side, Freeman cut neural connections in the frontal lobe. Psychologists had long observed that following high fever and seizures, the mentally ill were often symptom-free. That observation led to the 20th century development of techniques including insulin overdose, chemicals, microwaves, oxygen deprivation, and electric currents to induce brain seizures.
4. In 1952, a surgeon in Paris looking for a way to reduce surgical shock in his patients, made an accidental discovery that started a revolution in the care and treatment of the mentally ill. When patients facing surgery were given a dose of a strong drug called Thorazine, they were calm and less anxious. When tested on patients in psychiatric hospitals, Thorazine had a powerful calming and sedating effect there, too. Patients who had been restrained because of violent behavior could be unchained, and patients who stood without moving or speaking began to walk and talk normally.
5. Anti-psychotics, also called neuroleptics, are used to treat psychotic symptoms by blocking dopamine receptors. Anti-depressants treat depression by increasing the availability of norepinephrine and/or serotonin at neural receptor sites. Anxiolytics are used to treat anxiety symptoms and sleep difficulties by enhancing the activity of the neurotransmitter GABA. GABA has an inhibitory effect on motor neurons, so enhancing its activity effectively slows nerve impulses throughout the body. Mood stabilizers have anti-mania qualities and anti-depressant effects and are often used in the treatment of bipolar disorder.
6. From a worldview perspective, psychiatric drugs reflect the belief that psychological disorders are biological problems. From the perspective of naturalism, good psychological health and bad psychological health are both reducible to electrochemical brain activity. From that perspective, it is logical to look to science to produce chemical solutions to chemical problems. Critics of the biological (medication) approach to treatment suggest that the emphasis on medications provides a false hope that a "magic pill" will "fix" all of our problems. Critics suggest that the emphasis on alleviating symptoms with medications ignores underlying spiritual and social problems. Other people suggest that by treating the symptoms of psychological problems with medications, it allows people to then focus on their spiritual and social problems.
7. Psychopharmacology is the study of the relationship between drugs and mental processes.
8. The discovery of psychotropic medications allowed many patients to leave psychiatric institutions to live at home in the community. From 1955 to 1980, the population of psychiatric hospitals fell from over 500,000 to around 50,000 in a social movement that came to be called de-institutionalization. De-institutionalization refers to the wide-spread release of the mentally ill from mental hospitals to community-based treatment centers. Today people with mental illness cannot be hospitalized against their will unless they are an obvious threat to themselves or others.
9. The mentally ill were released to communities that were not prepared to care for them. The result was a rise in the number of homeless mentally ill in the 1970s and 1980s. There was also an increase in the number of mentally ill people in jails and prisons. Today, jails and homeless shelters serve as de facto mental institutions. The U. S. Justice Department estimates that over 200,000 people with severe mental illnesses are held in jails and prisons at any given time.
10. Counseling, therapy, psycho-therapy, talk therapy, and analysis are general terms that describe countless techniques by which therapists enter into relationships with a patient for the purpose of helping the patient with symptoms of mental illness, behavioral problems, or personal growth. Therapists meet patients face-to-face, over the telephone, or over the Internet. Therapy may be brief or extend over months or years. Clinical psychologists, social workers, marriage-family therapists, expressive therapists, trained nurses, psychiatrists, psycho-analysts, mental health counselors, school counselors,

and the clergy provide therapy. Therapy is used to help people with symptoms of serious mental illness, to help people choose a career path, to solve relationship problems, or to deal with trauma, abuse, neglect, grief, disappointment, anger, and stress. Therapy can help repair self-concept, ease fears and anxiety, resolve conflict, improve communication, or seek "the meaning of life."

11. Freud's approach to treating disorders, known as the talking cure, involved talking to patients while they reclined on his famous couch. Freudian psycho-analytic or psycho-dynamic therapies, still popular today, look to the unconscious to discover and treat psychological problems. Psycho-dynamic therapists help patients to bring unconscious motivations and conflicts to light, to confront beliefs and actions, and to examine memories, events, and feeling from the past for clues to current problems. Although there is a current trend toward brief therapy, Freudian psycho-analytic therapy typically lasted for several years.

12. Behavior therapy (also called behavior modification) refers to the systematic application of behavioral techniques to the treatment of psychological disorders. Behavior therapy presumes that psychological disorders are collections of learned responses. Behavior therapy establishes rewards and reinforcements to change unwanted thoughts, feelings, and behavior.

13. Cognitive therapy seeks to correct distorted thinking patterns that lead to unwanted feelings, and behaviors. Cognitive therapy presumes that irrational thoughts and beliefs underlie emotional and behavioral problems. The therapist helps a patient identify and change the way they think about things, their beliefs, and their expectations.

14. Humanistic therapy, also called person-centered therapy, seeks to help patients achieve self-actualization and high self-esteem. Humanistic therapy emphasizes Mankind's inborn "goodness" and potential. Humanistic counselors presume that in an accepting, non-judgmental, and non-directive environment of unconditional positive regard, the innate goodness in all Mankind will propel us toward our full potential.

15. Family therapy, also called systemic therapy and family systems therapy, focuses on relationships between people. Where other therapies focus on individuals, family therapists deal with interaction patterns within a family system. This approach emphasizes the importance of family relationships to mental health. From this perspective, abnormal thoughts, feelings, and behaviors in individuals are the expression of problems in the family system. By adjusting interactions within the family, the family functions more effectively, and the individual members experience symptom relief.

16. Spiritual treatments, in a broad sense, are treatments that rely on spiritual or religious means to treat psychological disorders.

17. Anti-psychology refers to a belief among some Christians that modern psychology, especially counseling psychology, is spiritually dangerous, that it is not a science, or that it is invalid because it relies on knowledge derived from sources other than the Bible. Many Christians denounce counseling psychology as idolatrous, heretical, and an ungodly rival "religion" that places Christians at risk of spiritual deception and demonic attack.

18. Many Christians believe that God reveals truths through the Bible and through psychological research. This approach, known as integration, presumes that valid findings of psychology and accurate interpretations of the Bible will not ultimately contradict – that psychological discoveries are not inherently anti-Christian, and that psychology can contribute, it its own way, to a comprehensive understanding of Mankind and to solutions to psychological disorders. From this perspective, the motto "all truth is God's truth" applies to counseling psychology, too. Integration presupposes truth in biblical revelation and in the "essential correctness" of scientific psychology. If all truth is God's truth, then a truth discovered by psychology can be translated for understanding and use by Christians. Integration means finding an approach to counseling psychology applying the unified truths of both psychology and the Bible.

19. While many Christians who are counselors consider their approach to counseling to be "biblical," the biblical counseling movement rejects the use of any extra-biblical sources to understand or to care for abnormal thoughts, feelings, and behaviors. Biblical counseling, also known as nouthetic counseling, emphasizes the redemptive and healing aspects of biblical admonition and instruction. A key characteristic of biblical counseling is the belief that an individual's psychological problems are caused by that individual's sinfulness, wrong patterns of thinking and living, and disunity with God. This approach sees the Bible as completely sufficient for dealing with all problems of living, including those described as mental illnesses. Nouthetic counselors discern sin and wrong patterns of thinking and living in the counselee, and use the Bible to admonish, confront, motivate, and provide spiritual direction. The goals of nouthetic counseling are confession, repentance, reconciliation and restoration, and support for the counselee's walk with God in order to produce maturity and Godly living in their life. Many biblical counselors believe that to use any technique, model, approach, theory, or method from modern psychology is compromise (at best) or heresy (at worst).

20. In addition to the models of treatment described in this chapter, there are hundreds, perhaps thousands of good-sounding "popular" approaches to treatment psychology described in books, magazines, tabloids, talk radio, and the internet that may not be supported by quality research or sound theology. Secular popular psychology offers advice for living, marriage counseling, child-rearing and relationship advice, and many other topics. However, popular approaches to treatment generally avoid academic and technical terms or references to theory and underlying assumptions. "Christian" popular "pop psychology" uncritically adopts anti-Christian worldview assumptions and disguises them by sprinkling in Jesus' name and a few verses of the New Testament. Christians spend millions of dollars annually on popular psychology titles. Though popular psychology may contain truths, they are likely to dangerously distort important biblical doctrines. Truths from popular psychology are only discernible from error at the worldview level.

Chapter 13 Quiz Answers

1) _____ refers to the systematic application of behavioral techniques to the treatment of psychological disorders.   a) Behavior therapy

2) _____ seeks to correct distorted thinking patterns that lead to unwanted thoughts, feelings and behaviors. b) Cognitive therapy

3) _____ combines a cognitive and behavioral approach to recognize and change distorted thought patterns and unwanted behaviors. c) Cognitive-behavioral therapy

4) _____ help patients achieve self-actualization and high self-esteem. d) Humanistic therapies

5) _____, also called systemic therapy, focuses on relationships between people. a) Family therapy

6) Beginning in the 19th century, a movement known as _____ saw the mentally ill not as immoral possessed animals, but as people who were "sick" and in need of treatment. d) moral management

7) The surgical procedure called _____ involves cutting neural connections between the frontal lobe and the rest of the brain. a) lobotomy

8) _____ is famous in the history of psychology for work as an advocate for the humane treatment of the mentally ill in the 19th century. a) Dorothea Dix

9) The pharmacological revolution started in 1954 with the approval of _____. b) Thorazine

10) _____ therapies used insulin overdose, chemicals, microwaves, oxygen deprivation, and electric currents to induce brain seizures. a) Convulsive

11) _____ is the study of drug-induced changes in perception, emotion, thinking, and behavior. b) Psychopharmacology

12) _____, also called neuroleptics, are used to treat psychotic symptoms. a) Anti-psychotics

13) _____ treat depression. b) Anti-depressants

14) _____ are used to treat anxiety symptoms and sleep difficulties. c) Anxiolytics

15) _____ have anti-mania qualities and anti-depressant effects and are often used in the treatment of bipolar disorder. d) Mood stabilizers

16) In Biblical counseling, which is NOT a key belief about the causes of psychological problems? d) low self-esteem

17) The goals of _____ are confession, repentance, reconciliation and restoration, and support for the counselee's walk with God to produce maturity and Godly living in their life. b) nouthetic counseling

Chapter 14 Social Psychology

Chapter 14 Learning Objectives

Describe interpersonal communication.
Describe the Shannon-Weaver model of communication.
Describe feedback, non-verbal communication, and proxemics.
Describe the characteristics of good listeners.
Describe social influence, social comparison, and social norms.
Describe attitudes, attitude formation, and attitude change.
Describe interpersonal attraction.
Describe group dynamics, group roles, and group norms, and group decision-making.
Describe groupthink.
Describe the Stanford Prison experiment.
Describe the Asch conformity study.
Describe Milgram's obedience study.
Describe Sherif's Robbers Cave study.
Describe conformity and obedience.
Discuss stereotypes, prejudice, and discrimination.

Key Concepts and People

Social cognition
Interpersonal communication
Shannon-Weaver model of communication
Non-verbal communication
Proxemics
Social context
Social influence
Social facilitation
Roles and norms
Role conflict

Asch conformity study
Milgram obedience study
Kitty Genovese
Norm of reciprocity
Attribution theory
Internal and external attribution
Attribution error
Actor-observer bias
Self-serving bias
Fundamental attribution error

Attitudes
Cognitive dissonance
Attraction
Diffusion of responsibility
Altruism
Groupthink
Group polarization
Stanford Prison experiment
Robber's Cave study

Short Essay Questions

1. Describe attitudes, attitude formation, and attitude change.
2. Describe interpersonal attraction.
3. Describe groupthink.
4. Describe conformity and obedience.
5. Discuss stereotypes, prejudice, and discrimination.

For Further Study

1. Video: A Class Divided. From FRONTLINE. One day in 1968, Jane Elliott, a teacher in a small, all-white town, divided her third-grade class into blue-eyed and brown-eyed group and gave them a daring lesson in discrimination. http://pbs.org/wgbh/pages/frontline/shows/divided
2. Read: Milgram Obedience study http://wadsworth.com/psychology_d/templates/student_resources/0155060678_rathus/ps/ps01.html
3. Read: When not to obey, by T. M. Moore https://www.ailbe.org/columns/pastortopastor/item/9209-submission-and-obedience
4. Web: Stanford Prison Experiment. Official site of the Stanford Prison Experiment. A simulation study of the psychology and imprisonment conducted at Sanford University http://prisonexp.org/

Topics for Discussion

1. Can you think of examples from your own life where you made the fundamental attribution error?
2. Give some examples of how Christians conform to secular society?
3. What makes it difficult for Christians to take a stand against society?
4. How might the results of the Good Samaritan study help you model appropriate behavior despite your busy schedule?

Chapter 14 Worldview Issues

Social psychology is the scientific study of human social interactions. It is about describing and explaining the complexities of human social life, group dynamics, how we form attitudes, how we are persuaded, and what attracts us to some people and repels us from others. What are we 'like' when we're around other people?

There are important worldview issues underlying social psychology. It can seem like learning lists of the ways we behave badly in social interactions. Why is human history filled with examples of humans treating each other terribly – prejudice, racism, wars, genocide, mass shootings, slavery, assault, harassment, and intimidation? Why are social interactions today often characterized by moral relativity, political correctness, hypersensitivity, trigger warnings, safe zones, and micro-aggressions? Why do we think too highly of ourselves, judge others unfairly, and love ourselves over others? Why are we distrustful, especially those who are different from us? Social psychology provides students important warnings about the power of the social forces on campus. For example, Stanford Prison experiment is an excellent example of the power of social pressure.

On the other hand, human history is filled with examples of great altruism and self-sacrifice. Every day, people treat each other with kindness. We form friendships and fall in love, we respect and get along with people of diverse backgrounds, and we cooperate. Sometimes, people will lay down their life for their friends. Why?

Students will feel pressure to conform to a belief that naturalism is the best answer. Naturalism assumes that social behavior, like individual behavior, is determined by outside forces. Social behavior, like individual behavior, evolved from simpler social behaviors, each serving a survival or reproductive advantage.

A Christian approach to begins with what Bible has to say about social influences and social interactions. The Bible teaches that God created us to be social. Social relationships are a primary part of His plan – a reason for our existence. But sin affects all areas of life – including social interactions. Part of spiritual growth is developing biblical social interactions and rising above the world's social influences. Social psychologists describe the factors that *do* influence social behavior. The Christian worldview describes the factors that *should* influence social behavior. Our social interactions and relationships should reflect Christ in us. We should be salt and light in the world. We should love our neighbor as ourselves and pray for those who persecute us. We should oppose, not just learn about. racism, greed, and violence. We should not conform to the ways of the world.

Study Guide Chapter 14

1. _____is the study of how the presence of other people influences the ways we think, feel, and behave.

2. _____is a professional and academic discipline interested in sociology and social psychology.

3. _____pursue social welfare, social change, and social justice. Social workers also seek to improve that quality of life for individuals in the context of their social relationships.

4. Communication can occur _____.

5. The messenger's _____ are powerful tools in communication.

6. _____ provides an indication that the message is getting through.

7. _____ (e.g., puzzled looks and folded arms) provides clues that the message is not getting through.

8. _____refers to the ways we organize, interpret, and understand social inputs.

9. _____are "mental short cuts" that we use in social interactions.

10. When we form _____of the people we meet, we tend to assume a great deal about someone based on very little information.

11. _____refers to the characteristics of the situations in which social interactions occur.

12. _____ is the study of personal space.

13. _____is the way we understand ourselves in relation to others.

14. _____refers to our tendency to compare ourselves to other people.

15. _____are explanations for the circumstances, thoughts, feelings, and behaviors of ourselves and others.

16. Attributions may be _____, based on our assumptions about internal personal characteristics, or _____ based on our observations and assumptions about external events and circumstances.

17. _____refers to an inference that a person is behaving in a certain way because of something about, or from inside the person, such as attitude, disposition, or personality trait.

18. Internal attribution refers to the inference that we behave the way we do because of our _____.

19. _____refers to an inference that a person is behaving a certain way because of something about the situation and circumstance the person is in.

20. An _____is an incorrect or distorted understanding of what happens around us.

21. The _____refers to the tendency to overestimate internal dispositional influences and underestimate external situational influences upon others' behavior.

22. The _____, a type of extension of the fundamental attribution error, describes the tendency to apply the negative behavior of a member of a group member to all the members of the group.

23. Attribution errors and biases can lead to _____, _____, and _____.

24. _____ are a type of biased schema; a mental shortcut used to characterize whole groups of people based on a false assumption that all members of a group share the same characteristics.
25. _____ is an attitude, positive or negative, about an individual based their membership in a group.
26. When one's behavior is affected by stereotyping or prejudice, the result is _____.
27. A _____ is a predisposition toward a particular attribution.
28. The _____refers to tendency to use a double standard when attributing meaning to our own circumstances.
29. The _____refers to our predisposition to make an external attribution to explain our own bad circumstances, but to make an internal attribution to explain the bad circumstances of others.
30. The _____, or the just-world hypothesis, refers to the tendency to believe that bad things happen to bad people – that people get what they deserve.
31. One explanation for stereotypes, prejudice, and discrimination is that they are attribution errors grounded in an _____.
32. _____refers to the tendency to have positive attitudes and give preferential treatment to people in the group to which we belong.
33. _____refers to the tendency to view negatively people who are not part of a group to which we belong.
34. _____ are defined by social psychologists as pre-dispositions, positive or negative, toward someone or something.
35. The _____describes our tendency to have a positive attitude toward familiar things. The more we are simply exposed to an object, the more likely we are to have a positive attitude toward that object.
36. Psychologist Leon Festinger defined _____as the discomfort caused by when our behavior and attitudes conflict.
37. _____ is a communication process by which attitude change.
38. Persuasive messages take two forms: _____ (the central route) or _____ (the peripheral route).
39. _____uses data, pros and cons, or other logical reasons in order to change someone's attitude.
40. _____uses fear, love, guilt, envy, affiliation, authority, or other emotional appeals.
41. The _____refers to our tendency to comply with a large request after first complying with a small one.
42. The _____refers to our tendency to grant a small request after first refusing a large one.
43. The _____refers to our tendency to think that when we do something nice to someone, they should do something nice in return.
44. _____ is defined as a powerful favorable attitude toward another person. Attraction theory refers to the ways we form attractions and the factors that affect attraction.
45. The strongest factor influencing the chance that people will like one another is _____.
46. Folk wisdom says that "opposites attract," but research suggests that _____ – the extent to which people are like us in terms of attitudes, values, personality, and physical qualities – is a most important factor in attraction.
47. _____ refers to the tendency to be attracted to people who are nice to us and who we believe are attracted to us. We tend to like those who like us and dislike those who dislike us.

48. Another factor influencing attraction is _____.

49. Philip Zimbardo is famous in the history of psychology for his 1971 study of social influences on behavior known as the _____.

50. _____ refer to the different patterns of behavior appropriate to various social situations.

51. _____ refers to situations in which two or more roles make conflicting demands on behavior.

52. _____ refer to unwritten, but generally accepted rules of appropriate behavior in various social situations or contexts.

53. _____ refers to the influence the presence of other people has on how well we perform various tasks.

54. Roles, norms, and context create _____, a powerful influence on behavior, and left unchecked, can lead to prejudice, discrimination, blind obedience, and violence.

55. _____ refers to perceived pressure to change one's thoughts, feelings, or behavior to match those of the group.

56. The pressure to conform is commonly known as _____.

57. The _____ is famous in the history of psychology for its demonstration of the power of social pressure to conform.

58. Stanley Milgram is famous in the history of psychology for his research on _____.

59. The _____, also called the Genovese syndrome, suggests that an individual's likelihood of helping someone in need is related to the number of other people present at the time.

60. _____ refers to the spreading of responsibility for a task across all members of the group.

61. Diffusion of responsibility, in the extreme, can lead to _____ – a loss of one's individual self-awareness, self-restraint, and moral values when in group situations that foster anonymity.

62. The _____ suggests that from an evolutionary standpoint, helping behavior is determined by the extent to which one perceives a genetic similarity between oneself and the person in need of help.

63. Social psychologists are interested in understanding the thoughts, feelings, and behaviors of people in group settings or _____.

64. _____ refers to the strength of the relationships between group members, agreement about group goals, and adherence to group norms.

65. _____ refers to a group decision-making process in which the group norms of harmony and cohesion actually override a realistic view of the alternatives.

66. _____ refers to a tendency of groups to drift toward and strengthen extreme positions – positions very different than group members would have taken individually.

Chapter 14 Quiz

1) _____ is a complex psychological process that takes place between two or more people.
   a) Interpersonal communication
   b) Language
   c) Listening
   d) Socialization

2) In communication, the mental process of converting ideas and emotions into a form suitable for the channel is called _____.
   a) Decoding
   b) Encoding
   c) Syntax
   d) Grammar

3) Which is not a characteristic of a good listener?
   a) Is attentive and alert to a speaker's verbal and nonverbal behavior
   b) Is patient and doesn't interrupt
   c) Provides little or no verbal or nonverbal feedback
   d) Is responsive and provides verbal and nonverbal feedback

4) _____ refers to the powerful effect the presence of other people has on the ways we think, feel, and behave
   a) Social perception
   b) Social norms
   c) Self-identity
   d) Social influence

5) _____ refers to the tendency to compare oneself to others.
   a) Social comparison
   b) Self-identity
   c) Social perception
   d) Norm of reciprocity

6) _____ refers to the ways we understand ourselves in relation to others.
   a) Social perception
   b) Self-identity
   c) Social norms
   d) Attributions

7) _____ refers to situations in which two or more roles make conflicting demands on behavior.
   a) Role conflict
   b) Internal attribution
   c) External attribution
   d) Self-identity

8) _____ refer to generally accepted rules of appropriate behavior in various social situations or social context.
   a) Bias
   b) Social perception
   c) Social norms
   d) Attributions

9) The _____ refers to the tendency of people will respond to each other in kind; treating those well who treat us well and treating those who treat us poorly in kind.
   a) prejudice
   b) Golden Rule
   c) just-world bias
   d) norm of reciprocity

10) _____ refers to the ways we organize, interpret, and give meaning to social experiences.
   a) Social perception
   b) Social comparison
   c) Attributions
   d) Self-identity

11) _____ are explanations for the circumstances, thoughts, feelings, and behaviors of ourselves and others.
   a) Interpretations
   b) Attributions
   c) Stereotypes
   d) Prejudices

12) _____ refers to an inference that a person is behaving in a certain way because of something about, or from inside the person, such as attitude, disposition, or personality trait.
   a) Internal attribution
   b) External attribution
   c) Fundamental attribution
   d) Ultimate attribution

13) _____ refers to an inference that a person is behaving a certain way because of something about the situation and circumstance the person is in.
   a) External attribution
   b) Internal attribution
   c) Fundamental attribution
   d) Ultimate attribution

14) An _____ is an incorrect or distorted understanding of the reasons for what happens around us.
   a) attribution error
   b) bias
   c) denial
   d) prejudice

15) The _____ refers to the tendency to overestimate internal dispositional influences and underestimate external situational influences upon others' behavior.
   a) self-serving bias
   b) fundamental attribution error
   c) out-group bias
   d) just-world bias

16) _____ are a type of biased schema; a mental shortcut used to characterize whole groups of people based on a false assumption that all members of a group share the same characteristics.
   a) Prejudice
   b) Stereotypes
   c) Bigotry
   d) Discrimination

17) _____ is an attitude, positive or negative, about an individual based their membership in a group.
   a) Prejudice
   b) Stereotypes
   c) Bigotry
   d) Discrimination

18) When one's behavior is affected by stereotyping or prejudice, the result is
_____.
   a) Prejudice
   b) Stereotypes
   c) Bigotry
   d) Discrimination

19) _____ refers to the tendency to have positive attitudes and give preferential treatment to people in the group to which we belong.
   a) In-group bias
   b) Out-group bias
   c) Actor-observer bias
   d) Self-serving bias

20) Psychologist Leon Festinger defined _____ as the discomfort caused by when our behavior and attitudes conflict.
   a) bias
   b) cognitive dissonance
   c) repression
   d) discrimination

21) _____ uses data, pros and cons, or other logical reasons in order to change someone's attitude.
   a) Central route persuasion
   b) Peripheral route persuasion

22) The _____ refers to our tendency to comply with a large request after first complying with a small one.
   a) norm of reciprocity
   b) door-in-the-face phenomenon
   c) foot-in-the-door phenomenon
   d) mere-exposure effect

23) The strongest factor influencing the chance that people will like one another is
_____.
   a) physical proximity.
   b) similarity
   c) reciprocity
   d) self-disclosure

24) _____ refer to the different patterns of behavior appropriate to various social situations.
   a) Role conflict
   b) Social roles
   c) Social facilitation
   d) Social pressure

25) _____ refers to the spreading of responsibility for a task across all members of the group.
   a) De-individualization
   b) Conformity
   c) Diffusion of responsibility
   d) Peer pressure

26) _____ refers to the strength of the relationships between group members, agreement about group goals, and adherence to group norms.
a) Groupthink
b) Group cohesion
c) Group polarization
d) Group dynamics

27) _____ refers to a group decision-making process in which the group norms of harmony and cohesion override a realistic view of the alternatives.
a) Groupthink
b) Group cohesion
c) Group polarization
d) Group dynamics

28) _____ refers to a tendency of groups to drift toward and strengthen extreme positions – positions very different than group members would have taken individually.
a) Groupthink
b) Group cohesion
c) Group polarization
d) Group dynamics

Answer Key Chapter 14

Chapter 14 Study Guide (Answers)

1. **Social psychology** is the study of how the presence of other people influences the ways we think, feel, and behave.
2. **Social work** is a professional and academic discipline interested in sociology and social psychology.
3. **Social workers** pursue social welfare, social change, and social justice. Social workers also seek to improve that quality of life for individuals in the context of their social relationships.
4. Communication can occur **verbally, non-verbally, intentionally, and unintentionally.**
5. The messenger's **facial expressions, tone of voice, gestures, body position,** and **movement** are powerful tools in communication.
6. **Positive feedback** (e.g., nods and "uh huhs") provides an indication that the message is getting through.
7. **Negative feedback** (e.g., puzzled looks and folded arms) provides clues that the message is not getting through.
8. **Social perception** refers to the ways we organize, interpret, and understand social inputs.
9. **Social schemas** are "mental short cuts" that we use in social interactions.
10. When we form **first impressions** of the people we meet, we tend to assume a great deal about someone based on very little information.
11. **Social context** refers to the characteristics of the situations in which social interactions occur.
12. **Proxemics** is the study of personal space.
13. **Self-identity** is the way we understand ourselves in relation to others.
14. **Social comparison** refers to our tendency to compare ourselves to other people.
15. **Attributions** are explanations for the circumstances, thoughts, feelings, and behaviors of ourselves and others.
16. Attributions may be **dispositional**, based on our assumptions about internal personal characteristics, or **situational**, based on our observations and assumptions about external events and circumstances.
17. **Internal attribution** refers to an inference that a person is behaving in a certain way because of something about, or from inside the person, such as attitude, disposition, or personality trait.
18. Internal attribution refers to the inference that we behave the way we do because of our **internal characteristics**.
19. **External attribution** refers to an inference that a person is behaving a certain way because of something about the situation and circumstance the person is in.
20. An **attribution error** is an incorrect or distorted understanding of what happens around us.
21. The **fundamental attribution error** refers to the tendency to overestimate internal dispositional influences and underestimate external situational influences upon others' behavior.
22. The **ultimate attribution error**, a type of extension of the fundamental attribution error, describes the tendency to apply the negative behavior of a member of a group member to all the members of the group.
23. Attribution errors and biases can lead to **stereotyping, prejudice,** and **discrimination.**
24. **Stereotypes** are a type of biased schema; a mental shortcut used to characterize whole groups of people based on a false assumption that all members of a group share the same characteristics.
25. **Prejudice** is an attitude, positive or negative, about an individual based their membership in a group.
26. When one's behavior is affected by stereotyping or prejudice, the result is **discrimination.**
27. A **bias** is a predisposition toward a particular attribution.
28. The **self-serving bias** refers to tendency to use a double standard when attributing meaning to our own circumstances.
29. The **actor-observer bias** refers to our predisposition to make an external attribution to explain our own bad circumstances, but to make an internal attribution to explain the bad circumstances of others.
30. The **just-world bias**, or the just-world hypothesis, refers to the tendency to believe that bad things happen to bad people – that people get what they deserve.
31. One explanation for stereotypes, prejudice, and discrimination is that they are attribution errors grounded in an **in-group/out-group bias**.
32. **In-group bias** refers to the tendency to have positive attitudes and give preferential treatment to people in the group to which we belong.
33. **Out-group bias** refers to the tendency to view negatively people who are not part of a group to which we belong.

34. **Attitudes** are defined by social psychologists as pre-dispositions, positive or negative, toward someone or something.

35. The **mere-exposure effect** describes our tendency to have a positive attitude toward familiar things. The more we are simply exposed to an object, the more likely we are to have a positive attitude toward that object.

36. Psychologist Leon Festinger defined **cognitive dissonance** as the discomfort caused by when our behavior and attitudes conflict.

37. **Persuasion** is a communication process by which attitude change.

38. Persuasive messages take two forms: **rational-logical** (the central route) or **emotional** (the peripheral route).

39. **Central route persuasion** uses data, pros and cons, or other logical reasons in order to change someone's attitude.

40. **Peripheral route persuasion** uses fear, love, guilt, envy, affiliation, authority, or other emotional appeals.

41. The **foot-in-the-door phenomenon** refers to our tendency to comply with a large request after first complying with a small one.

42. The **door-in-the-face phenomenon** refers to our tendency to grant a small request after first refusing a large one.

43. The **norm of reciprocity** refers to our tendency to think that when we do something nice to someone, they should do something nice in return.

44. **Attraction** is defined as a powerful favorable attitude toward another person. Attraction theory refers to the ways we form attractions and the factors that affect attraction.

45. The strongest factor influencing the chance that people will like one another is **physical proximity**.

46. Folk wisdom says that "opposites attract," but research suggests that **similarity** – the extent to which people are like us in terms of attitudes, values, personality, and physical qualities – is a most important factor in attraction.

47. **Reciprocity** refers to the tendency to be attracted to people who are nice to us and who we believe are attracted to us. We tend to like those who like us and dislike those who dislike us.

48. Another factor influencing attraction is **self-disclosure**.

49. Philip Zimbardo is famous in the history of psychology for his 1971 study of social influences on behavior known as the **Stanford Prison Experiment**.

50. **Social roles** refer to the different patterns of behavior appropriate to various social situations.

51. **Role conflict** refers to situations in which two or more roles make conflicting demands on behavior.

52. **Social norms** refer to unwritten, but generally accepted rules of appropriate behavior in various social situations or contexts.

53. **Social facilitation** refers to the influence the presence of other people has on how well we perform various tasks.

54. Roles, norms, and context create **social pressure**, a powerful influence on behavior, and left unchecked, can lead to prejudice, discrimination, blind obedience, and violence.

55. **Conformity** refers to perceived pressure to change one's thoughts, feelings, or behavior to match those of the group.

56. The pressure to conform is commonly known as **peer pressure**.

57. The **Asch conformity experiment** is famous in the history of psychology for its demonstration of the power of social pressure to conform.

58. Stanley Milgram is famous in the history of psychology for his research on **obedience to authority**.

59. The **bystander effect**, also called the Genovese syndrome, suggests that an individual's likelihood of helping someone in need is related to the number of other people present at the time.

60. **Diffusion of responsibility** refers to the spreading of responsibility for a task across all members of the group.

61. Diffusion of responsibility, in the extreme, can lead to **de-individualization** – a loss of one's individual self-awareness, self-restraint, and moral values when in group situations that foster anonymity.

62. The **kin selection theory of altruism** suggests that from an evolutionary standpoint, helping behavior is determined by the extent to which one perceives a genetic similarity between oneself and the person in need of help.

63. Social psychologists are interested in understanding the thoughts, feelings, and behaviors of people in group settings or **group dynamics.**

64. **Group cohesion** refers to the strength of the relationships between group members, agreement about group goals, and adherence to group norms.

65. **Groupthink** refers to a group decision-making process in which the group norms of harmony and cohesion actually override a realistic view of the alternatives.

66. **Group polarization** refers to a tendency of groups to drift toward and strengthen extreme positions – positions very different than group members would have taken individually.

Chapter 14 Short Essay Questions (Answers)

1. Attitudes are defined by social psychologists as pre-dispositions, positive or negative, toward someone or something. Attitudes are feelings, value judgments, evaluations, or opinions about something. An attitude requires an object – something or someone about which we have feelings (e.g., broccoli, rap music, homosexuality). Attitudes and emotions are both comprised of cognitive, emotional, and behavioral components. The cognitive component of attitudes refers to perceptions, beliefs, thoughts, and memories about the object. The emotional component includes our feelings about the object, and the behavioral component of attitudes refers to our actions toward the object. Most psychologists believe that attitudes are primarily learned. A Christian worldview understands that God can supernaturally change attitudes (i.e., a change of "heart"). Social psychologists, however, are interested in the interpersonal or social pressures that influence attitude changes. As mentioned previously, social context, roles, and norms create implicit social pressure on attitudes. A large part of all interpersonal communication is explicitly intended to change someone's mind or attitude about something by persuasion. Persuasion is a communication process, a social interaction, by which attitude change.

2. Attraction is defined as a powerful favorable attitude toward another person. Attraction theory refers to the ways we form attractions and the factors that affect attraction. The strongest factor influencing the chance that people will like one another is physical proximity. Although folk wisdom suggests that "absence makes the heart grow fonder," in another example of the mere-exposure effect, the more time we spend with someone; the more likely we are to like that person. Folk wisdom says that "opposites attract," but research suggests that similarity – the extent to which people are like us in terms of attitudes, values, personality, and physical qualities – is a most important factor in attraction. Reciprocity refers to the tendency to be attracted to people who are nice to us and who we believe are attracted to us. We tend to like those who like us and dislike those who dislike us. Another factor influencing attraction is self-disclosure. We tend to be more attracted to people about whom we have personal knowledge. Sharing personal information about yourself increases the likelihood that you will be found attractive by others, but good relationships require both parties to self-disclose.

3. Groupthink refers to a group decision-making process in which the group norms of harmony and cohesion actually override a realistic view of the alternatives. In groupthink, reaching a consensus trumps careful consideration of differing perspective. Groups suffering from groupthink are over confident, they rationalize away or avoid alternative perspectives, and they may pressure members to conform to the majority or leadership position. Groups that are isolated, groups with strong directive leaders, groups comprised of members with homogenous backgrounds, and groups under stress are at risk for groupthink. In these groups, members must find a way to establish new norms of creativity and openness to differing perspectives.

4. Conformity refers to perceived pressure to change one's thoughts, feelings, or behavior to match those of the group. We have a tendency to feel anxiety when we stand out from other people and we feel strong pressure to conform and fit in. The pressure to conform is commonly known as peer pressure. Obedience refers to changing one's behavior in response to a directive from an authority figure.

5. Attribution errors and biases can lead to stereotyping, prejudice, and discrimination. Stereotypes are a type of biased schema; a mental shortcut used to characterize whole groups of people based on a false assumption that all members of a group share the same characteristics. Stereotypes can be positive (e.g. all Asians are smart), but they are usually made up of negative characteristics (e.g., white men can't jump). Prejudice is an attitude, positive or negative, about an individual based their membership in a group. When one's behavior is affected by stereotyping or prejudice, the result is discrimination – treating someone differently because of their membership a group.

Chapter 14 Quiz Answers

1) _____ is a complex psychological process that takes place between two or more people.
a) Interpersonal communication
2) In communication, the mental process of converting ideas and emotions into a form suitable for the channel is called _____.   b) Encoding
3) Which is not a characteristic of a good listener?   c) Provides little or no verbal or nonverbal feedback
4) _____ refers to the powerful effect the presence of other people has on the ways we think, feel, and behave   d) Social influence
5) _____ refers to the tendency to compare oneself to others.   a) Social comparison
6) _____ refers to the ways we understand ourselves in relation to others.   b) Self-identity
7) _____ refers to situations in which two or more roles make conflicting demands on behavior.   a) Role conflict
8) _____ refer to generally accepted rules of appropriate behavior in various social situations or social context.   c) Social norms
9) The _____ refers to the tendency of people will respond to each other in kind; treating those well who treat us well and treating those who treat us poorly in kind.   d) norm of reciprocity

10) _____ refers to the ways we organize, interpret, and give meaning to social experiences.   a) Social perception

11) _____ are explanations for the circumstances, thoughts, feelings, and behaviors of ourselves and others.   b) Attributions

12) _____ refers to an inference that a person is behaving in a certain way because of something about, or from inside the person, such as attitude, disposition, or personality trait.   a) Internal attribution

13) _____ refers to an inference that a person is behaving a certain way because of something about the situation and circumstance the person is in.   a) External attribution

14) An _____ is an incorrect or distorted understanding of the reasons for what happens around us.   a) attribution error

15) The _____ refers to the tendency to overestimate internal dispositional influences and underestimate external situational influences upon others' behavior.   b) fundamental attribution error

16) _____ are a type of biased schema; a mental shortcut used to characterize whole groups of people based on a false assumption that all members of a group share the same characteristics.   b) Stereotypes

17) _____ is an attitude, positive or negative, about an individual based their membership in a group.   b) Stereotypes

18) When one's behavior is affected by stereotyping or prejudice, the result is _____.   d) Discrimination

19) _____ refers to the tendency to have positive attitudes and give preferential treatment to people in the group to which we belong.   a) In-group bias

20) Psychologist Leon Festinger defined _____ as the discomfort caused by when our behavior and attitudes conflict.   b) cognitive dissonance

21) _____ uses data, pros and cons, or other logical reasons in order to change someone's attitude.   a) Central route persuasion

22) The _____refers to our tendency to comply with a large request after first complying with a small one.   c) foot-in-the-door phenomenon

23) The strongest factor influencing the chance that people will like one another is _____.   a) physical proximity

24) _____ refer to the different patterns of behavior appropriate to various social situations.   b) Social roles

25) _____ refers to the spreading of responsibility for a task across all members of the group.   c) Diffusion of responsibility

26) _____ refers to the strength of the relationships between group members, agreement about group goals, and adherence to group norms.   b) Group cohesion

27) _____ refers to a group decision-making process in which the group norms of harmony and cohesion override a realistic view of the alternatives.   a) Groupthink

28) _____ refers to a tendency of groups to drift toward and strengthen extreme positions – positions very different than group members would have taken individually.   c) Group polarization

Chapter 15 Research Methods

Chapter 15 Learning Objectives

Describe the research strategies used by psychologists to explore human affect, behavior, and cognition.
Describe the term scientific method.
Describe and explain the elements of an experiment.
Explain the importance of sampling and random assignment in psychological research.
Explain and describe measures of central tendency and variability.
Describe the concept of correlation and explain how it is used in psychology.
Explain the purpose and basic concepts of descriptive and inferential statistics.
Describe ethical issues in research with human and other animals that are important to psychologists.
Describe and compare quantitative and qualitative research strategies.
Think critically about research conclusions.

Key Concepts & People

Scientific method
Empiricism
Christian theism as the foundation of modern science
Basic research
Applied research
Hypothesis
Standardization
Replicable
Variables

Nominal variables
Ordinal variables
Interval variables
Dependent variable
Independent variable
Cause-and-effect relationships
Reliability
Validity
Representative sample
Randomization

Qualitative designs
Quantitative designs
Quasi-experimental designs
Descriptive statistics
Inferential statistics
Measures of central tendency
Measures of variability
Institutional Review Board (IRB)

Short Essay Questions

Respond to the assertion that a Christian worldview is anti-science.
Describe empiricism as a worldview and an approach to science.
Describe the steps in the empirical method.
Why is standardization important in psychological research?
Name and describe nominal, ordinal, interval, and ratio variables.
Explain independent and dependent variables.
Explain why reliability and validity are important in psychological research.
Explain bias in research. Describe subject and experimenter bias and research designs to control for subject and experimenter bias.
Describe the Hawthorne effect.
Describe and contrast qualitative and quantitative research.
Describe correlation research and the correlation coefficient.
Describe the placebo effect.
Describe descriptive and inferential statistics.
Describe a normal distribution.
Describe ethical considerations of research using human and animal subjects.

For Further Study

1. Web: TeachPsychScience.org: Resources for Teaching Research Statistics in Psychology has enough resources to keep a student who is interested in research busy for a very long time. http://www.teachpsychscience.org/resource.asp?tier2=1
2. Read: Publication Manual of the American Psychological Association. http://www.apastyle.org/

3. Read: Prayer Letter by David G. Myers http://www.davidmyers.org/davidmyers/assets/prayer-letter.pdf
4. Read: This Thing Called Prayer by David G. Myers
   http://www.davidmyers.org/davidmyers/assets/Thing.Called.Prayer.pdf

Topics for Discussion

1. Cite a research study finding that is applicable to you living out your faith.
2. Are there areas of life in which scientific data are limited in what they can tell us?
3. When is it appropriate to change our beliefs as a result of scientific evidence?
4. Can science measure the effectiveness of prayer? Read and discuss, This Thing Called Prayer by Dr. David Myers.
5. Respond to the assertion that a Christian worldview is anti-science.

Chapter 15 Worldview Issues

God reveals Himself in nature, through the Bible, and ultimately in Jesus. God is revealed in design and operations of our Minds. That is what Research Psychology is about. Psychologists that we have made and will continue to make important discoveries by careful observation and experimentation. The Empirical Method, the Scientific Method, and Research Methods, all refer to the systematic approach to the design, execution, and evaluation of psychological research and psychological tests. The challenge for you is evaluating the quality of psychological research methods and conclusions.

Is the Bible a Psychology Textbook?

You may not think about it often, but a big part of your worldview has to do with epistemology – the study of truth and knowledge. How can we know truth with certainty? What sources and methods of gaining knowledge are trustworthy? Are there limits to what we can know?

One of the first chapters in most introductory psychology textbooks is research methods – the techniques used to study psychological phenomenon. Modern psychology's goal, since its beginning, was to use scientific methods to gain understanding – to be a 'hard' science like chemistry and physics. As scientific psychology matured, new methods were developed – quasi-experimental designs, correlation studies, descriptive studies, surveys, and more.

The Bible is the inspired Word of God, but is it a psychology textbook? The Bible is inspired, authoritative, and sufficient, but it is not scientific. So, in as much as psychology is a science, the Bible is not a psychology textbook.

But recall our big definition of psychology – of psuche. Psychology is about human nature. In as much as psychology is the study of human nature and the ways in which we're unique and spiritual, the Bible is most certainly a psychology textbook. The Bible says things about us that the techniques of science can never discover.

Students will feel pressure to conform to scientism, also called empiricism and logical positivism. Scientism is a philosophy, a belief that says, because the world operates only by natural processes, the only valid sources of knowledge are natural, too. From this perspective, the Bible has nothing to contribute to psychology. We can only know truth with certainty through scientific methods.

A Christian approach to psychology recognizes the importance of science, but it rejects the belief that scientific methods are the only way of discovering truth.

Study Guide Chapter 15

1. The Christian worldview and true science cannot ultimately conflict – there is no inherent

   _____.

2. Many of the founders of modern psychology wanted it to be a _____like physics and chemistry, so they adopted controlled empirical, or scientific methods for their research and limited their study to the "physics" of mental life.

3. Students should understand the limits of science and should be able to distinguish quality research from _____.

4. Often, under the banner of science, psychologists promote _____.

5. Modern psychology's dominant worldview, _____ (also called logical positivism) is a belief that the empirical method is the only valid source for any knowledge, including psychological knowledge.

6. Research methods refer to the _____ of psychological research and psychological tests.

7. Though there is no "official" empirical method, the term refers to systematic and standard ways of _____

   _____.

8. _____is designed to solve a particular problem.

9. _____seeks to expand our knowledge and understanding for its own sake.

10. A _____is any factor that corrupts or distorts research results.

11. A _____ is a testable prediction about a relationship between things.

12. A hypothesis must be stated in a way that makes it possible to find it false; it must be

    _____.

13. Hypotheses can be _____

14. A _____predicts that two variables are related.

15. A _____predicts that one variable causes or leads to the other. The hypothesis that children who play violent computer games will behave more violently is a causal hypothesis.

16. _____ is the process of assuring that experimental procedures and measurements are precisely defined and carefully controlled.

17. _____ refers to precisely defining key concepts, processes, and measurements.

18. A good experiment is described in such detail that subsequent researchers can

_____ the experiment in every meaningful way.

19. A _____ is any event, condition, or behavior that researchers can measure. Gender can be measured as male or female.

20. Psychologists measure four types of variables: _____

_____.

21. _____classify data according to category.

22. _____can be classified quantitatively in rankings.

23. _____can be ranked in order, and the difference between intervals is known and fixed.

24. _____can be ranked in order, the intervals are known and fixed, the measurements can be added or subtracted, and multiplication and division make sense.

25. In experiments there are three types of variables: _____

_____.

26. The variable that the researcher manipulates is called the _____.

27. The _____is the "effect" in cause-and-effect relationships – it is the result of the experimental treatment.

28. _____ refers to the extent to which a measurement tool gives the same result when administered to the same people at different times.

29. _____ refers to the extent to which the measurement measures what it is supposed to measure.

30. A _____is a relatively small group of participants selected from the population of all possible participants.

31. An experiment has _____ if the sample is not representative of the larger population for some characteristic.

32. In drug trials, subjects are divided into two groups. The _____receives the experimental treatment, and the _____ does not.

33. The single most important control psychologists take in designing experiments is

_____.

34. _____ means that every member of a population has the exact same chance of being selected to be part of the study sample as every other member.

35. _____means that each member of the sample has the same chance of being placed in the experimental as the control group.

36. _____ occurs when subjects know what the experiment is about.

37. In a _____design, the subjects do not know the true purpose of the experiment or whether they are in the experimental or the control group.

38. _____describes anything the experimenter does that influences the results.

39. To control for experimenter bias, researchers create a _____ procedure in which neither the experimenter nor the subject knows which subjects receive the treatment and which do not.

40. The _____ has come to describe the mental process by which believing or expecting that something is going to happen tends to make it happen.

41. _____ is descriptive; it describes the qualities and characteristics of psychological phenomena.

42. _____ seeks to discover cause-and-effect relationships and to measure the strength of relationships among psychological variables.

43. _____ observes and describes phenomena in the context of the "real world" or natural circumstances.

44. _____ encompass a number of qualitative research designs for learning about human behavior by watching human behavior.

45. _____ is observational research conducted in natural settings.

46. _____ are naturalist observations of entire cultures.

47. _____are a type of observation in which psychologists study a single subject, program, or event in depth.

48. _____ are types of observational research used to gather data about attitudes and opinions.

49. The goal of experimental or quantitative research is to systematically identify _____.

50. In simple _____, a single independent variable is manipulated and a single dependent variable is measured.

51. Unlike experimental designs which randomly assigns subjects and carefully controls for extraneous variables, _____lack some or many of those characteristics.

52. _____may lack random assignment, the participants may not be "blind," a control group may not be possible, or other controls may be missing.

53. _____ help psychologists describe, organize, summarize, interpret, and draw inferences from research data.

54. _____organize, describe, and summarize data.

55. Psychologists use _____to interpret and draw inferences from the research data.

56. _____ are things that occur together and make it possible to use the value of one variable to predict the value of another.

57. Psychologists measure the strength of correlation on a scale from negative one (-1) to positive one (+1) using a _____.

58. Measures of central tendency include the _____.

59. The _____ is the arithmetic average.

60. The _____ is the measurement in the exact middle of an ordered range of measures.

61. The _____ is the value that occurs most often. A population set can have more than one mode.

62. _____or dispersion examine how a variable is distributed and how it varies in a sample or population.

63. The _____ describes the difference between the lowest and highest values.

64. The _____ is a statistical tool psychologists use to describe the total variation in a set of measures.

65. A _____ is often shown graphically by a normal or bell curve.

66. Psychologists use _____to make generalizations and draw conclusions about a population based on data obtained from samples.

67. Psychologists calculate the _____, or the confidence level, that the results did not occur by chance.

68. Today psychologists conducting research using humans or animals must follow ethical standards established by the _____.

69. Colleges and universities conducting psychological research must have an _____to review and approve all research proposals in advance.

70. Human subjects must _____and must be _____ associated with participating in the study.

71. The APA permits _____ if it is justified by the research's scientific value and if non-deceptive alternatives are not feasible.

72. The APA requires that _____ be treated humanely, with minimal discomfort and pain.

Chapter 15 Quiz

1) Modern psychology's dominant worldview, _____ (also called logical positivism) is a belief that the empirical method is the only valid source of knowledge.
   a) empiricism
   b) atheism
   c) evolution
   d) humanism

2) Research methods refer to the _____ of psychological research and psychological tests.
   a) design
   b) execution
   c) evaluation
   d) all of the above

3) _____ is designed to solve a particular problem.
   a) Applied research
   b) Basic research

4) A _____ is a testable prediction about a relationship between things.
   a) theory
   b) hypothesis
   c) hunch
   d) experiment

5) A hypothesis must be stated in a way that makes it _____.
   a) falsifiable
   b) provable
   c) testable
   d) reliable

6) _____ variables classify data according to category.
   a) nominal
   b) ordinal
   c) interval
   d) ratio

7) _____ variables can be classified quantitatively in rankings.
   a) nominal
   b) ordinal
   c) interval
   d) ratio

8) _____ variables can be ranked in order, and the difference between intervals is known and fixed.
   a) nominal
   b) ordinal
   c) interval
   d) ratio

9) _____ variables can be ranked in order, the intervals are known and fixed, the measurements can be added or subtracted, and multiplication and division make sense.
   a) nominal
   b) ordinal
   c) interval
   d) ratio

10) In experiments there are three types of variables: independent variables, dependent variables, and confounding variables. The variable that the researcher manipulates is called the _____.
   a) independent variable
   b) dependent variable
   c) confounding variable
   d) nominal variable

11) The _____ is the "effect" in cause-and-effect relationships – it is the result of the experimental treatment.
   a) independent variable
   b) dependent variable
   c) confounding variable
   d) nominal variable

12) _____ refers to the extent to which a measurement tool gives the same result when administered to the same people at different times.
   a) Reliability
   b) Validity

13) A _____ is a relatively small group of participants selected from the population of all possible participants.
   a) random sample
   b) representative sample
   c) control group
   d) experimental group

14) The single most important control psychologists take in designing experiments is _____.
   a) informed consent
   b) randomization
   c) control group
   d) double-blind

15) To control for experimenter bias, researchers create a _____ procedure in which neither the experimenter nor the subject knows which subjects receive the treatment and which do not.
   a) single-blind
   b) double-blind

16) The _____ effect has come to describe the mental process by which believing or expecting that something is going to happen tends to make it happen.
   a) expectancy
   b) placebo
   c) bias
   d) random

17) _____ research is descriptive; it describes the qualities and characteristics of psychological phenomena.
   a) Qualitative
   b) Quantitative
   c) Observational
   d) Naturalistic

18) _____ research seeks to discover cause-and-effect relationships and to measure the strength of relationships among psychological variables.
   a) Qualitative
   b) Quantitative
   c) Observational
   d) Naturalistic

19) _____ research is a general term for research techniques to observe and describe phenomena in the context of the "real world" or natural circumstances.
   a) Qualitative
   b) Quantitative
   c) Observational
   d) Clinical

20) The goal of experimental or quantitative research is to systematically identify _____.
   a) cause-and-effect relationships
   b) correlations

21) _____ may lack random assignment, the participants may not be "blind," a control group may not be possible, or other controls may be missing.
   a) Quasi-experimental designs
   b) Experimental designs

22) _____ organize, describe, and summarize data.
   a) Descriptive statistics
   b) Inferential statistics

23) _____ are things that occur together and make it possible to use the value of one variable to predict the value of another.
   a) Hypothesis
   b) Theories
   c) Correlations
   d) Relational variables

24) The _____ is the arithmetic average.
   a) mean
   b) median
   c) mode
   d) range

25) The _____ is the measurement in the exact middle of an ordered range of measures.
   a) mean
   b) median
   c) mode
   d) range

26) The _____ is the value that occurs most often.
   a) mean
   b) median
   c) mode
   d) range

27) The _____ describes the difference between the lowest and highest values.
   a) mean
   b) median
   c) mode
   d) range

28) The _____ is a statistical tool that psychologists use to describe the total variation in a set of measures.
   a) mean
   b) range
   c) standard deviation
   d) correlation coefficient

29) A _____ is often shown graphically by a normal or bell curve.
   a) measure of variability
   b) normal distribution
   c) correlation coefficient
   d) positive correlation

30) Psychologists use _____ to generalize and draw conclusions about a population based on data obtained from samples.
   a) descriptive statistics
   b) inferential statistics

31) For research results, psychologists calculate the _____, or the confidence level, that the results did not occur by chance.
   a) measures of variability
   b) statistical significance

32) Today psychologists conducting research using humans or animals must follow ethical standards established by _____.
   a) the American Psychological Association
   b) congress
   c) the United Nations
   d) the Bible

33) Human subjects must _____ and must be informed of any risks associated with participating in the study.
   a) be properly compensated
   b) voluntarily consent
   c) deceived about purpose of study
   d) not be compensated

Chapter 15 Study Guide (Answers)

1. The Christian worldview and true science cannot ultimately conflict – there is no inherent **faith/science dichotomy**.
2. Many of the founders of modern psychology wanted it to be a **hard science** like physics and chemistry, so they adopted controlled empirical, or scientific methods for their research and limited their study to the "physics" of mental life.
3. Students should understand the limits of science and should be able to distinguish quality research from **junk science.**
4. Often, under the banner of science, psychologists promote **philosophies and worldview positions.**
5. Modern psychology's dominant worldview, **empiricism** (also called logical positivism) is a belief that the empirical method is the only valid source for any knowledge, including psychological knowledge.
6. Research methods refer to the **design, execution**, and **evaluation** of psychological research and psychological tests.
7. Though there is no "official" empirical method, the term refers to systematic and standard ways of **defining research questions, forming and testing hypotheses, analyzing and interpreting data, drawing conclusions, and publishing the results.**
8. **Applied research** is designed to solve a particular problem.
9. **Basic research** seeks to expand our knowledge and understanding for its own sake.
10. A **confounding variable** is any factor that corrupts or distorts research results.
11. A **hypothesis** is a testable prediction about a relationship between things.
12. A hypothesis must be stated in a way that makes it possible to find it false; it must be **falsifiable**.
13. Hypotheses can be **relational or causal**.
14. A **relational hypothesis** predicts that two variables are related.
15. A **causal hypothesis** predicts that one variable causes or leads to the other. The hypothesis that children who play violent computer games will behave more violently is a causal hypothesis.
16. **Standardization** is the process of assuring that experimental procedures and measurements are precisely defined and carefully controlled.
17. **Operationalizing** refers to precisely defining key concepts, processes, and measurements.
18. A good experiment is described in such detail that subsequent researchers can **replicate** the experiment in every meaningful way.
19. A **variable** is any event, condition, or behavior that researchers can measure. Gender can be measured as male or female.
20. Psychologists measure four types of variables: **nominal, ordinal, interval, and ratio.**
21. **Nominal variables** classify data according to category.
22. **Ordinal variables** can be classified quantitatively in rankings.
23. **Interval variables** can be ranked in order, and the difference between intervals is known and fixed.
24. **Ratio variables** can be ranked in order, the intervals are known and fixed, the measurements can be added or subtracted, and multiplication and division make sense.
25. In experiments there are three types of variables: **independent variables, dependent variables, and confounding variables**.
26. The variable that the researcher manipulates is called the **independent variable**.
27. The **dependent variable** is the "effect" in cause-and-effect relationships – it is the result of the experimental treatment.
28. **Reliability** refers to the extent to which a measurement tool gives the same result when administered to the same people at different times.
29. **Validity** refers to the extent to which the measurement measures what it is supposed to measure.
30. A **representative sample** is a relatively small group of participants selected from the population of all possible participants.
31. An experiment has **sample bias** if the sample is not representative of the larger population for some characteristic.
32. In drug trials, subjects are divided into two groups. The **experimental group** receives the experimental treatment, and the **control group** does not.
33. The single most important control psychologists take in designing experiments is **randomization**.
34. **Random selection** means that every member of a population has the exact same chance of being selected to be part of the study sample as every other member.
35. **Random assignment** means that each member of the sample has the same chance of being placed in the experimental as the control group.
36. **Subject Bias** occurs when subjects know what the experiment is about.
37. In a **single-blind** design, the subjects do not know the true purpose of the experiment or whether they are in the experimental or the control group.
38. **Experimenter bias** describes anything the experimenter does that influences the results.
39. To control for experimenter bias, researchers create a **double-blind** procedure in which neither the experimenter nor the subject knows which subjects receive the treatment and which do not.

40. The **placebo effect** has come to describe the mental process by which believing or expecting that something is going to happen tends to make it happen.
41. **Qualitative research** is descriptive; it describes the qualities and characteristics of psychological phenomena.
42. **Quantitative research** seeks to discover cause-and-effect relationships and to measure the strength of relationships among psychological variables.
43. **Qualitative research** observes and describes phenomena in the context of the "real world" or natural circumstances.
44. **Observation designs** encompass a number of qualitative research designs for learning about human behavior by watching human behavior.
45. **Naturalistic observation** is observational research conducted in natural settings.
46. **Ethnologies** are naturalist observations of entire cultures.
47. **Case studies** are a type of observation in which psychologists study a single subject, program, or event in depth.
48. **Surveys** and **polls** are types of observational research used to gather data about attitudes and opinions.
49. The goal of experimental or quantitative research is to systematically identify **cause-and-effect relationships**.
50. In simple **quantitative research designs**, a single independent variable is manipulated and a single dependent variable is measured.
51. Unlike experimental designs which randomly assigns subjects and carefully controls for extraneous variables, **quasi-experimental designs** lack some or many of those characteristics.
52. **Quasi-experimental designs** may lack random assignment, the participants may not be "blind," a control group may not be possible, or other controls may be missing.
53. **Statistics** help psychologists describe, organize, summarize, interpret, and draw inferences from research data.
54. **Descriptive statistics** organize, describe, and summarize data.
55. Psychologists use **inferential statistics** to interpret and draw inferences from the research data.
56. **Correlations** are things that occur together and make it possible to use the value of one variable to predict the value of another.
57. Psychologists measure the strength of correlation on a scale from negative one (-1) to positive one (+1) using a **correlation coefficient**.
58. Measures of central tendency include the **mean, median, and mode**.
59. The **mean** is the arithmetic average.
60. The **median** is the measurement in the exact middle of an ordered range of measures.
61. The **mode** is the value that occurs most often. A population set can have more than one mode.
62. **Measures of variability** or dispersion examine how a variable is distributed and how it varies in a sample or population.
63. The **range** describes the difference between the lowest and highest values.
64. The **standard deviation** is a statistical tool psychologists use to describe the total variation in a set of measures.
65. A **normal distribution** is often shown graphically by a normal or bell curve.
66. Psychologists use **inferential statistics** to make generalizations and draw conclusions about a population based on data obtained from samples.
67. Psychologists calculate the **statistical significance**, or the confidence level, that the results did not occur by chance.
68. Today psychologists conducting research using humans or animals must follow ethical standards established by the **American Psychological Association (APA)**.
69. Colleges and universities conducting psychological research must have an **Institutional Review Board (IRB)** to review and approve all research proposals in advance.
70. Human subjects must **voluntarily consent** and must be **informed of any risks** associated with participating in the study.
71. The APA permits **deceiving subjects** if it is justified by the research's scientific value and if non-deceptive alternatives are not feasible.
72. The APA requires that **animals used in research** be treated humanely, with minimal discomfort and pain.

Chapter 15 Short Essay Questions (Answers)

1. Many people believe that a Christian worldview and science are inherently in conflict. Many believe that the Bible has no place in science and that science is the Bible's enemy. In other words, they believe that there is a faith/science dichotomy. Some historians have made the case that the Church (especially the Catholic church), fought every new scientific idea. Though it is true that through history the Church disputed many major scientific discoveries, it is not correct that the Christian church is necessarily "anti-science." In fact, science (and by extension, psychology) was born of the Christian worldview. A Christian worldview sees God as immutable, sees the world as orderly and rational, and believes that we can and should seek to understand creation. The historical Christian approach to science (though not without exception) was that faith and science were complementary. The fathers of modern science, many of whom were Christians, were not surprised to discover, on the basis of reason, truths about the universe. They saw science as one tool to explore creation, to discover how God operates in natural processes, and to understand what it means to be human. Descartes, Bacon, Newton, and Galileo explored God's creation and then tested their ideas with scientific methods.

2. Empiricism (also called logical positivism), in its extreme, is a belief that the empirical method is the only valid source for any knowledge, including psychological knowledge. From this perspective, the only "things" we can know are "things" that can be observed with one of the senses. As you learned earlier, empiricism is part of a naturalistic worldview. Naturalism excludes the possibility of the supernatural.

3. Define the Question, Test the Hypothesis, Analyze and Interpret Data, Draw Conclusion, Publish Results.

4. Standardization is the process of assuring that experimental procedures and measurements are precisely defined and carefully controlled. Standardization minimizes the effects of that confounding variable.

5. Nominal variables classify data according to category. Ordinal variables can be classified quantitatively in rankings. Interval variables can be ranked in order and the difference between intervals is known and fixed. Ratio variables can be counted. It is meaningful to say that there is an absolute zero level of ratio variables, measures can be ranked in order, the intervals are known and fixed, and the measurements can be added, subtracted, multiplied, or divided.

6. The variable that the researcher manipulates is called the independent variable. The independent variable is the cause in cause-and-effect relationships. The dependent variable is the "effect" in cause-and-effect relationships – it is the result of the experimental treatment. The dependent variable is what the researcher measures; it is the answer to the research question.

7. If the measurements are not reliable and valid, the research conclusions are not valuable.

8. There are many types of bias in psychological research. A bias is a systematic error caused by the presences of an extraneous variables, including selection and measurement biases.

9. Between 1927 and 1932 researchers at the Western Electric Company's Hawthorne Plant tried to discover the relationship of working conditions to worker productivity. The researchers manipulated the lighting, humidity, work hours, break schedules, and a number of other factors in hopes of discovering which factors were associated with higher worker productivity. They were surprised to find that worker productivity improved with every change in the environment. In fact, the change in worker productivity was associated with the presence of the researchers and not with the specific environmental changes the researchers made. Workers worked faster when they were being watched. The researchers' presence was an extraneous variable.

10. Qualitative research is a generic term for a number of non-experimental research techniques. Qualitative research observes and describes phenomena in the context of the "real world" or natural circumstances. Qualitative research lacks careful controls, random assignment, control groups, and/or researcher-manipulated variables; it cannot establish cause-and-effect relationships. Instead it focuses on psychological phenomena in their "real-life" complexity and context. Qualitative research is descriptive, not experimental; it generates new questions, not answers; and it creates a narrative of information about a topic. Because of the subjective quality of qualitative research, it is viewed as an inferior source of knowledge by strict empirical psychologists. But in many ways, qualitative research is better-suited for psychological research than is quantitative research. The goal of experimental or quantitative research is to systematically identify cause-and-effect relationships. In simple quantitative research designs, a single independent variable is manipulated and a single dependent variable is measured. The ideal quantitative design involves two groups of subjects that are equal in every relevant characteristic. Both groups are measured on some variable. One group receives the experimental treatment and the other does not. Both groups are measured again on the same variable. Results from the two groups are statistically analyzed to determine if the observed difference between the groups is significant – if it was unlikely to have occurred by chance. If the dependent variable changes in the experimental treatment but not in the control group, we can conclude, all other things being equal, that the treatment caused that change. The challenge of quantitative research is in assuring that all other things are truly equal.

11. Correlations are things that occur together. Correlations make it possible to use the value of one variable to predict the value of another. Psychologists measure the strength of correlation on a scale from negative one (-1) to positive one (+1) using a correlation coefficient. Correlation coefficients close to -1 or +1 both indicate a strong relationship between variables. A correlation coefficient of zero indicates no relationship between the variables. A positive coefficient means that as one variable increases, so does the other. A negative correlation reflects an inverse relationship between variables.

12. The placebo effect is an example of subject bias. In drug trials both groups take pills. The experimental group's pills contain the active ingredient. The control group's pills are chemically inert placebos with no active ingredients. (Sugar pills). Placebos are not, however, psychologically inert. The placebo effect is real and measurable. The active ingredient in the medication is effective only to the extent that its effect exceeds that of the placebo. The placebo effect has come to describe the mental process by which believing or expecting that something is going to happen tends to make it happen.

13. Descriptive statistics organize, describe, and summarize data. Psychologists use inferential statistics to interpret and draw inferences from the research data. Statistical analyses can provide evidence that measurements were valid and reliable and that the effect of the experimental treatment was statistically significant and not likely to have occurred by chance. Statistics cannot, however, prove anything.

14. A normal distribution (or "a bell curve") is a statistical grouping of scores. In a normal distribution, the majority of scores fall in the middle, clustered around the mean. Fewer scores fall at the extreme ends. It is often called a "bell curve" because the shape of the graph resembles a bell. Many physical characteristics (i.e. height) are normally distributed. Many psychological characteristics (i.e. intelligence) are said to be normally distributed.

15. Today psychologists conducting research using humans or animals must follow ethical standards established by the American Psychological Association (APA). The APA provides ethical guidelines and a code of conduct for psychologists in clinical and research practice. Colleges and universities conducting psychological research must have an Institutional Review Board (IRB) to review and approve all research proposals in advance. The APA prohibits coercion and placing human subjects at risk of physical or psychological harm. Human subjects must voluntarily consent and must be informed of any risks associated with participating in the study. The APA permits deceiving subjects if it is justified by the research's scientific value and if non-deceptive alternatives are not feasible. Research participants must be debriefed and provided with ways to contact the researchers about the results. The APA requires that animals used in research be treated humanely, with minimal discomfort and pain.

Chapter 15 Quiz Answers

1) Modern psychology's dominant worldview, _____ (also called logical positivism) is a belief that the empirical method is the only valid source of knowledge. a) empiricism

2) Research methods refer to the _____ of psychological research and psychological tests. d) all of the above

3) _____ is designed to solve a particular problem. a) Applied research

4) A _____ is a testable prediction about a relationship between things. b) hypothesis

5) A hypothesis must be stated in a way that makes it _____. a) falsifiable

6) _____ variables classify data according to category. a) nominal

7) _____ variables can be classified quantitatively in rankings. b) ordinal

8) _____ variables can be ranked in order, and the difference between intervals is known and fixed.   c) interval

9) _____ variables can be ranked in order, the intervals are known and fixed, the measurements can be added or subtracted, and multiplication and division make sense.   d) ratio

10) In experiments there are three types of variables: independent variables, dependent variables, and confounding variables. The variable that the researcher manipulates is called the _____. a) independent variable

11) The _____ is the "effect" in cause-and-effect relationships – it is the result of the experimental treatment.   b) dependent variable

12) _____ refers to the extent to which a measurement tool gives the same result when administered to the same people at different times.   a) Reliability

13) A _____is a relatively small group of participants selected from the population of all possible participants.   b) representative sample

14) The single most important control psychologists take in designing experiments is _____.
b) randomization

15) To control for experimenter bias, researchers create a _____ procedure in which neither the experimenter nor the subject knows which subjects receive the treatment and which do not.
b) double-blind

16) The _____ effect has come to describe the mental process by which believing or expecting that something is going to happen tends to make it happen.   b) placebo

17) _____ research is descriptive; it describes the qualities and characteristics of psychological phenomena.   a) Qualitative

18) _____research seeks to discover cause-and-effect relationships and to measure the strength of relationships among psychological variables.   a) Qualitative

19) _____ research is a general term for research techniques to observe and describe phenomena in the context of the "real world" or natural circumstances.   a) Qualitative

20) The goal of experimental or quantitative research is to systematically identify _____.
a) cause-and-effect relationships

21) _____ may lack random assignment, the participants may not be "blind," a control group may not be possible, or other controls may be missing.   a) Quasi-experimental designs

22) _____ organize, describe, and summarize data.   a) Descriptive statistics

23) _____ are things that occur together and make it possible to use the value of one variable to predict the value of another.   c) Correlations

24) The _____is the arithmetic average.   a) mean

25) The _____ is the measurement in the exact middle of an ordered range of measures.   b) median

26) The _____ is the value that occurs most often. A population set can have more than one mode.   c) mode

27) The _____ describes the difference between the lowest and highest values.   d) range

28) The _____ is a statistical tool that psychologists use to describe the total variation in a set of measures.
c) standard deviation

29) A _____ is often shown graphically by a normal or bell curve.   b) normal distribution

30) Psychologists use _____ to generalize and draw conclusions about a population based on data obtained from samples.   b) inferential statistics

31) For research results, psychologists calculate the _____, or the confidence level, that the results did not occur by chance.   b) statistical significance

32) Today psychologists conducting research using humans or animals must follow ethical standards established by _____.   a) the American Psychological Association

33) Human subjects must _____ and must be informed of any risks associated with participating in the study.   b) voluntarily consent

Also by Tim Rice

Natty Rose was homeschooled her entire life, and State U. is exciting and intimidating at the same time. Natty Rose must grow to be the woman her parents raised her to be, but she must first overcome the pressures all freshmen face in modern college life. Natty Rose is forced to decide for herself what she really believes.

Join Dr. Rice's lectures. Live and interactive OR asynchronous and self-paced.

CPSIA information can be obtained
at www.ICGtesting.com
Printed in the USA
JSHW021713110819
1025JS00016B/17

9 780981 558738